Inter-firm Collaboration, Learning and Networks

Inter-firm relations are not new. But fast developments in technology and globalization have led to increased opportunities for international alliances, and an upsurge in the interest in inter-organizational relations. With the time ripe for a unified theory of collaboration, *Inter-firm Collaboration, Learning and Networks* surveys the current field, connects differing perspectives and answers questions about who should collaborate, why and how.

Emphasizing learning and innovation, this book offers an integrated account of the key issues in the design and management of inter-firm relations and networks. It takes a uniquely interdisciplinary approach, bringing together perspectives from economics, sociology and management to offer a new kind of book on this subject. Supporting theory, the book includes illustrative case examples taken from a variety of firm, network and industry types.

Coherent and wide-reaching, *Inter-firm Collaboration, Learning and Networks* provides students and academics in economics, business, sociology, social psychology and economic geography with the tools required to understand this topical and highly relevant subject.

Bart Nooteboom is Professor of Organization in the Rotterdam School of Management at the Erasmus University Rotterdam.

Inter-firm Collaboration, Learning and Networks

An integrated approach

Bart Nooteboom

Routledge
Taylor & Francis Group

LONDON AND NEW YORK

First published 2004
by Routledge
11 New Fetter Lane, London EC4P 4EE

Simultaneously published in the USA and Canada
by Routledge
29 West 35th Street, New York, NY 10001

Routledge is an imprint of the Taylor & Francis Group

Typeset in Perpetua and Bell Gothic by
Graphicraft Limited, Hong Kong
Printed and bound in Great Britain by
The Cromwell Press, Trowbridge, Wiltshire

British Library Cataloguing in Publication Data
A catalogue record for this book is available from the
British Library

Library of Congress Cataloging in Publication Data
Nooteboom, B.
   Inter-firm collaboration, learning and networks : an integrated
approach / by Bart Nooteboom. – 1st ed.
      p. cm.
   Includes bibliographical references and index.
      1. Strategic alliances (Business).   2. Business networks.   I. Title.
   HD69.S8N663 2004
   658′.044–dc21   2003014633

ISBN 0–415–32953–1 (hbk)
ISBN 0–415–32954–X (pbk)

Contents

List of illustrations   vii
Preface   ix

1   Introduction   **1**
Summary   1
Aims and scope   2
Concepts and theory   8
Advanced   26

2   Goals   **36**
Summary   36
Goals   37
Concepts and theory   46
Advanced   59

3   Structure   **66**
Summary   66
Forms   67
Choice   77
Concepts and theory   92
Advanced   94

4   Governance   **96**
Summary   96
Risk analysis   97
Instruments   104
Concepts and theory   111
Advanced   119

5   Process   **144**
Summary   144
Stages of relations   145

Networks for exploration and exploitation 155
Advanced 179

6   Summary and conclusions   **185**
Summary 185
Integrated theory 185
Dyads and networks 189
Goals of collaboration 191
Forms of collaboration 192
Governance 196
Process 200
Further research 203

Appendix   Specification of variables 205
Notes 208
References 210
Name index 223
Subject index 226

Illustrations

FIGURES

1.1	Optimal cognitive distance	27
2.1	Threshold cost	60
3.1	Hub and spoke	71
3.2	Supply pyramid	72
3.3	Concentration of ownership and control	75
3.4	Cobwebs of IOR profiles	77
4.1	Relational risk audit	101
4.2	Value of Y to X	119
4.3	Switching costs for X	123
4.4	Opportunities for opportunism, Y	125
4.5	Intent towards opportunism, Y	127
4.6	Integrated risk analysis	128
5.1	Opening game	179
5.2	Closing game	181

TABLES

2.1	Goals of collaboration	38
2.2	Goals of collaboration in the cycle of discovery	64
3.1	Reasons for a merger, acquisition or alliance	79
3.2	Arguments for and against licensing	87
3.3	Number of direct suppliers in the car industry in Japan, North America and Europe	90
3.4	Reduction of number of direct suppliers in the American car industry	90
3.5	Sources of improvement	91
4.1	Typology of strategy	106
4.2	Instruments of governance and their drawbacks	107

4.3	Detailed instruments	129
4.4	Effects of instruments	130
4.5	Detailed conditions of market and technology	131
4.6	Institutional conditions	132
4.7	Problems of governance	134
4.8	Tests of effects on dependence perceived by suppliers	138
4.9	Tests of effects of trust	142
5.1	Contingencies	163
5.2	Networks for exploration and exploitation	167

Preface

This book is intended as both a textbook for advanced level teaching and a monograph. Chapters are dedicated, fairly straightforwardly, to the goals, forms, governance and development process of collaboration between firms. For use in teaching, each chapter starts with the main points, then treats the relevant concepts and theories used, and subsequently moves on to advanced topics. The latter may appeal to researchers and scholars. In teaching, the advanced sections might be used for electives. The book could be used as a main text in courses on inter-firm alliances and networks, and as a supplementary text in courses on organization, strategy, innovation, international business and economic geography.

The book takes an integrated approach, combining issues of competence and governance, efficiency and learning, strategy and organization. There is an emphasis on learning and innovation as a goal of collaboration. The book also takes an interdisciplinary approach, employing elements from economics, sociology, cognitive science, social psychology and geography. It is aimed at students and scholars in economics, sociology, business/management and geography.

The book employs parts from a previous book, published by Routledge, with the title *Inter-firm Alliances: Analysis and Design*, but the set-up is different. It also goes much deeper into network effects, the process of relationship development and network dynamics.

The book is built on some fifteen years of teaching and research, and next to the use of a wide range of literature, it employs results from a large number of publications by the author. I wish to thank a number of colleagues for our collaboration in past research that has contributed to this book. In particular, I wish to acknowledge contributions by Niels Noorderhaven, Hans Berger, Rosalinde Klein Woolthuis, Gjalt de Jong, Victor Gilsing, Frédérique Six and Bob Kijkuit. I am also indebted to countless others who offered critical response, at conferences, many workshops, mostly in Europe, and in the reviews of many publications.

Bart Nooteboom, The Hague, May 2003

Chapter 1

Introduction

- ■ Aims and scope
  - ● Questions
  - ● Scope
  - ● Disciplines
- ■ Concepts and theory
  - ● Competence
  - ● Knowledge
  - ● Decision heuristics
  - ● Organization
  - ● Institutions
  - ● Complementary cognition
  - ● Tacit knowledge, absorptive capacity and firm size
  - ● Knowledge transfer to small firms
  - ● Governance
- ■ Advanced
  - ● Cognitive distance
  - ● Empirical tests
  - ● Evolutionary psychology
  - ● Institutions and evolution
  - ● Methodological interactionism
  - ● Incommensurability

SUMMARY

This introductory chapter presents the aims and scope of this book, outlines its content, indicates its special features and discusses some of the basic concepts used. First, it indicates the questions dealt with in this book, in subsequent chapters: why should one collaborate (goals), in what form of organization and network (structure), how (governance) and how does collaboration develop (process). Second, this chapter indicates the scope of the book, in terms of themes, perspectives and disciplines used. The book analyses bilateral relationships as well as networks in which they are embedded. It lays an emphasis on dynamics: learning and innovation as a goal of inter-organizational relationships (IORs), and the development of relationships and networks. It aims to give a comprehensive treatment, integrating a variety of perspectives and disciplines. In particular, it integrates perspectives of competence (especially competence development, learning) and governance (how to manage relations, in particular 'relational risk'). This chapter briefly indicates what elements are used from what disciplines: economics, sociology, social psychology, business studies, geography and cognitive science. Subsequently it discusses some of the basic notions to be used: competence, knowledge, decision heuristics (taken from social psychology), organizations and institutions, governance and some features of cognition and knowledge transfer. In the advanced section (p. 26), it further discusses the notion of 'optimal cognitive distance', empirical tests of that, some evolutionary origins of cognition, the notion of 'co-evolution', the methodological stance of 'methodological interactionism' and the problem of 'incommensurable paradigms'.

AIMS AND SCOPE

This section discusses the notion of IORs and what is new about them. It specifies the questions addressed in this book, the perspectives from which the analysis is conducted and the disciplines that are used.

Questions

Outsourcing, inter-organizational collaboration and networks are forms of inter-organizational relationships (IORs). In this book, that generic term is adopted from Christine Oliver (1990). The term 'organizations' goes beyond 'firms', but while the analysis is aimed at organizations in general, in this book the focus is on firms.

Inter-*firm* relations are not new. They go back at least as far as Adam Smith's argument for division of labour between firms, for the sake of productive efficiencies of specialization. Such specialization in firms by definition entails outsourcing of the production of inputs, upwards in the *supply chain*, and the distribution and use of products downwards in the supply chain. That entails inter-organizational relations and networks. Collaboration entails mutual adjustment, needed for the utilization of complementary resources from different organizations. Collaboration does not always entail balance of mutual value, dependence and power. Often, there is both collaboration and conflict of interest, in rivalry or even outright competition. This tension between collaboration and conflict of interest, and how to deal with it, in the governance of relations, is a central theme of this book.

The upsurge of renewed interest in inter-organizational relations is due to developments in technology and markets. In technology, there is fast development and proliferation of novel opportunities, e.g. in information and communication technology (ICT), micro-mechanics, optics, sensors, their combination in robotization, biotechnology, new materials and surface technologies. In markets, there is renewed globalization,[1] partly as a result of new opportunities offered by ICT. Globalization does not necessarily lead to convergence of 'business systems' (Whitley 1999). It does entail that there are new opportunities for entering foreign markets, of both products and inputs, new threats of competition from abroad and new needs and opportunities for international alliances. ICT offers new opportunities for co-ordinating activities across markets and organizations. Such effects of ICT are taken for granted, and will not be analysed in any detail.

As usual, in this book the term *product* includes anything that has added value, including both physical *goods* and more or less intangible *services*.

As a result of emerging complexity and rapid change of markets and technology, competition has increasingly become a 'race to the market' with new or improved products. To have any chance of winning such a race, one needs to shed activities, as much as strategically possible, that are not part of the 'core competencies' (Prahalad and Hamel 1990) that constitute competitive advantage. Other, complementary, competences must then be sought from outside partners. Such outside sourcing also maximizes the flexibility in configurations of activities that is needed under rapid change. For example, in order to reduce development times of new products and to reduce risks of maladjustment to customer needs, suppliers should be brought in as partners in developing and launching a new product.

The sourcing decision – what to make and what to buy – is a special case of the more general decision what to do inside one's own organization, and what to do outside, in collaboration with other organizations. Sourcing entails vertical collaboration, in the supply chain, including marketing and distribution. Relations may also be horizontal, with competitors, or lateral, with firms in other industries.

A famous example of horizontal collaboration between competitors is the co-operation between Sony and Philips in setting the standard for the compact audio disc (CD). While Philips and Sony co-operated in setting the technical standard for the CD, in other markets they kept on competing, and they resumed competition in CDs once the standard had been set. This co-operation was based on their experience from the debacle in the market for video-recorders. There they both had technically superior products (the Betamax of Sony and the Video 2000 of Philips), but the competing VHS system (operated by JVC and Matsushita) won by achieving a breakthrough in market acceptance. This type of effect obtains especially in markets with 'network externality', where the usefulness of a piece of equipment depends on how many others have equipment of the same technical standard. The VHS system won due to a better fit to market demand in the supply of software (video-tapes) that was compatible only with the VHS standard built into the hardware (recorders). This included length of play for recording baseball games, and more extensive distribution of recorded tapes for hire. This gave a head start in the market, with supply according to that standard reinforcing itself, so that a consumer choosing an alternative from Sony or Philips ran an accelerating risk that the supply of appropriate software would fall back and stop.

Next to the question *what* to do inside or outside, and *why*, there are the questions *with whom* to collaborate, and *how*: in what *forms of organization*, with what *instruments for governance*, and in what kind of *process*. These are the questions addressed in this book. The focus is on strategy and organization rather than on operational matters of partner selection and evaluation, project design and management, staffing, accounting and control.

Scope

The time is ripe for a unified theory, connecting and integrating perspectives and arguments that have emerged in recent advances, from different disciplines. This book is intended as a comprehensive survey. It aims to provide an integrated text for students, scholars and practitioners. Most of the elements of the book are not new. What is new is the attempt to integrate, in a coherent fashion, elements from a widely dispersed literature.

The book does not take the customary approach of first giving an introduction to theory and a survey of the (very large) literature on IORs, prior to application. In each chapter it goes directly into a discussion of the different features of collaboration. These features are: goals of collaboration (Chapter 2), the structure of its organization, in firms and networks (Chapter 3), governance (Chapter 4) and the process of relationship development (Chapter 5). After a summary of the feature, what follows, in each chapter, is a summary of concepts and theory used at that point. These are needed for proper understanding and application. Much of it will be familiar to scholars and advanced students. For them, there is a subsequent discussion of 'advanced topics', which in teaching can be taken as electives. References to literature will also be given where they are relevant. Illustrative examples are inserted in the text, to aid recognition, understanding and application.

The account is integrated in several respects, as follows:

1 It considers a wide variety of goals and types of inter-organizational relations. It includes sourcing and distribution, in 'vertical' relations, 'horizontal' collaboration between firms in the same industries, and 'lateral' relations between firms in different industries. It includes goals of efficiency (scale, scope), positioning in markets, learning and innovation. It considers different degrees of integration, from mergers/acquisitions, through equity joint ventures, and non-equity alliances, to *ad hoc* contracting. It includes a variety of scope and strength of ties.

2 It combines a 'competence' and a 'governance' perspective. In the first, it analyses inter-organizational relations for pooling competences, and for developing competences, in learning and innovation. In takes a governance perspective for the analysis of 'relational risk'. It offers a toolbox of instruments for design and governance of relations, and contingencies for their selection.

3 It looks not only at the positive but also at the negative side of relationships; at both collaboration and conflict. Ongoing relations may create rigidities that block innovation. There is a need to look not only at how a relation is to be set up, but also at how it is to be adapted to changing conditions, and how it is to be ended.

4 For theses purposes, the book integrates insights from different disciplines: economics, sociology, social psychology, cognitive science, business studies and (some) economic geography. It looks at considerations of rational design as well as social and psychological aspects of motivation, cognition and relational dynamics.

5 It incorporates strategy, design, management and development of relations.

6 Beyond dyads of collaborating firms, it includes effects of network structure and position.

Of course, such an integrated approach runs the risk of becoming eclectic, incoherent or even contradictory. However, the claim of this book is that it yields a coherent whole. This claim is reviewed at the end, in the final chapter, in the summary and conclusions. There are several opportunities for such coherence. One, in particular, lies in an underlying theory of knowledge, which will be discussed in this chapter. For an adequate understanding, there is an urgent need for integration. In particular, there is a need to combine perspectives of competence and governance (Nooteboom 1992; Williamson 1999). From the competence perspective, there has been a focus on the development of competences and learning, with a neglect of relational risk and its governance. Transaction cost economics (TCE) has focused on relational risk (of 'hold-up') and the hazards of opportunism. However, while transaction cost economics focuses on

5

static efficiency, trading off production costs, transaction costs and costs of organization, given a certain state of knowledge, technology and preferences, a perspective of dynamic efficiency or innovation is also needed, incorporating shifts of knowledge, technology and preferences. It is now a priority for firms to develop 'dynamic capabilities'.

In the literature, important new insights have been generated, but they tend to focus on few aspects, resulting in one-sided conclusions. For example, opinion seems to have settled on a rather extreme view in favour of outsourcing everything that is not part of 'core competences'. However, that may go too far (Teece 1986; Bettis *et al.* 1992; Chesbrough and Teece 1996). The question of course is what, exactly, is to be seen as part of core competence, and what is meant by the qualification, given above, that one should outsource as much as 'strategically possible'. When is something not to be outsourced even if it is not part of core competence?

Philips Electronics is a user of chips (semiconductors) as components in many kinds of consumer electronics. A compact disc player, for example, requires a combination of mechanics, laser technology, electro-technology, control technology and informatics. Should Philips make its own chips, or contract them from specialist producers? The production of chips entails high-tech surface technology, to affect, at a microscopic level, the conducting properties of a silicon disc by means of sophisticated physical and chemical processes. That does not seem to fit with Philips's core competences. So, according to the maxim of sticking to core competences, it seems reasonable to have it contracted out. But there are strategic complications. The first is that the world-class producers of chips are the same Japanese companies that compete with Philips in the market for consumer electronics. Should one become dependent for supply on one's main competitors? The second complication is that the development of technology and markets is very rapid, and new products often arise from novel combinations of existing technologies, and often one needs to react fast to novel opportunities. The 'window of opportunity' is narrow and passes fast. For this reason one may need to maintain competence in an area that in a static situation one should surrender. The production of semiconductors requires sophisticated (miniaturized, uncontaminated and perfectly accurate) technology, with physical and chemical processes for etching micro-patterns on the surface of silicon slices, and modifying conductive properties in those patterns. Similar technology can also be used for the deposition of thin layers on surfaces for other purposes, such as hardening materials, coating photovoltaic cells or the production of sensors. Thus the technology of chip production is a 'platform' technology, which contributes to other products than chips, which might fit well in Philips's product portfolio. To keep such future options open, chip production may have to be seen as part of core competence.

Disciplines

From economics this book employs notions of efficiency, such as effects of scale and scope, trade-off between opportunities and costs, including costs of opportunities forgone (opportunity costs), 'sunk costs', effects of market structure from industrial organization economics, some results from game-theoretic analysis of strategic interaction (including what one might call the 'temporal embeddedness' of relationships), elements from transaction cost economics, evolutionary economics, institutional economics and from a range of innovation studies.

From sociology it takes insights from network analysis, for 'structural embeddedness', and from theories of social exchange and social learning, for 'relational embeddedness'. The latter is necessary, in particular, for the analysis of trust. Outside network studies in sociology there still is a tendency to look only at pairs of organizations (dyads). This chapter also looks at network effects of multiple partners and indirect linkages (Granovetter 1973; Coleman 1988; Powell 1990; Burt 1992; Uzzi 1996). It matters greatly how organizations are embedded, in terms of network structure, position in that structure, and types of ties between organizations. Organizations often gain access to resources, and risk loss of resources, in indirect relations. Structure and types and strength of ties have important implications for both competence and governance. In various literatures a variety of definitions of networks have been given, and they will not be enumerated here. In this book, the term 'network' simply means that more than two organizational actors are involved, with both direct and indirect linkages.

From social psychology this book takes heuristics people use in decision making, and in their attribution of characteristics (competences, intentions) to people and organizations, on the basis of observed events. This is needed, in particular, to analyse the development and breakdown of trust.

From business studies this book takes insights from strategic management, organization and internationalization of business. However, while the analysis is conducted in the context of internationalization, it does not aim to give an exhaustive, specialized treatment of international alliances.

From geography this book takes certain notions such as externalities of location, and certain themes such as the role of distance and the development of 'industrial districts'.

From cognitive science it takes insights from 'situated action' or 'activity' theory of knowledge. This will be discussed below.

Finally, this book avoids claims of universal best practice. What forms of organization and governance are appropriate in IORs depends upon a range of conditions, such as the goals of participants, their experience in IORs, characteristics of technology and knowledge, the institutional environment, the history of relationships and stages of their development. The institutional environment includes features such as legal and educational systems, physical infrastructure, intermediaries, norm systems and reputation systems. These are important, in particular, for governance, as discussed in Chapter 4.

An example of the effect of institutions on organizational integration or disintegration in the history of the US system of innovation is the effect of anti-trust regulation (Mowery and Rosenberg 1993). At first it was lax, which stimulated large firms to grow and innovate by taking over innovative small firms. When anti-trust policy shifted to restrict this, there was more growth of small, entrepreneurial firms. The entry of such firms was further enabled by a liberal regime of property rights protection, which allowed small firms to enter market niches, an active venture capital market, and military procurement policies that were open to small firms. A weakness in the United States, identified by Mowery and Rosenberg, is lack of diffusion of innovations, particularly in robotics and computer-integrated manufacturing. Mowery and Rosenberg detect changes in the US system – a lesser importance of military procurement and a more liberal anti-trust policy since the Reagan administration – which may shift the emphasis back away from small entrants towards larger firms. This is expected to be enhanced by a policy aimed at more appropriability of innovations, which yields fewer entry opportunities and may exacerbate the lack of diffusion.

CONCEPTS AND THEORY

This section discusses some of the concepts and theories used above, which will also be used later in the book. It discusses the notions of competence, knowledge, and their implications for the theory of organization and of inter-organizational relations, institutions and governance. It discusses some problems and solutions in knowledge transfer, especially to small firms. Of fundamental importance, in particular, is the theory of knowledge used, which forms the main basis for integrating different perspectives and disciplines. Concepts of efficiency and learning are discussed in the analysis of the goals of IORs, in Chapter 2. Networks are discussed in the analysis of forms of IORs, in Chapter 3. Issues of dependence and power, and instruments for governance, including trust, are discussed in the analysis of governance, in Chapter 4. Process issues, in the development of relationships, are discussed in Chapter 5.

Competence

The competence view, which is close to the 'resource-based' view, goes back to the work of Edith Penrose (1959). Following that lead, the book analyses the use and development of resources and competences, in interaction between firms, in networks. That approach was pioneered in the 1970s and 1980s by a number of Swedish scholars, from the perspective of industrial (business to business) marketing (Håkansson 1982, 1987, 1989; Johanson and Mattson 1987; Håkansson and Snehota 1995; Laage-Hellman 1997).

The notion of 'resource' is a broad one. Resources have a potential to generate value. There are many forms: physical assets, finance, access to markets (of inputs and outputs), brand name and reputation, human resources, organizational structure and culture, positions in networks and abilities/capabilities/competences. This view of resources is consistent with the 'resource dependence' view (Pfeffer and Salancik 1978), which states that those stakeholders in an organization have most power who control the resources that are critical for the organization, i.e. are scarce and necessary for survival, at a given time. Note that resources include 'positional advantage' (Stoelhorst 1997), with respect to markets and competition. They also include competences.

In the literature, the notion of competence is somewhat ambiguous. No survey is given here of all the conceptualizations that have been proposed. In this book competence is seen as itself a resource, because it contributes to value creation, but it is a resource of a special kind. Unlike some other resources (such as assets), it entails repertoires of action. Here, it is defined as the (individual and organizational) ability to efficiently employ, acquire or develop other resources.[2] Among other things, this includes the ability to learn and innovate. This includes, among other things, 'absorptive capacity' (Cohen and Levinthal 1990), i.e. the ability to absorb knowledge from outside an organization. On the level of an organization, absorptive capacity entails a combination of individual and organizational capabilities. Competence goes beyond technical ability, and includes the power, authority and legitimacy to exercise abilities.

The competence view emphasizes differences of competence between organizations. Competition is seen not only, and not primarily, as competing on the price of a homogeneous product, i.e. a product that can be closely substituted by users between different suppliers, but also, and primarily, as an attempt to maintain competences that are scarce and difficult to imitate by potential competitors (Lippman and Rumelt 1982).

Clearly, resources and competences do not operate in isolation, but in configurations. The utilization and further development of core competences may require access to 'complementary assets' (Teece 1986). The question then is how 'separable' those complementary assets (or resources, more generally) are from core competences. Separability can be technical, organizational or strategic. For example, access to a distribution channel may be strategically crucial, there may be only one alternative to choose from, and it may be controlled by a competitor. Then, it may be strategically desirable to build proprietary access to markets, even if technically and organizationally it would be separable.

9

Recall the example of Philips, above. Technically and organizationally, the production of chips, needed for consumer electronics, could be separated off. However, if that means that they have to be procured from competitors, this may constitute a strategic obstacle.

An important question is to what extent an investment in an asset, or in resources more generally (including competences), is 'sunk' in a given market or field of activity, i.e. cannot be deployed elsewhere. This creates exit barriers, or, equivalently, switching costs. To switch to a new activity, where the resource cannot be deployed, would require a new investment, with loss of the old one. This notion of sunk costs in industries or markets is familiar from industrial organization economics. An exit barrier becomes an entry barrier: knowing that exit would entail switching costs, and hence lack of flexibility, and hence dependence, one hesitates to enter that market or industry. Such entry barriers limit the threat of competition to firms already in the market ('incumbents').

Consider a job opportunity for a scholar at a provincial university that is far away from alternative job opportunities, so that once one is employed, and one's family is locally rooted, in their jobs, schools and social relations, it is difficult to switch. Being aware of that, one may hesitate to take that job. Thus, the exit barrier yields an entry barrier. This may lower competitiveness among the staff at that university, and may lower its overall quality.

A crucial notion from transaction cost economics is that of a 'transaction-specific' investment. That is an investment that is sunk in a transaction. In inter-organizational relations it is more useful to take the relation, rather than a transaction, as the unit of analysis, and to speak of 'relation-specific' investments. When a relation breaks, an investment would have to be made anew in another relation.

A classic example of a relation-specific investment is the die (mould) in which part of a car (door, bonnet) is stamped into shape. It has the shape of the part and is therefore as 'specific' as anything can get. It is also expensive because it is large and made of hard, durable material, to survive the force of stamping and maintain a constant shape. The investment in the die is not recouped until a large number of items have been stamped, and that requires a minimal number or duration of production. If production is stopped, the die has no more than scrap value.

More attention will be paid to relation-specific assets later, in the discussion of governance, in Chapter 4.

Knowledge

This book pays much attention to innovation and learning in IORs. For that, a theory of knowledge is needed. The theory employed here forms a cornerstone for an integrative theory of IORs.

It is important to note that this book takes the notions of knowledge and cognition in a wide sense, including perception, interpretation and evaluation, which include emotion-laden value judgements. In other words, cognition and emotion (such as fear, suspicion, grief, excitement) are seen as linked. The Cartesian separation of mind and body is rejected (Merleau-Ponty 1964; Damasio 1995). Note the difference between urges (such as hunger, sex) and emotions. As noted by Nussbaum (2001), in contrast to urges, emotions are directed not at generalized but at specific objects. Also, emotions are informed by cognition in more detail than urges. For example, fear of something is informed by its perception, by attribution of characteristics, interpretation of events, and causal inferences of threat (Nussbaum 2001).

We are more afraid of tigers than of cows because we know things about them. Tigers eat meat, cows grass. In contrast with cows, tigers are fast and have claws.

As argued by Herbert Simon, due to bounded rationality, in the sense of limited cognitive capacity, much behaviour is routinized, and 'automatic', in the sense of unreflected, and largely based on tacit knowledge, in 'subsidiary' rather than 'focal' awareness (Polanyi 1962, 1966, 1969). Routinized behaviour is rational in the sense of being 'adaptive': it helps us to function and survive in a world of uncertainty and bounded rationality. Activity becomes routinized when it has proved to be consistently adequate, or 'satisficing'. The routine is relegated to subsidiary awareness. The down side of routines is that they may become dysfunctional in new circumstances. When this yields a perceived threat, due to malfunction, routinized behaviour may be shifted from subsidiary to focal awareness, for critical, deliberative reflection. As argued by Simon (1983) emotions, such as fear, caused by malfunction, serve to trigger such a shift. This is one reason why emotions are part of rationality, in the sense of adaptiveness.

It is a truism to say that information is not the same as knowledge: to become knowledge, information needs to be interpreted and understood in a cognitive framework. Similarly, to most researchers in this area, this book employs an 'interactionist', 'constructivist' theory of knowledge, and language, which descends from 'symbolic interactionism' in sociology (G. H. Mead), and the view, taken from cognitive psychology, that intelligence is internalized action (Vygotsky 1962; Piaget 1970, 1974; Bruner 1979). That is why it has also been called an 'activity theory' of cognition (Blackler 1995).

In contrast with the dominant 'computational representational' view in cognitive science, this leads to the view of knowledge in terms of 'situated action'. Knowledge and the meaning of words are not independent from context. Neither are they completely determined by context. They lie partly in the context of use, and they shift from one context to another. One may still speak of mental 'representations', but only on the understanding that they are mentally constructed, in an embedding in existing cognitive structures, and are not 'given' as any 'mirror image' of reality. Even 'recall' from 'memory' is not simple retrieval, but reconstruction, affected by the context at hand. For a more detailed recent analysis, see Nooteboom (2000a).

Mental categories or schemata are more or less routinized and tacit. This applies, for example, to pattern recognition. That arises in many areas, such as shapes of objects or drawings, physiognomy, practices, conditions and motives of behaviour.

In discussions of tacit knowledge there is a tendency to see tacit and codified knowledge as substitutes, as when tacit knowledge is 'externalized' (Nonaka and Takeuchi 1995) into codified knowledge. However, there is also complementarity. Underlying, tacit categories are needed to interpret information (externalized knowledge) transmitted in communication. People properly understand each other only if they sufficiently share underlying categories. When those are tacit and incongruent, there is a problem. They may then first have to develop shared categories, by interaction in a 'community of practice' (Brown and Duguid 1996).

This process of knowledge construction precludes objective knowledge (or at least any certain knowledge whether or to what extent knowledge is objective). We cannot 'descend from our mind to check how our knowledge is hooked on to the world'. Personal knowledge is embedded in a system of largely tacit, routinized mental categories that constitute absorptive capacity.

Knowledge can have different *forms*: more or less tacit, in particular. It can have different *contents*: professional expertise, skill, work perception and attitude, operation of projects, organization, markets (customers, competition), modes of conflict resolution and 'meta-knowledge' on the location and reliability of sources of knowledge (Wegner *et al.* 1985). It can have different *scope*: generic knowledge, beyond specific applications, or specific, for a given project or practice.

Decision heuristics

As noted above, cognition and emotions are intertwined. Next to cognition in the narrow sense of rational evaluation, there are also more emotion-laden and instinct-based considerations from social psychology. Such instincts are inherited, emerging, at least in part, from evolution. Elements from evolutionary psychology are discussed in the 'advanced' section of this chapter.

We infer causes of behaviour and we attribute characteristics and motives to people according to mental categories or schemata. We can identify with people to the extent that there is similarity of such behavioural schemata. Empathy entails knowledge of other people's cognition, without sharing it. Empathy helps to attribute motives and capabilities correctly, and thereby arrive at a more reliable assessment of trustworthiness. Identification leads to sympathize with them and perhaps tolerate disappointments. We entertain more or less tacit categories of justice, and trust depends on the extent that others share them. Absorptive capacity may be limited by cognitive dissonance: we may subconsciously resist information that is in conflict with established and cherished views or convictions, particularly if it would require an admission of mistaken choices in the past. Past acts have to be justified to oneself and to others, even at the cost of distorting facts or construing artificial arguments.

Social psychology offers a number of insights into instinct-related decision heuristics that people use. In a survey, Bazerman (1998) specifies the following heuristics:

1 *Availability*. People assess the probability and likely causes of an event by the degree to which instances of it are 'readily available' in memory, i.e. are vivid, laden with emotion, recent and recognizable. Less available events and causes are neglected.
2 *Representativeness*. The likelihood of an event is assessed by its similarity to stereotypes of similar occurrences.
3 *Anchoring and adjustment*. Judgement is based on some initial or base value ('anchor') from previous experience or social comparison, plus incremental adjustment from that value. People have been shown to stay close even to random anchors that bear no systematic relation to the issue at hand. First impressions can influence the development of a relation for a long time.

These heuristics are not rational in a calculative sense (*calculative rationality*). However, they are 'adaptively rational' in the sense of contributing to survival under uncertainty and bounded rationality, and the need, in many situations, to decide and act quickly (*adaptive rationality*). Concerning the availability heuristic, in the above analysis of routines the importance was noted of an emotional identification of a suspicious event to trigger awareness of the routine and to subject it to rational scrutiny. Perhaps this is connected with the availability heuristic: we pay attention only when triggers are emotion laden. If we did not apply such filters our consciousness would likely be overloaded.

Concerning the representativeness heuristic, there is a connection with the role of 'prototypes' or 'exemplars' in language and categorization (Rosch 1977; Nooteboom 2000a). Since definitions can seldom offer necessary and sufficient conditions for categorization, and meaning is context-dependent and open-ended, allowing variation and change, we need prototypes. Prototypes are salient exemplars of a class that guide categorization by assessing similarity to the prototype. The root meaning of a 'paradigm', in science, is 'exemplar'. This also explains the role of cultural features such as myths and role models. The mechanism of attributing unobserved characteristics upon recognition of observed ones enables pattern recognition, which is conducive to survival. However, they also yield prejudice.

Concerning anchoring and adjustment, under uncertainty cognition does need such an anchor, and taking the most recent value of a variable, or a value observed in behaviour of people in similar conditions, with whom one can empathize, may well be rational. The notion of a default entails that one adapts past guidelines for behaviour on the basis of new evidence. Incremental adjustment can be inadequate, but so can fast adjustment. Studies of learning and adjustment have shown that hasty and large departures from existing practices can yield chaotic behaviour (Lounamaa and March 1987; March 1991).

As will be discussed later, in Chapters 4 and 5, these heuristics are highly relevant to trust and its development, because they affect attribution of characteristics and expectations of trustworthiness. According to the heuristics, one would develop expectations, explain broken expectations and attribute trustworthiness according to what is 'available' in the mind, stereotypes, existing norms or recent experience. Note, however, that although these heuristics are rational in the adaptive sense, they can yield errors of myopia, prejudice and inertia. As a result, while trust is feasible and viable, it can go wrong.

Another psychological phenomenon is that people are found to have difficulty in choosing between immediate gratification and long-term benefit, yielding a problem of 'the weakness of the will'. This has been explained in terms of people having multiple selves that are at odds with each other, or as a visceral drive competing with a rational inclination. Another interpretation follows the availability heuristic: immediate gratification is more 'available'. Studies of behaviour under uncertainty have shown that people may assess delay in gratification differently when it is near from when it is far ahead, and that sometimes time discounting of future penalties or rewards seems to take place not according to an exponential but according to a hyperbolic function. According to that function, the negative utility of a delay of gratification increases as the decision moves to the present. As a result, preferences may reverse at some point in time. The relevance of this phenomenon to collaborative relations is also clear, in the trade-off between fairness or 'benevolence' to a partner, which may be in one's long-term interest, and the temptation to opportunism that offers more advantage in the short term. One may honestly think one is able to withstand that temptation in the future, and yet succumb to it when it nears. Again, we cannot unequivocally judge that this psychological mechanism is maladaptive. As noted also by Bazerman (1998), the impulse of temptation may also entail the vision of entrepreneurial opportunity, and too much repression of it may suppress innovation.

'Prospect theory' (Tversky and Kahneman 1983) has demonstrated that people are not risk-neutral, but can be risk-taking when a decision is framed in terms of loss, and risk-averse when it is framed in terms of gain. This 'framing' entails, among other things, that in a relation people will accept a greater risk of conflict when they stand to incur a loss than when they stand to obtain a benefit. Related to this effect is the 'endowment effect': people often demand more money to sell what they have than they would be prepared to pay to get it. In the first case one wants to cover for loss. This may contribute to loyalty and stable relations, as follows. Relations typically end when one of the partners encounters a more attractive alternative, while the other partner wants to continue the relation. The first partner is confronted with a gain frame, the second with a loss frame. This may cause the second partner to engage in more aggressive, risky behaviour, to maintain the relation, than the first partner, who may be more willing to forgo his profit and run less risk of a harmful separation procedure. The ending of relations is discussed in more detail in Chapter 5.

Earlier, the importance was noted of identification on the basis of shared categories concerning motives and conditions of behaviour. This is clearly related to the availability heuristic: behaviour that one can identify with is more 'available'. This affects both one's own trustworthiness, in the willingness to make sacrifices for others, and one's trust, in the tolerance of behaviour that deviates from expectations. One will more easily help someone when one can identify with his need. One can more easily forgive someone's breach of trust or reliance when one can identify with the lack of competence or the motive that caused it. One can more easily accept the blame for oneself. Since one can identify with him, one may sympathize with his action, seeing, perhaps, that his action was in fact a just response to one's own previous actions.

Another reason to attribute blame to oneself when someone else is in fact to blame is to reduce uncertainty or establish a sense of control. This works as follows. If it is perceived to be impossible or very difficult to influence someone's behaviour in order to prevent or redress damage from broken expectations, one may attribute blame to oneself. By doing that, one relieves the stress of feeling subjected to the power of others. For people with little self-confidence or a low self-image, this is a move of desperation, and self-blame fits with the preconception one had of oneself. For people with self-confidence, self-blame may yield a sense of control: if the cause lies with oneself, one can more easily deal with it. Of course, that may be an illusion, due to overconfidence in oneself.

15

Another mechanism is that of a belief in a just world, which gives reassurance. By enacting justice, even anonymously, one confirms its existence by contributing to it, and thereby maintains a sense of security. However, when the sacrifice for another would be too high to accept, in the view of self-interest, then to avoid a self-perception of callousness one may convince oneself that the other's hardship is his own fault.

Yet another psychological mechanism is that in violation of rational behaviour sunk costs, such as sacrifices made in a relationship, are not seen as bygones that should be ignored in an assessment of future costs and benefits. They are seen as sacrifices that would be seen as in vain if one pulled out after having incurred them. This yields what is known as 'non-rational escalation of commitment'. It is associated with cognitive dissonance: cutting one's losses and pulling out would entail an admission of failure, of having made a bad decision in the past. The phenomenon is confirmed in empirical research, which shows that when the decision is made by someone not involved in the initial decision, or when the threat of an admission of failure is removed, the rational decision to pull out is made. Again, one cannot say that this mechanism is always bad, because it also demonstrates perseverance in the face of setbacks, which can be a good thing, and is in fact a trait of many a successful innovating entrepreneur.

This phenomenon can also be connected with the effect of a loss frame versus a gain frame, proposed in prospect theory. The person, or group, that made the initial decision experiences a loss frame, with the inclination to accept further risk in order to prevent acceptance of the loss. The decision maker who enters fresh experiences a gain frame, to make a decision that will offer profit in the future, regardless of past sunk costs, and will be less inclined to accept the high risk of continuing losses from sticking to past decisions. The mechanism of non-rational escalation can contribute to the continuation of a relationship where it is not beneficial.

Organization

In a broad sense, the notion of organization could include natural forms, such as biological organisms or stellar systems. This book looks at organizations in the social sense, such as firms. The basic features of such organizations include a *structure* of *elements* (subsidiaries, divisions, teams, individual people) that have resources and *repertoires of action* (competences), with *decision rules* that govern *choice* from those repertoires, to achieve *goals*, in *co-ordination* (which includes governance) between those elements. Co-ordination is needed to the extent that elements are connected, i.e. their actions, in both their selection and performance, depend on each other. The position that an element has in a structure, i.e. its pattern of ties with other elements, constitutes its *role* in the organization (Nooteboom and Bogenrieder 2002).

Note that there may be different levels of repertoires, including those for the development of repertoires (learning). In organizations, many actions and decision rules or heuristics are routinized, and may have a large tacit component. In other words, they constitute organizational routines (Nelson and Winter 1982). The rationale of routinization was argued above. Decision rules may or may not be rationally designed, and they include the decision heuristics from social psychology that were discussed in a previous section. Goals also may be largely tacit.

Different elements in the organization may or may not know or understand some or all of each other's actions and repertoires, and may or may not agree on each others' goals. In other words, there may be differences in semantics and values, and some of those may even be irreconcilable. This touches upon the difficult issue of 'incommensurable paradigms', within organizations, and within the theory of organizations (Essers 2003), that has been on the agenda of the philosophy of science since the work of Thomas Kuhn. This issue will be briefly discussed in the 'advanced' section of this chapter (p. 26).

However that may be, it will be argued, later in the present section, that an organization requires a certain 'focus', of some shared views of the world, goals and ways of doing things, in order to function and survive as a collective. This focus may be wide, allowing much diversity, or narrow, depending on a variety of conditions. In other words, an organization puts limits, somewhere, to cognitive diversity.

There are a number of familiar arguments for the existence of organizations. A legal argument for organization derives from the need for a legal identity of a group of people working together, to regulate ownership of assets, conditions of employment, liability and accountability. In the literature on IORs, there are claims that boundaries of firms are blurring, in forms of organization 'between market and hierarchy'. This is correct in the sense that in IORs forms of governance extend across boundaries of the firm, in forms of semi-integration. In the legal sense, however, boundaries remain clear (Hodgson 2002). In other words, boundaries of organization as forms of co-ordination do indeed blur, but boundaries of organizations as legal entities do not. The legal perspective does not, however, specify what activities have to be combined in an organization, and why.

Economics has given a variety of arguments for integrating different activities in an organization. One is technical: when complementary activities are technically inseparable, they need to be integrated by definition. A second type of economic theory derives from the need to align incentives in complementary activities, in the face of possible problems of monitoring, due to asymmetric information. One branch of that theory is 'principal–agent' theory. It will not be used in this book, because it puts the analysis of collaboration on the wrong foot, with its assumption that there is a clear, independent principal

17

('boss') on one side, and a dependent agent on the other side, who is driven to satisfy the demands of the principal. In IORs, dependence and power are often not balanced, but nevertheless, in collaboration agents are to be seen as each others' principals and agents at the same time. One of the main obstacles in collaboration is that people tend to take a one-sided principal–agent view.[3]

Another branch of this type of economic theory is transaction cost economics. In spite of justified criticism of that theory, mainly of the fact that it neglects learning and innovation as well as the potential of trust, elements of the theory are still useful, as will be discussed later.

Informed more by sociology and social psychology, organization theory has focused on forms of mutual dependence in organizations (Thompson 1967), and on how to co-ordinate activities (Mintzberg 1983). Here, motivation goes beyond incentives as understood by economists. In particular, next to extrinsic motivation, it includes intrinsic motivation (Frey 2002). People may voluntarily align behaviour on the basis of shared norms, based on shared values obtained by socialization into organizational culture. In this branch of organization theory, arguments for integrating activities remain more implicit, or are taken for granted: when activities are connected, they need to be co-ordinated, and this is what organizations are for. Clearly, this view is related to the notion of 'inseparability' of activities, in economics, discussed above.

Next to these familiar notions of organization, the theory of knowledge set out above yields a relatively new, cognitive argument for organization. Recall that here cognition is meant in a broad sense, including emotion-laden value judgements. Since according to the interactionist, constructivist theory of knowledge mental categories have developed on the basis of interaction with others, in a string of contexts that make up experience, knowledge is path-dependent. There will be 'cognitive distance' (Nooteboom 1992, 1999a) between people with different experience, and cognitive similarity to the extent that people have interacted, in shared experience. Cognitive distance yields both a problem and an opportunity. The opportunity is that we learn from others only when they see and know things differently. The problem is, however, that owing to cognitive distance people may not understand each other, and have to invest in mutual understanding.

In view of this, organizations need to reduce cognitive distance, i.e. achieve a sufficient alignment of mental categories to understand each other, utilize complementary capabilities, achieve common goals and have trust. This yields the notion of organization as a 'focusing device' (Nooteboom 2000a). That notion is similar to the notions of organization as a 'sensemaking system' (Weick 1979, 1995), 'system of shared meaning' (Smircich 1983) or 'interpretation system' (Choo 1998).

In an organization, people need to achieve a common purpose, and for this they need some more or less tacit shared ways of seeing and interpreting the world. In view of incentive problems, in monitoring and controlling work, especially in contemporary organizations of more or less autonomous professionals, people in organizations also need to share more or less tacit values and norms, to align objectives, govern relational risk and to provide a basis for conflict resolution. As currently recognized also by economists, due to uncertainty concerning contingencies of collaboration, and limited opportunities for monitoring, ex-ante measures of governance are seldom complete, and need to be supplemented with ex-post adaptation. Organizational focus, provided by organizational culture, yields an epistemological and normative 'substrate' to achieve this, as a basis for shared processes of attribution, mutual adaptation and decision making. In other words, cognitive distance needs to be restricted for the sake of co-ordination. Organizational culture incorporates fundamental views and intuitions regarding the relation between the firm and its environment, attitude to risk, the nature of knowledge, the nature of man and of relations between people, which inform content and process of strategy, organizational structure, and styles of decision making and co-ordination (Schein 1985). One aspect of entrepreneurship, which links with Schumpeter's notion of the entrepreneur as a charismatic figure, is that it is his central task to achieve this: to align perceptions, understandings, goals and motives.

While transaction cost considerations contribute to decisions whether an activity should be integrated within a firm or be left outside, it is proposed here that the present cognitive considerations are more fundamental and more general. The argument from TCE is that problems of opportunism and hold-up can be better governed within than between firms, since under the generalized authority of an employment relationship one can demand more information, for monitoring, and impose decisions to resolve conflict, than one could between firms. However, also within firms monitoring can be problematic, and there can be strong principal–agent problems within organizations. This is especially the case since labour has become more professionalized and knowledge-based, whereby superiors can find it hard to assess performance even if information were readily provided. Some shared cognitive focus, including normative categories of behaviour, is needed to understand observed behaviour, to establish processes for resolution of conflict and to generate intrinsic motivation for compliance and collaboration.

Note that the notion of focus does not entail the need for people to agree on everything, or see everything the same way. Indeed, such lack of diversity would prevent both division of labour and innovation. However, there are some things they may have to agree on, and some views they need to share, on goals, values and ways of doing things.

Organizational focus needs to be tight, in the sense of allowing little ambiguity and variety of meanings and standards, if the productive system of a firm, or the focal part of the firm, is 'systemic', as opposed to 'stand-alone' (Langlois and

Robertson 1995). Here, 'systemic' is defined as follows: a complex division of labour, i.e. with many activities and a dense structure of relations between them, with tight constraints on their interfaces. An example is an oil refinery. In more stand-alone systems, elements of the system are connected with few other elements, and connections are loose, with limited constraints on interfaces, allowing autonomy of elements. An example is a consultancy firm. An intermediate system, between systematic and stand-alone, is a modular system. Here, there are also multiple, more or less densely connected elements, as in the systemic case, but the standards on interfaces allow flexibility, where different modules can be plugged into the system.

Focus arises on different levels of an organization: in the organization overall, and in more specialized forms within the organization, in 'communities' (Brown and Duguid 1996). As we go 'down' to more specialized subunits in the organization, the focus is sharper, and cognitive distance is less. However, even at the lowest level people will not have identical perceptions, interpretations and value judgements.

Institutions

Some scholars (e.g. Williamson) maintain that organizations are institutions, while others (e.g. North 1990) maintain that organizations are players in a field of institutions. North and Thomas (1973) proposed a distinction between the 'institutional environment' and the 'institutional arrangements' of organizations within it. In institutional economics, notably in the work of North (1990), a distinction is made between formal and informal institutions. In more recent work (e.g. the work of North) institutions are seen to have not only a regulative (constraining, enabling) but also a cognitive aspect. To deal with the cognitive aspect in general, and with the relation between regulative and cognitive institutions in particular, a theory of knowledge is needed, as presented above.

Nooteboom (2000a) tried to resolve the definitional issue by giving not an ontological definition of institutions, in a universally applicable list of institutional entities, but a functional one, on the basis of what institutions do. In any specific context, this may then generate a list of context-specific institutional entities. The definition is as follows. Institutions both constrain and enable action, they are the (cumulative) result of earlier actions, they are relatively stable, compared with the actions they enable, and they are more or less binding, i.e. it is difficult to dodge or violate them without losing legitimation and acceptance. Note that institutions can be more or less tight and constraining.

This characterization is sufficiently sharp to discriminate and sufficiently flexible to allow for a multitude of institutions, on different levels. Within the wider institutional environment organizations constitute more specialized institutional arrangements, and develop their own specialized semiotic niches: cognitive frames, language, symbols, metaphors, myths and rituals, in an organization-specific focus. This is what we call organizational culture. Organizational culture differs between organizations to the extent that they have accumulated different experiences, in different industries, technologies and markets. An organization is also itself an institution regarding the actions within the firm. Within the firm, a team or 'community of practice' (Brown and Duguid 1996) is subject to organizational institutions and is itself an institution for the workers in the team.

On different levels, institutions apply to different ranges of action. For national institutions it is the country, for industry institutions the industry (which increasingly crosses national boundaries), for organizational institutions it is the actions within it. Those ranges overlap. For example, a firm is faced with both national and industry institutions. An important point now is that the larger the range of an institution the more it will be subject to conservatism or 'inertia'. When a local practice requires a change of an institution, that will have more repercussions to the extent that change would affect other activities, and force them to adapt to institutional change. Thus, higher-level institutions will change more slowly than lower-level ones. Such rational resistance to change yields an incentive to disintegrate, uncouple or unbundle systems, to yield more allowance for local variety, with different foci and corresponding institutional arrangements. That yields another argument why economic systems need to be cut up into different organizations.

Complementary cognition

Diversity is a crucial condition for learning and innovation, to produce 'novel combinations', as argued by Joseph Schumpeter, and demonstrated in evolutionary economics (Nelson and Winter 1982). Diversity is associated with the number of agents (people, firms) with different knowledge and/or skills, who are involved in a process of learning or innovation by interaction. However, next to the number of agents involved, a second dimension of diversity is the degree to which their knowledge or skills are different. This connects with the notion of 'cognitive distance'.

As a result of the need to achieve organizational focus, discussed above, there is a risk of myopia: relevant threats and opportunities to the firm are not perceived. To compensate for this, people, and firms, need complementary sources of outside intelligence, to utilize 'external economy of cognitive scope' (Nooteboom 1992). Next to the familiar goals of inter-organizational relations, to be discussed in Chapter 2, this yields a novel perspective.

The different foci of firms entail cognitive distance between firms. In processes of learning and innovation, in interaction between firms, this yields both an opportunity and a problem. The opportunity lies in diversity: the novelty value

21

of a relation increases with cognitive distance. However, mutual understanding decreases with cognitive distance. A trade-off arises between cognitive distance, for the sake of novelty, and cognitive proximity, for the sake of understanding and utilization of complementary knowledge. The merit of novelty increases but the comprehensibility decreases with cognitive distance. Absorptive capacity is the ability to 'cross' cognitive distance. The difference between there being distance and crossing it is related to the difference between empathy and identification (Lewicki and Bunker 1996). Absorptive capacity entails the ability to empathize, i.e. the generalized, non-relation-specific ability to access the thinking of others without thinking alike. Or more loosely: to speak their language next to one's own. Identification entails a relation-specific commonality of thought, with shared mental categories. Or in other words: a shared language. Identification arises, and cognitive distance is reduced, to the extent that agents have engaged in continued interaction (McAllister 1995; Lewicki and Bunker 1996). In other words, their foci start to overlap, in a shared epistemological and normative framework. This reduces the novelty value of a partner's cognition.

Note that in view of the problem of possible incommensurability of cognitive perspectives ('paradigms'), it may not always be possible to cross cognitive distance, no matter how much effort is put in trying to develop mutual absorptive capacity.

Tacit knowledge, absorptive capacity and firm size

It is well recognized that there is an obstacle in knowledge transfer when the knowledge to be transferred is wholly or partly tacit. Tacit knowledge hinders clear expression by the source of knowledge. A problem that is not well recognized in the literature is that there is also a problem when the knowledge that is to be replaced is tacit. Tacit knowledge reduces absorptive capacity for the receiver. As discussed before, it is especially background knowledge, or cognitive categories, that tend to be tacit. The deeper or more fundamental categories are, the more tacit they are. One's own tacit knowledge is taken for granted, as self-evident, and is difficult to replace by new knowledge on the basis of rational argument. For rational criticism knowledge must first be made explicit, externalized by intellectual midwifery or *maieutics*. This entails such questioning and answering that the person holding the knowledge becomes aware of it and is able to externalize it to a sufficient extent that it can become susceptible to rational criticism (Nooteboom 1993b). Socrates was a master at it, as exhibited in Plato's dialogues.

In smaller organizations knowledge tends to be more tacit than in large ones. The reason is that co-ordination of work in small 'simple structures' (Mintzberg 1983) can be based on direct supervision, with the entrepreneur taking part in the primary processes of production, on the workshop floor, transferring tacit knowledge by personal interaction. This makes formal, codified forms of co-ordination unnecessary (such as specification of work processes, in- and outputs or skills; cf. Mintzberg 1983). This yields the potential of flexibility as a strength of small firms. It also has disadvantages. First, when knowledge is tacit, and embodied in individual people or firms, and has never been codified, it gets lost when the carriers of knowledge are lost, due to accident, poaching or other personnel turnover. Second, tacit knowledge reduces absorptive capacity, as argued above.

Knowledge transfer to small firms

In the 1980s an advisory committee on technology policy of the Dutch Ministry of Economic Affairs noted that innovation yields prosperity only if it is diffused widely, and that small firms, which constitute the majority of firms, and some 60 per cent of total employment in the market sector, were lagging behind in the adoption of new technology. To remedy this, the committee advised the ministry to institute a regional network of what were then called the 'Innovation Centres' (now they are called 'Syntens'), for the transfer of technology to small firms, and this advice was implemented. One source of inspiration for the centres was experience in Germany with the Fraunhofer Institute. Part of the idea was that the centres should be regionally embedded, in order to reach small firms. These institutes ran into problems of technology transfer. The preceding analysis and the following discussion are informed by experience with this.

If tacit knowledge forms an obstacle to the absorption of novelty, what can be done? It was noted above that there are two problems. One problem was that tacit knowledge is self-evident and therefore not subject to critical reflection and debate. For that, tacit knowledge first has to be externalized by means of intellectual midwifery or *maieutics*. How is this to be done? A knowledgeable outsider is not credible for the very reason that he is subjecting to doubt what to the insider is evident, and thereby he supplies nothing but perceived evidence of his incompetence. An approach that has proved successful in practice is the following. The key insight for it is that only challenge from insiders, i.e. colleagues, is relevant, and only evidence from them is credible. The way to do it is to arrange a round-table discussion between colleagues, preferably including a few who have already adopted the innovation in question, and act as facilitator for them to exchange experience and thereby externalize, at least to some extent, their tacit knowledge. The trick is not to participate in the debate but to facilitate it. Above all: like Socrates, don't tell other people what to think, but elicit thought that will reveal its own error. For this debate to occur, the participants should be sufficiently different not to be direct competitors, and to yield interesting new insights, while they should be sufficiently close to make sense to each other. In other words, their cognitive distance should be just right.

23

Another problem was that for lack of codification tacit knowledge could be transferred only by comparatively lengthy, direct, on-line, real-time interaction, with demonstration, trial, error and correction. A remedy then is to transfer knowledge embodied in a worker, who then carries it into the firm while practising it, and transfers it on the basis of the ongoing interaction needed. Note that at the same time this also solves the previous problem of limited openness to rational criticism. New knowledge is assimilated in practice rather than adopted by design. This solution has been applied in the Netherlands, in a programme called 'Knowledge bearers in small and medium-sized business' (KIM). The scheme worked as follows. Graduates, mainly from polytechnics, could volunteer for the programme, and then followed a crash course on the peculiarities of small firms. Entrepreneurs could volunteer, and would receive a subsidy of part of the wage costs for a trial period, provided there was a prospect of permanent employment of the graduate after the trial period. The regional Innovation Centre counselled the project. A trial project was deemed a success, and the scheme was implemented nationally. A secondary purpose of the programme had been to stimulate employment of graduates, among whom there was substantial unemployment at the time the programme was started. However, the programme has been maintained for its success after employment increased. Apparently, a similar scheme is now under consideration in Denmark.

Governance

Governance is the management, or literally the 'steering' (the original meaning of the word in classical Greek) of behaviour. It entails the enabling, guiding and constraining of behaviour. This does not necessarily entail that there is a leader in charge. Governance can occur in mutual adjustment. In corporate governance, it entails the steering of behaviour of corporate management in order to satisfy demands of organizational stakeholders. In IORs, governance is aimed to realize the potential of relations. In particular, it is aimed to control relational risk.

The goals of IORs, to be discussed in Chapter 2, represent the positive side of collaboration, but there is also a down side, in risks that it may entail. There are four forms of such risk:

1 loss of resources;
2 hold-up risk;
3 spill-over risk;
4 psychological/social risk.

By outsourcing one may surrender the ability to assess the value of the offering of suppliers (Beije 1998). Another problem is that one may drop a resource that later turns out to be crucial in order to utilize or replace elements of core competence. Teece (1986) proposed that the appropriation of returns on core competences might require access to 'complementary assets'. Even if those are not part of core competence, they may have to be integrated in the firm. One may therefore have to see such complementary assets as attached to core competence. Recall the example, given above, of Philips. In fact, some people argue that because of these problems outsourcing does not increase flexibility, as is often argued, but decreases it (Bettis *et al.* 1992; Mol 2001).

However, there are ways to mitigate these problems. One is to make use of a benchmarking service, so that one can compare a supplier's offering with best practice. A second is to maintain sufficient R&D in the outsourced activity to maintain 'absorptive capacity', i.e. the ability to judge developments in the field. This may also help to retain the option of re-entry later, to retain options for future core competences, perhaps as a second mover, but still fast enough to be a serious player. This is reflected in empirical evidence that firms retain an R&D capability in activities that were outsourced (Granstrand *et al.* 1997). However, such R&D can perhaps be done in collaboration with others, in an R&D consortium. One may also try to retain the required openings in distribution channels by means of alliances. In other words, outside collaboration may also be used to retain options for the utilization or modification of core competences. Here, the flexibility of outside collaboration returns: one may use it to maintain more flexibility also in options for future core competence.

As defined in TCE, the problem of hold-up results from dependence, in the form of switching costs: one incurs a loss if the relationship breaks. Part of that is the loss of relation-specific investments, and the need for new ones in another relationship. As also argued by TCE, one may lose a hostage. There are also opportunity costs: the loss of the value that the current partner offers relative to the next best alternative. This depends on the availability of alternative partners, or the possibility of conducting an activity oneself, and the extent that the partner offers something unique. In other words, it depends on the extent that a partner has a monopoly in his offering, or monopsony in his access to markets. The partner may achieve this by engaging in specific investments, to establish a unique offer. The 'hold-up' risk is that the partner may opportunistically use asymmetric dependence to demand a higher share of jointly produced added value, under the threat of exiting from the relationship.

A refinement is needed. Specificity of products does not necessarily entail specificity of the assets needed to produce them (Nooteboom 1993a). If production technology is flexible, one can produce specific, differentiated products with generic assets. This is important, because one of the effects of ICT is that a number of processes in design, production and marketing have become more flexible, thereby reducing the problem of specific investments. For example, in production one can change the program in a computer-numerically-controlled

(CNC) machine relatively easily, to craft different shapes and functions. Virtual specification and testing of prototypes yields much more flexibility and speed of development than real, physical prototyping and testing.

Spill-over yields another kind of risk. It entails that knowledge that constitutes competitive advantage, as part of core competence, reaches competitors *and* is used by them for imitation. Note the addition that the knowledge is appropriated by competition. Sometimes the term 'spill-over' is used only to indicate that knowledge has spread, regardless of the implications for competition. Note also that spill-over risk is not the same as the loss of a resource, mentioned before. Under spill-over one still has the knowledge, but it is no longer exclusive. Spill-over risk may be direct, in the partner becoming a competitor, or indirect, in a network, with knowledge spilling over to a competitor via a partner. Spill-over risk is closely related to the notion of 'free riding'. This entails that in collaboration one benefits from partners without (fully) contributing to collaboration. In knowledge exchange this entails that one gets knowledge but contributes little. That problem is limited if one needs to contribute to joint knowledge development in order to build up the absorptive capacity needed to understand and utilize the information contributed by others.

A fourth type of risk is psychological (Edmonson 1999) and social, and entails a risk of legitimation. It applies especially in personal relations, but may also apply in IORs, if only because those are mediated by individuals. In knowledge sharing, one may also expose one's lack of knowledge, which may detract from self-image, social legitimation and reputation. The latter may destroy options for future relations.

ADVANCED

This section adds some depth of analysis. It elaborates on the notion of cognitive distance, with a simple mathematical formalization, and discusses some preliminary empirical tests. It gives some evolutionary considerations of psychology and institutions. It summarizes a fundamental methodological view of interactionism, to replace both the methodological individualism of economics and the methodological collectivism of (some) sociology. Finally, it gives a brief discussion of the issues of 'incommensurable paradigms', since that has implications for absorptive capacity and the ability to cross cognitive distance.

Cognitive distance

This section deepens the analysis of cognitive distance, and provides a mathematical model. Here, the problem of incommensurability is not taken into account. That is discussed in a separate section.

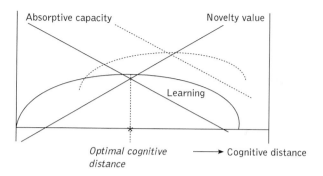

Figure 1.1 *Optimal cognitive distance*

If effectiveness of learning by interaction is the mathematical product of novelty value and understandability, the result is an inverse U-shaped relation with cognitive distance. Optimal cognitive distance lies at the maximum of the curve. This is illustrated in Figure 1.1.

In Figure 1.1 the downward-sloping line represents absorptive capacity (Cohen and Levinthal 1990): the ability to understand others at different levels of cognitive distance, i.e. to 'cross' cognitive distance. The generalized ability to communicate with agents who perceive and think differently can be raised, in an upward shift of absorptive capacity, which increases optimal cognitive distance and raises the optimal level of learning efficiency, as illustrated with the dotted lines in Figure 1.1. Absorptive capacity can be raised in several ways. When the knowledge involved is highly codified, it may be raised by maintaining R&D in areas outside the focus of the firm. When knowledge is more tacit, the hypothesis is that absorptive capacity is raised by cumulative experience in communicating and interacting with agents who think differently.

As a relation proceeds in time, with long, frequent and intensive interaction, cognitive distance may decrease, as a result of identification, with a reduction of the performance of learning below the optimum. This applies in particular if the relation is exclusive, i.e. a partner is barred from interaction with third parties, in some specific field of activity. That limits his access to new knowledge and experience, which detracts from his value as a source of learning. This yields a derived hypothesis: in ongoing, frequent and exclusive relations, cognitive distance decreases and innovative performance declines.

Empirical tests

The hypothesis concerning 'external economy of cognitive scope' entails that greater uncertainty in an industry, in terms of the volatility of technology and markets, yields a greater need to engage in outside relations with other organizations, to correct for the myopia of organizational focus. Thus, the hypothesis entails that in such industries there will be more outside relations, in inter-firm alliances for innovation and technical development. This is contrary to the hypothesis from transaction cost economics that in the presence of transaction-specific investments increased uncertainty yields an incentive to integrate activities under a single 'hierarchy' (Williamson 1975, 1985). The argument from TCE is that the dependence resulting from specific investments yields a risk of hold-up, which is difficult to control between firms under conditions of uncertainty concerning contingencies of contract execution, and easier to control under conditions of managerial fiat, in a hierarchy, which yields more scope for demanding information for monitoring, and for resolving conflicts of hold-up. That argument is not denied here. However, from the theory of knowledge set out above, there may be an overriding argument in favour of outside relations, for the sake of external economy of cognitive scope. The problem of hold-up that may arise from specific investments then has to be resolved by relational governance, which reconnects our theory with TCE. The hypothesis of an increased need of alliances under conditions of volatility has been confirmed by Colombo and Garrone (1998). They found that in technologically volatile industries, as measured by patent intensity, the likelihood of alliances is higher than in the absence of such volatility.

Concerning cognitive distance, most scholars expect an effect only in one direction: the success of collaboration increases with similarity between partners (see e.g. Fey and Beamish 2001 for a study of organizational climate similarity). Few studies test for the hypothesis of a curvilinear effect, where innovative success in particular first increases and then decreases with similarity or cognitive proximity. A direct test of the hypothesis of optimal cognitive distance requires a measure of cognitive distance and of learning or innovative performance. One way to measure cognitive distance is to calculate the distance between two points in an n-dimensional space spanned by characteristics of knowledge and technical ability derived from patent information (Jaffe 1986; Los 1999). The outcome of learning can be measured as the number of radical innovations that arise from collaboration.

Wuyts *et al.* (2003) conducted several indirect tests. In a first test, they employed data on relations between pharmaceutical companies and biotech companies. These included a measure of radical innovation output in the form of the number of 'FDA priority drugs', which yield substantial improvement in therapeutic performance over previous drugs in the same therapeutic class. The data did not, however, include a direct measure of cognitive distance. They did yield a measure related to the duration of ongoing collaboration. Combined with the subsidiary hypothesis, indicated above, that such ongoing collaboration reduces cognitive distance, the derived hypothesis could be tested that innovative performance has an inverse U-shaped relation with the duration of collaboration. This hypothesis was confirmed. A second test was performed on data on alliances in ICT-related industries. Those data offered several measures of cognitive distance. One was based on patent characteristics, as suggested above. However, there was no measure of relation-specific innovative performance. With the subsidiary hypothesis that firms enter into collaborative relations in order to maximize innovative output, the derived hypothesis could be tested that the likelihood of an alliance has an inverse U-shaped relation with cognitive distance. This hypothesis makes a strong assumption of insight in cognitive distance and its effect, so that firms are able to select partners at, or close to, optimal distance. For this to be consistent with the earlier hypothesis, it also implies that when cognitive distance is reduced below the optimal level, firms break relations and seek new partners. These conditions may be strong, which raises doubts about the likelihood of the hypothesis being confirmed. Nevertheless the hypothesis was confirmed for some measures of cognitive distance (related to differences in organization).

Evolutionary psychology

In the discussion of decision heuristics, taken from social psychology, it was suggested that they are based, at least in part, on mental processes, or predilections, inherited from evolution. That idea is further explored in this section.

In the section on theory of knowledge (p. 11) it was proposed that cognitive or mental categories develop in interaction with the physical and social environment. That does not necessarily entail that it applies to all mental categories or processes, and that at birth the mind is a *tabula rasa*, without any innate mental structures. Evolutionary psychologists claim that certain psychological features or mechanisms are 'in our genes' as a result of evolution (Barkow *et al.* 1992). They emerged as features that gave selective or reproductive advantage, over the millions of years that the human species evolved in hunter-gatherer societies. These form a shared heritage, in the form of common basic psychological and cognitive mechanisms. These are plausible to the extent that they were conducive to survival and procreation in ancient times. For example, survival required the basic ability to identify objects and movement, to categorize natural kinds (plants, animals), distinguish the animate from the inanimate, natural kinds from artefacts (Tooby and Cosmides 1992: 71). On top of that it requires the ability to recognize objects, judge speed and distance, to avoid predators and to catch prey (Tooby and Cosmides 1992: 110). Survival also requires mother–infant emotion communication signals (Tooby and Cosmides 1992: 39).

Of importance for the later discussion of trust is the claim that survival in hunter-gatherer societies was also furthered by sociality. The variance of yields, in gathering edible plants, roots, nuts, etc., and even more in hunting, together with problems of durable storage, entails an evolutionary advantage in the willingness to surrender part of one's yield to others in need, in the expectation of receiving from them when they are successful (Cosmides and Tooby 1992: 212). This is enhanced by the ability to assess such willingness among others, in 'cheater detection mechanism', and to signal a credible threat to sanction lack of reciprocity. As explained by Frank (1988), an emotionally based commitment to retaliation or revenge, and the ability to signal this, would help to make such threats credible when revenge would carry a cost disproportional to its economic gain and would hence be implausible on the basis of rational choice. It also entails an ability to 'read' facial expressions of emotion (Tooby and Cosmides 1992: 70), and to attribute, with some validity, motives to people on the basis of observed behaviour and verbal and other expression. All this may yield an evolutionary basis for social reciprocity and trust. Of course, if this evolutionary argument is true, we also have to take the bad with the good, including the adverse effects of a drive towards emotion-laden retaliation or revenge.

However, less basic, 'higher-level' cognitive categories of perception, interpretation and evaluation have to be geared to a world that is unrecognizably different from ancient hunter-gatherer societies. This requires a plasticity in the formation of cognitive structures, tacked on to deeper-level ones derived from evolution, that are apt for the world one is in. In fact, this is based on an evolutionary argument as well: without such plasticity we would not have been able to evolve as we have. In other words, while underlying cognitive abilities, urges and inclinations may be instinctive, inherited from a shared evolution, the superstructure of cognitive categories is developed in interaction with one's current, more individual environment.

The inference of evolutionary causes from existing characteristics, in the 'functionalist' argument that since the characteristics exist they have survived evolution and therefore must have contributed to it, is a dangerous one. Survival depends on complex interaction effects of inherited characteristics, and the manifestation of them depends on the context. Furthermore, not all characteristics that survive are necessarily conducive to survival. They may be neutral to it, neither contributing nor detracting from 'fitness'.

On the other hand, it is plausible that some mental features result from evolution. If it is accepted that mind and body are intertwined, as claimed in the section on knowledge, then why should it be plausible that bodily features result from evolution, and not that mental features may do so?

The section on decision heuristics discussed, among other things, that people judge and decide differently in loss frames than in gain frames. With all the caution needed for evolutionary inference, indicated above, it is tempting to speculate whether this may have had an adaptive rationale. Could that be that it reduces defection and thereby stabilizes relationships, as discussed?[4]

Institutions and evolution

Institutions form both the basis and the result of processes of interaction. The underlying intuition derives from the notion of structuration (Giddens 1984; Archer 1995), according to which structure enables (and constrains) action, and action (re)constructs structure.

From an evolutionary perspective, the institutional environment is often seen as a selection environment, with activities of firms (such as routines, as suggested by Nelson and Winter 1982) as the units of selection. In the dominant approach taken in the literature on learning and innovation, the institutional environment is often considered as exogenous; it is assumed that institutions determine the learning and innovation patterns in an industry (Pavitt 1984; Dosi et al. 1988; Nelson 1993; Whitley 1999). These studies strongly focus on how selection processes take place, and neglect the generation of variety and the reciprocal causation, often called 'co-evolution', between the institutional environment and the units of selection. In terms of the structure/agency issue in sociology, the question here is how the process of structuration works: how structure affects action and how action feeds back into structure.

A question is how we can causally connect 'macro' institutions, in national systems, with the 'micro' level of organizations, and, within organizations, how we can connect organizational institutions with the 'micro-micro' level of the people in it. That goes beyond the purpose of the present book.

Methodological interactionism

This section is of interest only for readers interested in methodology, in the sense of philosophy of science. It discusses methodological issues that result from the interactionist, constructivist theory of knowledge discussed above. Parts of this text are taken from Nooteboom (2000a), and a more detailed discussion can be found there.

The theory of knowledge set out above yields an intermediate methodological position between the 'methodological individualism' of economics and the 'methodological collectivism' of (some) sociology. In other words, it avoids both under- and over-socialization (Etzioni 1988). People preserve their individuality in the construction of their more or less idiosyncratic cognition, including its emotional content, in interaction with their environment, in their individual life histories. This is, however, a social process, since cognition is constructed in interaction with others, who share few or many social, cultural conditions.

According to this theory of knowledge, cognitive construction builds on our bodily and neural make-up, as developed in biological evolution. Cognition is rooted in the body (Merleau-Ponty 1964; Lakoff and Johnson 1999). Neural structures develop tentatively, and to some extent randomly, and are selected and reinforced on the basis of success in the physical and social environment (Edelman 1987, 1992). This connects with the pragmatic (or 'pragmaticist') view of knowledge (Peirce 1957) that truth and meaning are based on what works, rather than on untestable claims of coherence with objective reality. It also links with Wittgenstein's (1976) idea that meaning and correct reference are based on viable use, reflected in 'rules of the game'.

This epistemological view underpins the competence view of the firm, discussed above: it is because of such idiosyncrasy and path-dependence of thought that the competences of firms cannot immediately be copied and firms can enjoy a temporary, partial monopoly. It also underpins the notion of absorptive capacity (Cohen and Levinthal 1990): people, and firms, can understand only what fits into their idiosyncratic, path-dependent mental categories.

A difficult methodological question now arises. Doesn't a social constructivist theory of knowledge inevitably lead to relativism, in which any theory is as good as any other, and the surrender of any debate in terms of 'truth'? The answer is that it does yield a brand of relativism. But it is not the radical relativism of most postmodernism. Since cognition is constructed in interaction with the world it is not arbitrary, and is constrained and enabled by reality, at least as a material cause. In that sense it 'embodies' reality (Lakoff and Johnson 1999). Lakoff and Johnson argued that since our cognitive construction is rooted in the body, and people share bodily processes as an inheritance from evolution, their cognitive processes and constructions are bound to be similar to some extent. This is reflected in the fact that basic metaphors in thought are shared across widely different cultures. Another argument is that the physical environment, which is part of the environment in interaction with which we construct cognition, is also shared and subject to universal laws of nature. However, that does not detract from the fact that categories are constructed and that we are unable to descend from our mind to inspect how our ideas are hooked on to the world. Constructed categories enable but at the same time constrain cognition. 'Higher-level' cognitive constructs are built largely on social interaction, and the environment for that varies greatly with differences in culture. Thus, within constraints there is variety of cognition. Note that it is precisely because we cannot climb down from our minds to see how our knowledge is hooked on to the world, and because other people perceive and interpret the world differently, that we must listen to other people in search of truth, or the best approximation to it that we can achieve. Short of the long-term selection effects that reflect reality, at any point in time other people are the only source we have for finding out about our prejudices and errors. Critical debate is more important than ever.

How, then, can critical debate proceed? Karl Popper made his falsificationist methodology consistent with the fact that, as he granted, observation statements that form the basis for falsification are 'theory-laden'. To the extent that we can agree about observation statements, in spite of differences in theoretical view, we can agree about the falsifiers, so that the procedure of falsification can work. Popper underplayed the possibility that differences in theoretical perspective are so fundamental that no such agreement about 'the facts' can be reached, and that different perspectives or 'paradigms' may be 'incommensurable', as Thomas Kuhn (1970) called it. Popper claimed that we can 'at any time' step out of the prison of our categories. Consider the following quotation (Popper 1976: 56):

> I do admit that at any moment we are prisoners caught in the framework of our theories; our expectations; our language. But we are prisoners in a Pickwickian sense: if we try, we can break out of our framework at any time. Admittedly, we shall find ourselves again in a framework, but it will be a better and roomier one; and we can at any moment break out of it again.

This seems too optimistic. We cannot in that way pull ourselves out of the swamp by our own hair, like Baron Münchausen. Incommensurability still is an issue.

Incommensurability

As argued by Essers (2003), incommensurability has two dimensions: semantic (incommensurability of meaning) and 'axiological' (incommensurability of goals and underlying values). The latter, he argued, is the most serious. From the perspective of different theoretical frameworks ('paradigms'), terms that sound the same may have different meanings, in the sense of both extension or reference (the set of entities a term refers to), and intension or sense (how entities are identified as members of a set).[5] In that sense, different theories may speak different languages. However, even if one cannot fully translate one language into another, it is possible that people understand each other because they are familiar with both languages. This book, for example, attempts to speak economics, sociology and management. However, differences in goals and values are more difficult to resolve.

For example, economists typically analyse equilibria, while management scholars mostly analyse processes. For many economists the clarity, parsimony and rigour of mathematical formalization are elementary for their scientific values, while many organization scholars find that such aims are not adequate for the richness, variability and ambiguity of organizational phenomena. Underlying this difference is a basic difference of methodology, in the sense of philosophy of science. Economists do not claim realism for their theories, in any sense, and may indeed reject the very notion of realistic theory, while organization theorists often do claim realism, in some sense.

33

This gap is very difficult to bridge. Incidentally, the present book aims at a realistic account of organizations and their processes, and accepts ambiguities of meaning in both organizations and theories about them. Yet, when formalization is feasible without violating that aim, that opportunity will be taken.

The methodological gap between (most) economists and (most) organization scholars is a fundamental one. The seventeenth-century French philosopher/mathematician Blaise Pascal (1670) recognized it as the duality of the *esprit de géométrie* and *esprit de finesse*. *Géometrie* is described as difficult in its move of abstraction, turning one's regard away from the complex world as we see it, but easy once that has been done, in the analytical grip it affords in an inexorable march of logic. *Finesse* is characterized as easy, because one does not have to turn away from the world as we see it, but then it is difficult to reason without error in the face of all that nuance and complexity. And indeed, economists and management scholars mutually accuse each other of taking too easy a route. They are both correct, but mean different things. Pascal concluded that we need both *géometrie* and *finesse*. We cannot integrate them, but we can move to and fro between them.

Traditionally, people have felt uncomfortable with incommensurability, feeling that differences of insight can always be rationally resolved by empirical or logical argument. In their view, lack of reconciliation demonstrates lack of rationality. Kuhn claimed that a conflict between two perspectives could be *rationally* undecidable: from their different perspectives both have good arguments. This clearly complicates debate, but that does not mean it is bad. Incommensurability seems to be inevitable for radical innovation. Different theoretical perspectives disagree not only on the content of theory, but also on whether incommensurability is a problem or not. As analysed by Essers (2003), in organization theory this leads to a stand-off between integrationists, who claim that conflicts can be resolved in an integrative framework, and isolationists, who claim that such integration will squash heterodox views, which legitimates their isolation from prevailing doctrine. The author of this book grants that such isolation can be legitimate, and is indeed often needed to generate radical innovation (Nooteboom 2000a).

However, the problem of incommensurability, though present in principle, and often in fact, can be exaggerated. While there may be, and often is, incommensurability of some perspectives, it does not necessarily extend to all views people may have, and does not by definition exclude all collaboration. There may be areas of mutual understanding and shared goals left. By working together, people may increase their mutual understanding and agreement. Not just in spite of the constructivist view, but indeed following from it, people will agree on the facts to the extent that they have constructed their categories in a common physical and cultural environment. Thus a theory can be deemed realistic in the sense that it takes into account the facts as people construct them inter-subjectively. As Popper indicated, this does not give us any 'rock bottom' foundation, since we may be individually and collectively mistaken in our facts, but they are generally more stable and more reliable than theoretical hypotheses.

In sum, reconciliation and escape from mental prisons may not always be feasible, as Popper suggested, but it need not always fail either, as some interpretations of Kuhn suggest.

However that may be, the problem of incommensurability does limit ability to cross cognitive distance. It was said earlier that such crossing may require investment in mutual understanding, and that such investment may be relation-specific. Here, it is necessary to add that the investment may not be available, or may fail.

Chapter 2

Goals

- Goals
  - Efficiency
  - Competence
  - Positioning
  - Performance
- Concepts and theory
  - Economies of scale and scope
  - Economies of time
  - Innovation
  - Learning, exploration and exploitation
  - Communities of practice
  - Internationalization
- Advanced
  - Threshold costs
  - Cycle of discovery
  - Learning by internationalization

SUMMARY

This chapter specifies and discusses the possible goals of inter-firm collaboration. They are grouped in three categories: static efficiency in the exploitation of resources (e.g. economies of scale, scope and time), development of new competences (especially learning) and 'positioning' in markets (especially entry into new markets). Subsequently, it discusses the notions and theory involved: of scale, scope and time, innovation, organizational learning, the notion of 'communities of practice' and internationalization of firms. The notion of economy of scale, for example, entails a variety of different forms. The advanced section further discusses one of the lesser-known forms of scale, due to 'threshold costs', which are important especially in different kinds of service industries. Next, it summarizes a 'theory of discovery', in which exploration and exploitation build on each other. This gives a further perspective, for example, on entrepreneurial 'spin-offs' from firms. It also gives a perspective on the internationalization process of firms as a process of learning.

GOALS

The literature offers a variety of goals of IORs (e.g. Killing 1983; Anderson and Gatignon 1986; Porter and Fuller 1986; Contractor and Lorange 1988; Hennart 1988; Jarillo 1988; Ohmae 1989; Lamming 1993; Faulkner 1995; Doz and Hamel 1998; Child and Faulkner 1999; Nooteboom 1999a). Table 2.1 gives a survey. The goals are grouped into considerations of efficiency, competence and 'positional advantage' (Stoelhorst 1997). The three types of goals are briefly discussed. Note that the identification of possible goals does not necessarily imply that they are always chosen rationally. Not all goals may be feasible, their choice may be constrained, or indeed imposed by conditions, actors may not be aware of all possible goals, goals may arise as experience accrues, and goals may be reached unintentionally.

Efficiency is mainly aimed at exploitation, i.e. the efficient utilization of existing assets and competences. Competence is mainly aimed at exploration, i.e. learning, innovation and the development of new competences. Positional advantage may be aimed at both exploitation and exploration. Where it is aimed at entry into new markets, exploitation in novel conditions may lead to exploration (Nooteboom 2000a).

Goals are linked with the aspect of networks. Most goals allow for more than two participants, or even imply multiple participants by definition. This applies, in particular, to joint support systems (E2), risk spreading (E4), combination of products (E5), externalities of location (C3), cartels (P8) and blocking entry or exit (P9). Different forms for such network collaboration are discussed in Chapter 3. The development of networks, for exploration and exploitation, is discussed in Chapter 5.

Efficiency

Economics recognizes two forms of static efficiency, i.e. efficiency at a given state of technology and demand: *allocative* efficiency, in the use of scarce resources for matching demand and supply in different markets, and *productive* efficiency, in the use of economies of scale, scope and time. This book does not go into considerations of overall welfare of economic systems, and therefore does not consider allocative efficiency. It does look at productive efficiency. Economics also recognizes *dynamic* or innovative efficiency. Here, that is included in the second category, in Table 2.1, in the creation of new competences.

Economies of scale yield lower costs per unit of production at a larger volume of production (more of the same) per unit of time. Note that here

37

Table 2.1 Goals of collaboration

Efficiency

E1   Economies of scale, scope

E2   Joint support systems

E3   Capacity utilization, economies of time

E4   Spread risk

E5   Combine or swap products

E6   Utilize unequal prices for products and inputs

E7   Transport costs

Competences

C1   Complementary competences, skill substitution

C2   Learning by interaction

C3   Externalities of location

C4   Flexibility of configuration

Positioning

Political conditions:

P1   Satisfy demands from local government on local content, repatriation of profits, use of expatriates

Market access:

P2   Fast access to new markets of products and inputs

P3   Adjustment of products, technology or inputs to local market conditions

P4   Follow the customer

P5   Establish a standard in the market

Competition:

P6   Attack a competitor in his home market

P7   Block a competitor's access to resources

P8   Establish a cartel

P9   Blocking entry or exit

---

capacity is variable. It is not to be confused with the effect of improved utilization of a given capacity. Economies of scope yield lower costs per unit when different, complementary activities are combined, in the joint utilization or production of resources (E1). Further details on economies of scale, scope and time are given in the section on concepts and theories (p. 46).

Note that economy of scale may yield an argument for both integration of activities in an organization, and dis-integration by outsourcing. The first applies to core activities in which the organization is specialized, according to core competences. The second applies to activities one chooses to outsource to outside, specialized producers. Thus, one would in general expect vertical disintegration and horizontal integration.

A classic example of scope is the combination of diverse products from different producers in one distribution channel (e.g. a grocery shop). The combined package of products exerts a pull on a wider area of customers, yielding larger sales and better utilization of labour and shop capacity. Here, economy of scope has led to the development of retailing as an independent link in the supply chain. In other cases, firms may pool products to better utilize the distribution channel owned by one of them, or to better leverage the brand name of one of them. An example of the latter is Dunhill, who produced pipes and tobacco, and then included after-shave and sports apparel, especially for golf. They do not produce the latter themselves, but offer the advantage of their brand name to outside producers.

A special case of economy of scale that may merit separate attention is the use of joint systems of support, in an industry association or consortium for political lobbying, training programmes, standard setting, export promotion, marketing, etc. (E2).

Other issues of efficiency are associated with capacity utilization and effects of time (E3). There may be uneven capacity utilization (in production or distribution systems), due to demand that fluctuates as a result of seasonal effects or cycles in the economy. This is most problematic when there are high fixed costs, due to fixed capacity that cannot easily be adjusted to demand fluctuation. Here, it is advantageous, in order to avoid under-utilization, to outsource peak production to producers who suffer less from fluctuations, or whose cycles run counter to one's own (their peaks coinciding with one's own troughs).

Economies of time entail a range of effects of time on the utilization or creation of resources. One is the reduction of idle time of people, installations, or goods in stock, and set-up or switching times of production systems. 'Business process engineering' has shown that there can be high losses of efficiency in the transfer of goods, information or customers between different stations in the value chain, due to mismatches, distortions of information and delays in waiting. This can yield problems especially in IORs. However, such relations may also be used to increase efficiencies of time. For example, just-in-time delivery by suppliers reduces idle time of stocks of inputs for the user. By pooling logistics, firms may minimize idle time or unused capacity of transport facilities. Greater flexibility of production technology, e.g. in programmable machinery, reduces set-up time in switching between product forms.

Other effects of scale and time relate to so-called 'threshold' and set-up costs, and effects of experience and learning, which are discussed in the section on concepts and theory.

One may also need collaboration to spread risks (E4). A classic example is stock markets. Here, stockholders spread risks across a portfolio of firms. Organizations may share risks of research, development, establishment of a technical or commercial standard, access to a new market, exchange rates, political risk, etc.

An example of both economy of scale and spread of risk is (the now defunct) Fokker aircraft company. It specialized in the production of middle-range passenger aircraft. Due to increased opportunities, costs and complexity of technology, development cost increased too far to recoup on the relatively small number of planes that Fokker could expect to sell. The same applies to the increased cost of maintaining a worldwide service system. These are problems of scale. Both technological and commercial risk in developing a new model are high, and one failure or serious delay would bankrupt the company. Third, producing in the Netherlands and selling in dollars, Fokker was subject to high currency risk. Fokker should have developed partnerships to share development costs and risks, and currency risk. It did engage in such endeavour, but too late.

One may want to combine or swap products (E5). Combination of products, for example in product bundling, joint bidding and code sharing (airlines), can yield better opportunities for entering markets, pooling power or serving customers, and may reduce costs. By pooling products one may increase the utilization of distribution capacity, and here the effect overlaps with a previous category (E3), or one may achieve economies of scope (E1). By pooling products or competences one may gain access to large projects, in joint bidding, and one may improve services to a large, multinational industrial customer by jointly offering a portfolio of services, or providing a global service. In the market entry argument, this approaches the third category of 'positioning', in Table 2.1. Product swapping arises, for example, in cross-licensing, when the outcomes of R&D are unpredictable and turn out to yield products that do not fit in production or distribution.

An example is pharmaceutical products. This explains the phenomenon of cross-licensing between such companies. On the face of it, this may seem odd. Why put a lot of money in R&D, and then sell the outcome to competitors? The explanation is that the outcome of R&D is uncertain, and may yield products that do not fit in one's production or distribution structure, or brand name. This also applies to competing producers, so that licence swapping makes sense. Another example is the publication of literature. Here, books from unpredictable authors may turn out in unexpected ways that better fit a competitor's list.

The unpredictability of R&D is called the 'King Saul effect' (Mokyr 1990: 286). Examples are the following. Looking for a better dynamo for bicycle lights, Philips hit upon the development of an electric shaver. Gasoline at first was a useless by-product of deriving lubricants from crude oil, before it was developed into a fuel for the internal combustion motor. Bessemer invented his steel-making process while trying to solve problems of a spinning cannon shell (Mokyr 1990: 116).

Another familiar argument of efficiency for IORs is that some firms have access to markets with high product prices, while others have access to cheap production factors, such as labour, capital or land (E6).

The typical set-up here, often found in fashion goods, is that of one company doing the design and marketing, in advanced markets, and other firms, in low-wage countries, doing the production. One well-known case is Nike.

Finally, an efficiency argument concerns transport costs, taking into account bulk and weight of products, which have to be incorporated in cost–benefit considerations in the location of production (E7). At high cost of transport there is an incentive to produce close to markets, and for this one may need a local partner.

A curious case is Heineken beer. Most brewers produce in the country of destination, because export entails the transport of what is mostly water. Nevertheless, Heineken stuck to export. The reason was the maintenance of the Heineken image of an original premium beer from Holland.

In sum, classic arguments of efficiency for IORs are: the sharing among similar producers of costs, facilities, brand name, or the pooling of effort to achieve efficiency, spread risk or exert power. This happens, for example, in franchising, purchasing co-operatives, production co-operatives, trade associations.

41

Competence

For competences, one may need to use complementary competences of others that one could not oneself develop fast enough (C1). Another, somewhat narrower, term for this is 'skill substitution' (Child and Faulkner 1999). A crucial question concerns the configuration of goals of different participants: can they be reconciled, are they complementary or, preferably, mutually reinforcing? The following configurations are paradigm cases of successful collaboration, and embrace most of the cases discussed in the literature:

1   *The technology–design collaboration:* one side has the scientific/technological and the other the application/design capability for a product. For example: university–business collaboration. Another example is the alliance between Honda and Rover, where Honda supplied the technology and Rover the knowledge of British taste and design preferences (Faulkner 1995).

2   *The production–product collaboration:* one side has a good product and the other has the appropriate production technology. For example: a Japanese company contributes efficient production to a European product design. That also was part of the Honda–Rover collaboration.

3   *The product–market collaboration:* one side has a competence in product and production and the other has access to a market. For example: an American producer requires a Japanese company to access Japanese product and labour markets, such as Xerox, who supplied a product to be marketed in Japan by Fuji (Lorange and Roos 1992); a Japanese producer requires a European partner to overcome EU import restrictions, such as Mitsubishi, who teamed up with Volvo and the remainder of the Dutch car producer DAF in the joint venture NEDCAR, in the Netherlands.

4   *The product–product collaboration:* one pools products, to offer a more integrated portfolio of products to a joint customer. An example is the combination of ICT hardware, software and service firms supplying a joint, tailor-made package, in different countries, for a large MNC.

5   *The collaboration in complementary know-how:* in R&D, production, service, marketing. For example: R&D alliances, production consortia.

A new point, discussed in Chapter 1, concerns the development of new cognitive competence, with the need to prevent organizational myopia by supplementing perspectives from others, for extending 'cognitive scope' (C2). Note the related issues, discussed in Chapter 1. One may have to invest in mutual understanding, in order to 'cross cognitive distance', and when interaction is close, ongoing and exclusive, cognitive distance may fall, in a process of mutual identification, by which the potential for learning and innovation declines. This is part of the wider subject of learning by interaction, to be discussed under 'Concepts and theory' (p. 46).

One's competences can be enhanced by conditions of location ('external-ities'), and this may affect the choice of partnerships (C3). There is a large literature in geography, in studies of regional innovation systems (RIS), on the effects of locality and agglomeration on innovation (Jacobs 1968, 1984; Krugman 1991; Maskell and Malmberg 1999). This goes back to Alfred Marshall's (1920) ideas about 'industrial districts'. This literature will not be reviewed here, but the main points arising from it are that agglomeration yields advantages in a local accumulation of specialized labour skills, specialized suppliers, know-ledge spill-over, reputation mechanisms, and variety for the development of Schumpeterian novel combinations.

There is also an important argument of flexibility: one can more easily reconfigure outside relations than build up and scrap activities within an organiza-tion (C4). Note that there are institutional differences here between different economies. In the United States it is easier to hire and fire and to buy and sell parts of firms than it is in mainland Europe, which in many cases maintains protection devices against take-overs and labour lay-offs.[1] As a result, the need for outside collaboration is greater in (continental) Europe than in the United States, resulting more in 'networked economies' (Nooteboom 2000b).

Positioning

An important class of goals of collaboration concerns 'positional advantage' (Stoelhorst 1997) with respect to political conditions, demand and competition, for both products (sales) and inputs (sourcing). Often, these are foreign markets.

Especially in foreign markets, one may encounter political constraints (P1), which may all yield reasons to seek a local partner, such as:

1 import restrictions in the form of quota and duties;
2 restrictions on the repatriation of local profits;
3 demands for a minimum share of added value from local employment ('local content');
4 need to gain the image of a local producer to obtain better product acceptance and access to distribution channels;
5 requirement of local consortia, e.g. in defence industries.

Entering a market, one might, in principle, have the option to build up one's own presence, by foreign direct investment (FDI), but often that would be too slow, and one needs local partners for fast entry (P2). One may also need local knowledge of markets to make the necessary adjustment of products (P3).

A producer of copying machines (Xerox) sold its American product in Japan, until it found out that the shorter Japanese had to climb on to boxes to reach the buttons. Thus, the product had to be differentiated. McDonald's, on the other hand, takes extreme care to make hamburgers the same the world over, so that anyone anywhere knows precisely what he will get (Lorange and Roos 1992).

There may be collaboration between a firm in an emerging industry with one in the industry which it is substituting: this allows the newcomer to tap existing distribution channels, gives the incumbent firm a stake in the future and reduces his resistance to substitution (Porter and Fuller 1986: 334).

A producer may have to follow a customer in his process of internationalization (P4).

Toyota started to produce in the United States in order to avoid import restrictions. The Japanese tyre producer Bridgestone had Toyota as its main customer, and had to go along. Tyres are expensive to transport. If Bridgestone did not go along, American producers would take over the replacement-tyre market for Toyota, and from there perhaps also the new-tyre sales and perhaps even sales in the Japanese home market (Daniels and Radebaugh 1995).

Collaboration even between competitors may be desirable for developing and setting a joint standard in the market (P5). Earlier, the example was given of collaboration between Philips and Sony in setting the market standard for the audio compact disc. Similar 'standards battles' have been going on in the market for mobile telephone communications.

A reason for strategic positioning may be to 'pre-empt' a foreign competitor by attacking him in his home market and thereby weaken his basis for competition elsewhere. One might do this by taking over one of his local partners. In this way, one may kill two birds with one stone, taking away a partner's access to resources and gaining speedy access to his home market (P6). One may employ partners to block a competitor's access to resources (P7). For example: a producer of aluminium achieved a monopoly by taking over all the main sources of bauxite (the raw material of aluminium). One may seek partners to establishing a cartel, for price fixing or dividing the market between competitors (P8). One may also band together to block entry of new competitors that may threaten an oligopoly, or create exit barriers to prevent spill-over (P9). Law forbids such actions that limit competition, but firms may still try them when they get the opportunity.

Performance

Goal achievement is part of performance. Performance also includes outcomes that were not intended as part of goals but may nevertheless be beneficial. Increasingly, the literature has recognized that the measurement of perform-ance is problematic (Geringer and Hebert 1989). Measurement by return on investment (ROI) is problematic owing to problems of accounting: often invest-ments are made by one partner, but the corresponding profit is partly absorbed by the other partner, yielding investments without full returns, and returns without investments (Ohmae 1989). Return on sales is better (Hagedoorn and Schakenraad 1994), since it copes with such separation of profits and invest-ments. But financial measures generally are problematic when the objective of collaboration is long-term (as in building competence), so that their realization does not appear in short-term profits, or when the objective is risk reduction rather than profit, or is not directly related to profit (obstructing competition, satisfying political demands). Using financial measures can yield a systematic negative bias for Japanese companies, which are less oriented towards short-term profits.

Performance has been measured by the duration of a relation, but this is problematic because especially non-equity alliances may be designed only for a short duration (Kogut 1988). For example: to set up and complete a joint project, as in a consortium for building a refinery. There is also the famous case of Philips and Sony joining forces to get a technical standard established in the market, and then separating in order to compete with it. A relationship may also be deliberately temporary in order to assess the value of a firm prior to acquisition (Mody 1993).

This has been argued to be the reason for a short joint venture in white goods (washing machines and the like) between Philips and Whirlpool: for the latter to have time to assess the true value of Philips's white goods division, in spite of the set-up and governance costs expended on the joint venture.

A relation may also be experimental in that a potential is seen for a long-term relation, but it is considered wise to start small as a means of exploration.

In conclusion, it is often better to assess the achievement of objectives more widely, and to a large extent qualitatively, on the basis of participants' perceived objectives and their realization (Killing 1983; Beamish 1985; Bleeke and Ernst 1991).

45

CONCEPTS AND THEORY

This section discusses a number of concepts used above and in later chapters: economies of scale, scope and time, innovation, organizational learning and internationalization.

Economies of scale and scope

One form of economy of scale is division of labour: because people specialize in a specific part of production they can perform the work more efficiently. Note that here the distinction between economies of scale and scope becomes somewhat ambiguous. One can speak of economy of scale in the sense that a large volume of the same product is produced. One can speak of economy of scope in the sense that different, complementary activities are distinguished, in specialization.

Economy of scale by specialization applies, for example, to an assembly line. This is associated with large, hierarchically composed, vertically integrated firms. The system is often termed 'Fordism' after Henry Ford, who introduced the assembly line to the car industry. This source of scale has been subject to considerable erosion, because it also detracts from motivation and the value of team work, where workers are able to adjust to each other, to survey an integral part of the production system, and to come up with improvements, in 'communities of practice' (Brown and Duguid 1996). This is more important to the extent that work becomes more professional and innovative, and products become more differentiated or made to measure. The term 'post-Fordism' has been used to indicate this departure from Fordism. However, there are some misleading simplifications connected with that term (Amin 1989; Amin and Dietrich 1991). One of them is that effects of scale have disappeared, and that we are entering a period where the small firm will prevail ('small is beautiful').

Indeed, in some areas of production, effects of scale and scope have diminished (and small can be beautiful). For example, this is the case in information technology. This is partly due to the miniaturization of hardware, and its lessened sensitivity to location (temperature, dust, vibrations), making it cheaper and eliminating the need for specialized, large rooms. Partly it is also due to increasing availability of user-friendly and powerful software, eliminating the need for specialized staff to utilize ICT. However, Ohmae (1989) argued that since the turn of corporate ICT to (local and wide-area) networks, fixed costs have risen again. But there can be some doubt here: threshold expenditures in setting up or participating in a network appear to be small. For a small network one can employ a small network server, terminals are not expensive and there are many firms providing services of hardware, software and installation.

Another form of scale economy is due to the mathematical fact that the content of a sphere is proportional to the cube of the radius, and its surface is proportional to its square, while content yields production capacity and surface is connected with costs of material, weight and air resistance and hence transport costs, costs of cleaning, costs of heat loss. As a result, the revenue per unit of cost increases in proportion to size of production. It can easily be calculated that a doubling of size (production volume) yields a 20 per cent reduction of per-unit cost.[2] The effect has therefore been called an 'engineering' economy of scale. It applies to process industries (oil, chemicals, some pharmaceuticals, some food industries), where it has been called the 'pots and pans effect', but it applies also to trucks and aircraft. The 20 per cent reduction of cost at a doubling of volume is a familiar rule in those industries. This form of scale effect is undiminished.

It also applies to the shape of animals. Why are warm-blooded animals at the North Pole large and bulbous (polar bears, walruses and whales)? Because heat loss occurs through the skin, and the ratio between skin and volume is least for large bulbous shapes. How about penguins at the South Pole? They are not warm-blooded. Why do we also find large, bulbous shapes in tropical regions (elephants, hippopotamuses)? For the same reason, but in reverse: here, the outside temperature is higher than body temperature, and it is the relative temperature that matters. A large bulbous shape minimizes the entry of heat from outside. How, then, about the long, slim shapes of hyenas, large cat-like animals, antelopes, etc.? For their food they have to run fast, yielding spurts of excess heat they need to lose. Animals with no digestive tract, which excrete waste through the skin, and animals that absorb food, energy or air through the skin, cannot afford to be large and bulbous, and must be either flat or small, to allow sufficient exchange with the environment relative to their mass.

Further effects of scale arise in markets, in 'network externalities', 'bandwagon effects' and 'contagion effects'. In network externality (also called the 'telephone effect'), the utility of some product depends on the number of others who choose a product with the same, or a compatible, technical standard. This can yield a 'snowballing effect' of a new standard that gains a head start before competing standards. This is a case of 'first mover advantage'.

The standard example is the telephone: it is useful to the extent that others have a telephone that is compatible, in order to call and be called. Another example is the celebrated case of video-recorders, discussed before. Initially there were three alternatives: Philips's Video 2000 system, Sony's Betamax and the VHS system of a consortium of other Japanese companies (JVC, Matsushita). The latter system won, owing to a better fit to market demand in the supply of the software (video-tapes) that

47

was compatible only with the VHS standard built into the hardware (recorders): length of play for recording baseball games, and more extensive distribution of recorded tapes for hire. This gave VHS a head start in the market, with supply according to that technology reinforcing itself, so that the choice of an alternative entailed an accelerating risk that the supply of appropriate software would fall back and stop. This yielded dominance to VHS, even though technically it was inferior.

Other scale effects associated with networks are discussed later, in the chapter on forms of IORs (Chapter 3).

In the 'bandwagon effect', consumers (or voters, politicians or managers) copy each other's choices. In the 'snob effect' it is the other way round: choices of others are avoided. In the diffusion of a new product, early adopters exert a demonstration effect upon potential later adopters ('contagion'). This yields the familiar S-shaped ('logistic') curve of diffusion. Such contagion may occur at a distance or, mostly with stronger effect, in direct contact, by 'word of mouth'. Here, it matters who the source is. One is more inclined to follow people in similar positions or roles (role equivalence or equivalence in network position; cf. Burt 1987).

Economy of scope follows from different activities using the same resources, in different ways, or at different times, and thereby improving their utilization, or from different activities complementing each other in the production of resources.

The classic example of scope by joint utilization of resources is an orchard with sheep. For the sake of light and air, the trees need to be spaced out, and the resulting space between the trees is utilized for grazing sheep. Earlier, the example was given of combining different products in a distribution channel. An example of scope by complementarity in production is a surgical team. Here, scope shades into effects of scale by specialization, as indicated before.

As discussed in Chapter 1, economy of scope yields an argument for combining activities in an organization only if the effect of scope is inseparable.

Hide and meat are inseparable in the living animal. Now consider the process of slaughter. After separation of hide and meat, the former can be separated off in the leather industry, and the latter in meat processing.

There may also be (in)separability in place and time.

Consider a steel factory. After melting the steel, it saves energy to directly process it in the rolling of steel, which requires, preventing heat loss, that the rolling plant is located next to the melting plant. The heat that comes off the subsequent cooling of steel plates may be used for other processes, such as heating hothouses for plants, which then are also most economically located near the steelworks.

Economies of time

The effect of economic cycles on capacity utilization tends to be multiplied upwards in a supply chain. A small decline of demand at the downward end of the chain requires some time to register and adjust to, in the next upward link, which then needs to reduce activity more sharply, and this effect is multiplied up the chain. This has been called the 'car queue' effect: a slight deceleration can build up to a sharp brake, or a collision, further up the queue. As a result, firms up the chain, e.g. in the production of raw materials, suffer from cycles most.

When under-utilization of capacity is endemic, and widespread across producers, the need arises to reduce fixed costs. This is especially important in process industries, where fixed costs are high and furthermore 'sunk' in the market, and thereby create exit barriers. In such cases, there is a threat of ruinous price competition under conditions of excess supply, because assets cannot be reduced or sold off. Therefore the emergence of excess capacity should be avoided. A problem here is that in some industries (oil, basic chemicals) for strategic reasons governments, not to become dependent on other nations in times of crises, stimulate domestic production capacity. This yields all the more reason not to create even more excess capacity when entering some country, but to utilize existing capacity. Sometimes firms, often supported by governments, co-operate to rationalize a process industry with excess capacity by a balanced reduction of capacity. An example is a joint venture between British ICI and Italian Enichem in the PVC industry (Faulkner 1995).

Another time effect, which yields an economy of scale and scope, is due to the presence of fixed 'threshold' costs. These may be due to the fact that productive capacity is not feasible or viable below some minimum level (is indivisible), such as a person or a machine. They may also be due to minimum set-up costs, for an installation for physical production, a research facility or some service capacity. Such thresholds arise, in particular, at service facilities such as a point of sale in a shop, a call desk, the driver of a truck, a teacher before a class, specialist support staff in a firm. For staff (attendant, driver, teacher), the threshold cost is one person during availability of the service, for each separately staffed service point. Threshold staff or facilities are under-utilized during low levels of demand (few customer visits, empty truck, low class attendance), and this yields a scale effect. At higher levels of demand, additional labour may be added part-time, during peak hours only.

Operating an aeroplane combines two effects of scale and time. First there is the scale effect due the mathematical ratio of surface to volume. A large plane, con-structed to be as bulbous as it can get, consistent with properties needed for flying, as in a jumbo jet, offers more passenger space relative to costs of materials and costs of movement. Second, there is a threshold effect due to the need for a basic crew, regardless of plane size.

Threshold costs have increased dramatically. This is the case, for example, in research and development of advanced technology, and as a result of that in the development and production of many products that employ such technology, such as semiconductors, aircraft, cars, consumer electronics, biotechnology.

Formerly, products in consumer electronics could be made with low fixed costs and cheap labour, in the manual assembly of components in boxes. With the onset of miniaturization, this practice was no longer viable, and had to be replaced with the use of robots for assembly, which entails considerable threshold cost.

In marketing also, there are substantial 'threshold costs': in distribution chan-nels and brand names. In distribution there are set-up costs of laying a pipeline or track, building a warehouse, building a station or airport, having an attendant at a service point, sending a truck along a certain route. For the development of a brand name one must invest heavily in advertising and other forms of promotion. The fixed cost of an ad on national television is more easily recouped for a product that is marketed nationwide than for a local product. The need to market a specialized product worldwide, in order to gain sufficient economy of scale to compete, creates a need for a worldwide brand name, with corres-pondingly higher fixed costs.

Relatively novel effects of scale have been reported to arise in the insurance business: novel opportunities arise in direct marketing and telemarketing, but this requires large threshold outlays for hardware, software and the building up of data bases.

Another economy related to time arises in experience effects. According to the 'experience curve', unit cost declines as experience, measured as cumulative (uninterrupted) production, increases. This is due to increasing skill, better division and co-ordination of work, the fine tuning of processes by elimination of redundancies, and other process improvements. Such an experience effect can also become a liability, by acting as an exit barrier to new, competence-destroying technology, thus locking a firm into existing practice.

A special form of experience derives from learning. According to the interactionist/constructivist theory of knowledge set out in Chapter 1, learning is based on existing mental categories, which are in turn based on past learning. As a result, learning is cumulative, with increasing returns to experience.

That is why liberalization of markets is not a sufficient condition for developing countries to catch up. Since they are behind in their knowledge, they cannot compete in the utilization of opportunities from liberalization, and, owing to the cumulative nature of knowledge, this gap can only widen.

There are also several scale effects in transaction costs (Nooteboom 1993b). One is due to 'threshold costs' of contact (search costs) and contract (evaluation and setting up a contract or other agreement), which weigh more heavily at small firm sizes. Furthermore, to the extent that knowledge is tacit there is less documentation as a basis for assessment and evaluation of competences, needs, reliability, etc. As discussed in Chapter 1, tacit knowledge also reduces absorptive capacity, and knowledge is especially tacit in small firms. When knowledge is tacit, it tends to be self-evident, and not subject to rational criticism, until it has been sufficiently externalized in codified knowledge. Note that thus tacit knowledge gives a double jeopardy: less information for evaluation and control, and a lesser basis for critical reflection and debate. As discussed, there is limited absorptive capacity until tacit knowledge is made explicit, and this is not always possible. However, tacit knowledge also has the advantage that it does not spill over as easily as codified knowledge. That is an advantage especially to small firms, since it is relatively difficult for them to protect their innovations. Patents, for example, are relatively expensive for them. This is discussed further in Chapter 3.

The analysis explains the familiar phenomenon, identified in the small business literature, of how difficult it is to obtain an audience for the adoption of innovations among small firms, and their inclination to reject it as 'impractical'. A complication is that often it is in fact the case that an innovation that was developed in or for a large firm oes not satisfy the operational conditions of a small firm. The point here is that even if it is appropriate, it may still be rejected owing to the blindness induced by tacit knowledge.

Innovation

In the literature on innovation, much attention has been given to the process that follows the chaotic beginnings of novelty, with a multiplicity of new tentative forms (prototypes), in the convergence towards a 'dominant design' (Abernathy 1978; Abernathy and Utterback 1978). This is called the 'life cycle' theory of innovation. The literature describes how in technologies novelty is selected, improved and diffused along 'technological trajectories', sets 'technological guideposts' and constitutes a 'technological regime', according to a 'technological paradigm' (Nelson and Winter 1977; Sahal 1981; Dosi 1982; Teece 1988). In industry it leads to an 'industry recipe' (Spender 1989). In a dominant design, the overall architecture of the innovation has been established, and attention shifts to organization, in the optimization of elements and linkages within that architecture (Henderson and Clark 1990). The dominant design of the technology is followed by a 'dominant logic' of organization (Bettis and Prahalad 1995).

In this literature, the origins of novelty remain a mystery. The Schumpeterian term 'novel combinations' merely labels our ignorance. No one has explained by what path such combinations come about. Hence, the literature on innovation and innovation systems is mostly oriented towards incremental change, building on existing competences, moving along a 'technical trajectory'.

Incremental change is interspersed with more radical innovations, yielding novel competences and technical trajectories, or paradigm breaks, in Schumpeterian 'creative destruction'.Such phenomena of relative stability (trajectories, paradigms) interrupted by more radical change have also been characterized as 'punctuated equilibria' (Tushman and Romanelli 1985; Gersick 1991; Romanelli and Tushman 1994). However, this also is no more than a label of a phenomenon. How radical innovation, paradigm switches or punctuation arise remains unexplained. Even in neo-Schumpeterian theory radical innovation drops in unexplained: a stone thrown in the tranquil pond of equilibrium. The resulting ripples can be studied, but the origin of the stone remains a mystery. Some would say that the search for the sources of innovation would be a search for the philosopher's stone: if we could explain innovation, we could predict it, and that would deny that it is a true innovation. But that is mistaken: one can very well develop a 'logic' or 'heuristic' of discovery without claiming to be able to predict its outcomes.

An empirical puzzle is that in fact the process of consolidation does not always follow, but often precedes the emergence of chaotic novelty. To proceed, we need a theory of organizational learning, to explain how novelty arises. We need to develop a true cycle that leads back to new beginnings.

Learning, exploration and exploitation

The *content* of learning in organizations may be joint production, problem solving, the development of new practices or products, exchanging experience from different projects, sharing codified knowledge, the development of skills, training, attitude development, management development, organizational change.

The literature on organizational learning proposes two different *levels* of learning. On one level, people learn individually by *adopting* knowledge from others, in 'knowledge sharing'. On another level, people jointly *develop* knowledge that is new to an organization. The literature on knowledge management tends to focus only on knowledge sharing. That can be counterproductive, because measures taken to support knowledge sharing may impose uniformity of meanings and procedures that limit the variety needed for the development of new knowledge. Thus, we need to look at both knowledge sharing and knowledge production. However, the distinction between the two is not as clear as it may seem.

Recall from the discussion of knowledge in Chapter 1 that knowledge sharing is not like the simple transfer of a physical commodity. Knowledge loses tacit content and intent in its expression by the 'sender', and has to be reconstructed and re-embedded in tacit knowledge by the 'receiver'. As a result, knowledge 'received' is never identical to knowledge 'sent'. Another form of learning is the joint construction, in interaction between people, of knowledge that is new to both. As discussed in Chapter 1, this requires the crossing of cognitive distance. Without such distance, partners would have nothing new to say to each other. Note that the distinction between these two types of learning is not sharp, since 'transfer' entails reconstruction of knowledge, by the receiver, and in communication the sender may also reconstruct the knowledge he intends to transfer. This is particularly the case since meaning and knowledge are also context-dependent. How the sender expresses his knowledge, and what the receiver makes of it, depend on the context.

One definition of learning is the ability to respond differently to the same stimuli that obtained before, selecting from a given repertoire of responses. However, one might also learn to respond to new stimuli, with new repertoires of action. This is related to the distinction between learning to do existing things better, and learning to do new things. In this book, this distinction is called the *depth* of learning. The first has variously been called first-order, single-loop learning or learning for exploitation, and the second has been called second-order, double-loop or exploratory learning (Bateson 1973; Holland 1975; Hedberg *et al*. 1976; Argyris and Schön 1978; Fiol and Lyles 1985; March 1991). Efficient exploitation of resources is needed to survive in the short term, and

53

exploration of new resources is needed to survive in the long term. While this conceptual distinction can be made, in the process of learning the two kinds of learning do not stand apart from each other. Exploitation is based on exploration, and vice versa. We exploit what we have explored, and it is on the basis of exploitation that we explore. According to the activity theory of knowledge, set out in Chapter 1, learning forms the bridge between practice and innovation. A central task of organizations is to find ways of combining the two. Arguably, this is the central challenge for management.

March (1991) demonstrated, by means of a simple simulation model, how exploitation and exploration could be combined by separating workers into two groups. One adapts fast to existing ways of working. (Learning here entails adjustment to current procedures.) This is good for exploitation. The second group adopts slowly, to allow existing procedures to adapt to their ideas, brought in from outside experience. This is good for exploration. That is further enhanced by staff turnover, with new staff bringing in outside experience. This is more needed to the extent that the environment is subject to faster change. Note how this argument fits the notion of cognitive distance, discussed in Chapter 1.

However, what is the relation, in such a scheme, between the exploiters and the explorers? Can they work together, or do they have to be separated, in time or place? If they were not separated, wouldn't the exploration disturb exploitation, or vice versa? If they are separated, how does one ensure that the novelty from the explorers is workable, and based on experience in exploitation, and is indeed adopted by the exploiters?

Here, one recognizes the familiar problems between the functional areas of production (exploitation task), R&D (exploration task) and marketing (tasks of both exploitation, in customer service, and exploration, in research into new customer needs). R&D complains that Production is conservative, and does not want to disturb the efficiency of current production (recall the earlier discussion of the experience curve), and thereby misses new opportunities. Production complains that R&D has no sense of workable production.

The question in what organizational forms exploitation and exploration can be combined, with what separations in time and place, will be taken up in more detail in the analysis of forms of IORs, in Chapter 3.

Generally, the combination of exploitation and exploration is not easy. Exploitation generally entails stable standards and meanings of terms, and stable relations in division of labour. Exploration typically requires the reverse: the loosening and change of standards, meanings, and organizational structures and

54

processes. How difficult the combination is depends on how systemic, modular or stand-alone the exploitation system is. These notions were discussed in Chapter 1.

In a highly systemic production system, with, by definition, many linkages between many elements in the system, with tight constraints on the interfaces, there is limited scope for exploration, in deviation from those constraints, in the component activities. Think, for example, of a refinery. The scope for exploration, in any component activity, is limited by the tightness and number of constraints on ties with other, complementary component activities. This may still allow exploration, depending on the modularity of activities within the component activity. When multiple and narrowly constrained ties constrain exploration too much, exploration will have to take place outside the exploitation system, with the resulting problems of connecting exploitation and exploration, indicated above. When exploration outside the existing systemic order of exploitation yields interesting results, in a particular component activity, there is a large probability, in view of the systematicity of the exploitation system, that its introduction would destroy the integrity of the system, with unknown repercussions for other elements of the system, and the relations between them. When the exploitation system is modular, this means, by definition, that constraints on interfaces between parts of the system allow for a range of substitutions of parts that do not endanger the integrity of exploitation. It is largely for this reason that firms have been trying to modularize their production, in order to facilitate the combination of exploitation and exploration (Langlois and Robertson 1995).

When the exploitation system is stand-alone, elements of the production system are more or less autonomous, and they can more freely explore while exploiting their individual competences. Take, for example, a high-level management consultancy firm. Its consultants, often in teams of varying composition, are highly autonomous, employing their individual knowledge, skill and creativity to provide custom-made advice. Such a case would be most likely *not* to yield a problem in the combination of exploration and exploitation. Thus, if the problem did occur there also, this would present a strong test of the existence of the problem. Indeed, the problem does appear there also.

Communities of practice

The autonomy of individual consultants, or teams of them, offers broad scope for exploring new forms of consultancy, in strong interaction with a variety of clients, where exploration may be inspired from opportunities and needs for novelty that arise from exploitation, in the practice of giving tailor-made advice. Of course, even there measures are taken to safeguard professional standards and quality. For example, this is needed to ensure consistent quality across different

55

locations of a multinational customer. Nevertheless, the scope for exploration is as wide as it can get. However, here the problem is not how to make exploitation explorative, but the reverse, how to ensure efficient exploitation of what autonomous units find out, in their exploration. The question is what measures can be taken to ensure that different consultants make use of each other's innovations, not to reinvent the wheel all the time. There are different ways to do this.

One form, encountered in the former consultancy branch of the accountancy/consultancy firm Arthur Andersen, is as follows.[3] Consultants were required to contribute their experience to a common pool. A restriction encountered here was that customers would not like confidential information and experience derived from them to benefit competitors. Therefore, specific experience had to be abstracted to generic logics of consultancy practice that rose above the confidentiality of individual advice. Knowledge sharing required an incentive system for consultants to volunteer their experience to the common pool. They might not do that automatically, because colleagues were also competitors in careers and customer prospects. A system was introduced whereby they were remunerated and promoted at least in part on the basis of their contributions to the common pool. Later, the firm realized that it is not the contributions that count, but their fruitful use by colleagues, and the system was changed to weight contributions by their use by colleagues. There is a parallel here with the assessment of research performance at universities, which first took place by publication counts, and was subsequently replaced by the count of citations by colleagues. Next, this system, for the sake of exploitation, yielded a problem for exploration. The common knowledge pool required a certain minimal amount of standardization of concepts and procedures in a thesaurus. That fixity of meanings and categories hampered exploration. The most radically new innovations did not fit in the semantic structure. This required special measures to allow and prepare for shifts of meaning. Misfits in the system had to be reported to a committee that from time to time adapted the semantic structure of the knowledge pool to allow for more radical novelties. Of course, this system lagged behind such innovations, particularly because to fulfil its function the semantic system could not be revised too frequently. As a result, the more radically innovative proposals faced a delay in the rewards for referral. Also, the revision of the semantic structure of the knowledge pool can yield deep problems of linguistics, as a result of which it may not be possible to do this in a cumulative fashion, without more fundamental revision of the basic thesaurus and logics of composition.

An issue in the theory of organizational learning is the relation between learning by people and learning on the level of the organization (Cook and Yanow 1996; Weick and Westley 1996). The link between the two levels arises in teams, groups or 'communities', such as communities of practice (Brown and Duguid 1996; Wenger and Snyder 2000).

In their account of communities of practice, Brown and Duguid (1996: 60) employ the activity theory of knowledge (Blackler 1995), which is also used in the present book, as discussed in Chapter 1. They also see knowledge and practice as interacting, with 'learning as a bridge between working and innovation'. They employ the notion of 'canonical' and 'non-canonical' or 'procedural' knowledge (Cohen and Bacdayan 1996). Canonical knowledge entails decontextualized, codified and formalized rules for operation. Inevitably, such rules cannot cover the richness and the variability of practical contexts. It is by context-dependent deviations from canonical rules, with the ensuing need for improvisation and experimentation (Brown and Duguid employ Levi-Strauss's concept of *bricolage*), that learning arises, in interaction between members of the community. This is based on 'storytelling', to capture and share context-bound experience, to guide experimentation. As a result, communities emerge from shared work practice rather than being designed ex-ante.

The notion of communities of practice is useful, but is also too expansive, including a wide range of different kinds of activity. One can distinguish a variety of different 'learning groups' within organizations, with different configurations of characteristics, in terms of structural features, type and strength of ties within those groups, according to different features of structure and ties to be discussed in Chapter 3. Specific configurations, in different groups, depend on the purpose of a group (improvement of specific projects, development of generic skills or knowledge), the type of learning (more explorative or more exploitative), the type of knowledge involved (more codified or more tacit), the possible need to first build mutual absorptive capacity, specific investments to build absorptive capacity and trust, types of risk involved (hold-up, spill-over, psychological and career risks), type of market, and organizational features (institutions) that enable and constrain conduct. However, since this book focuses on inter-organizational rather than intra-organizational relationships, and external rather than internal networks, that line of analysis will not be pursued here. For a discussion, see Bogenrieder and Nooteboom (2003).

Yet, it is worth adding one further illustrative case. It is interesting to contrast the case of knowledge sharing in Arthur Andersen, discussed above, with the case of Cap Gemini, a consultancy firm in the area of IT.[4] While Arthur Andersen developed a formal, top-down system of knowledge sharing, described above, Cap Gemini sought to stimulate an informal bottom-up system. The basic idea was that it was in the interest of consultants themselves to compose 'communities of practice' in which they could benefit from cross-fertilization of experience. This would help them to perform well and obtain new customer prospects, which would contribute to their income and internal career prospects, so that no separate, formal system of rewards for knowledge pooling would be needed. Internal free riding within such communities was discouraged by internal social control and inclusion or exclusion from profitable communities. However, the problem that arose here was that such communities started to perceive each other as competitors, and were inclined to close themselves off from spill-over between them, in separate 'islands of expertise'. In other words, the threat of individual consultants isolating themselves now reappeared at the level of communities. This imposed limits on both exploitation and exploration from interaction and exchange between communities. Management then had to take measures to establish a movement of staff across communities. So here, also, the problem of combining exploration and exploration arises again, in a new form.

Internationalization

The motives for firms to 'go foreign' are discussed extensively in any textbook on international business (e.g. Daniels and Radebaugh 1995; Griffin and Pustay 1996). They are included in the survey of goals for IORs discussed above, since most motives for going international may also yield motives to seek partners for it. A summary of steps in internationalization is given below. The idea behind these stages is that one should not take a big step until one has found out in small steps that big steps are worth while and one has gained the requisite experience and confidence. However, that procedure may be too slow, and one may need partners to speed it up.

The logical first step in internationalization of the firm is 'indirect' export, through a trade corporation or by supplying to a customer who then exports it together with his own product, in 'piggy back' export. Another possibility is selling a licence of a product, for others to produce elsewhere. In direct export of one's own product one can use a local agent or distributor, before one takes the step of setting up one's own sales office. A next step is to set up such a sales office or, as a further step, production abroad, with more extensive foreign direct investment.

Another aspect of the internationalization process is that one starts with markets at a limited 'psychological distance' (difference in language, infrastructure and institutions), and proceeds to greater distances as one gets accustomed to dealing with them (Johanson and Vahlne 1977, 1990; Welch and Luostarinen 1988). Clearly, this notion is similar to the notion of cognitive distance, discussed in Chapter 1, and the need to cross such distance. However, there distance was seen not only as a problem, but also as an opportunity, as a source of the variety needed for learning. Here, the resulting hypothesis would be that, for the purpose of innovation, there is an optimal psychological distance in internationalization.

How one goes about internationalization depends crucially on whether one chooses a global or a multinational strategy. In the first one chooses to maintain a constant product all over the world, to utilize economies of scale, with perhaps adaptations only in appearance, advertising, packaging and distribution. In a multinational strategy one adapts the product to local tastes and other conditions (production, distribution). What strategy is the best depends on a trade-off between effects of scale and the degree to which product differentiation is possible and needed, while taking transport costs into account. This may yield several production centres in a few different regions across the world, to limit transaction costs and have some proximity to markets, while maintaining sufficient volume to achieve economy of scale.

Differentiability is a matter not only of technology, taste and conditions of use, but also of the importance of a constant product to reduce 'search costs' for customers, so that on the basis of a brand name the consumer can be certain of a fixed quality everywhere. That is important when customers travel across the world. This applies, for example, to McDonald's, which has taken great trouble to ensure constant quality across the world.

Another idea from the internationalization literature is that of the 'international product cycle' (Vernon 1966). Supposedly, new products arise in developed countries, with advanced technology and sophisticated customers. Next, when in that new market competition increases, with new entrants, profit margins decrease, and the market gets saturated, the product is shifted to less developed countries, where demand lags behind and production costs are lower. This view has been criticized on several grounds. One is that nowadays, with globalization, products may be immediately introduced worldwide. A new perspective on the internationalization process is that it may serve as a strategy of learning. This is discussed in the advanced section of this chapter.

ADVANCED

This section gives a more in-depth analysis of threshold costs, a theory of discovery by combining exploitation and exploration, and its application to internationalization of firms.

Threshold costs

In consumer services, the phenomenon of threshold costs at service points can be further elaborated, as follows. For labour costs, the threshold equals the sum of service/opening times across all independently staffed service units. With the use of queuing theory, it can be shown that under certain assumptions, namely that average queuing time of customers is roughly equal to average service time per customer, and perfect adaptation of additional, part-time staff capacity to

59

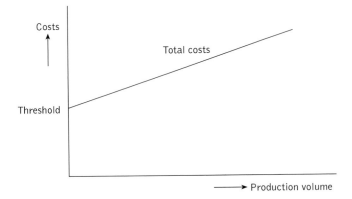

Figure 2.1 *Threshold cost*

intensity of demand, the curve of labour volume as a function of sales volume is a straight line, with threshold cost as an intercept (Nooteboom 1982). This is illustrated in Figure 2.1. With a linear cost curve, threshold cost entails an economy of scale and scope: at higher sales volumes, threshold costs are spread over larger sales. Higher sales volume can be achieved by higher sales volume of a given product (scale) or by combining goods and services that are complementary in the service function (scope).

Service units can also achieve lower costs by letting customers queue longer, and by staffing different service points jointly (with attendants switching stations as customers arrive). Alternatively, utilization of staff can be improved by letting them conduct activities that are independent of customer arrivals (such as cleaning, stocking, administrative work), during low rates of arrival. Yet another alternative is to increase average queuing time, but help customers to utilize it by entertainment, or making their wait agreeable in other ways (music, television).

Cycle of discovery

As noted, the combination of exploitation and exploration is more difficult to the extent that the technology of the production system is systemic. This includes linkages on multiple levels: within and between organizations, in distribution systems, industry structures and in the wider institutional environment. Thus, the problem often arises that in order to explore, one has to move outside the prevailing system, which has developed 'dominant designs' in technology, organization and institutional environment. Nooteboom (2000a) proposed a 'cycle of discovery', to show how exploitation may be maintained for as long as possible, while nevertheless setting out on a path of exploration. Briefly summed up, it works as follows. By taking existing practice outside current areas of application (in 'generalization'), one obtains:

1 Tolerance of deviance, since it no longer threatens current dominant designs.
2 New experience, in a new context, which generates new insights into the limits of validity of existing practice. Accumulation of failures, in the new context, provides acceptance of a need for change. This reflects a general idea that learning will occur only under pressure of failure, where survival requires it.
3 Minor adaptations (called 'differentiation') of existing practice to the new context (to preserve exploitation as long as possible), with recourse to prior experience, recalled from the development of current practice, and earlier experience with differentiations.
4 Insights into how things might be done differently, inspired by how other things work well in the new environment, where one's own practice fails. Here, hybrid structures are built, with elements of old practice and new practices encountered in the new context, while maintaining, as much as possible, the overall architecture (Henderson and Clark 1990) of old practice (called *reciprocation*). Again, this is to preserve the structure of exploitation for as long as possible.
5 These hybrids are often inefficient, with a mixing of incompatible elements, redundancies, overlaps, and difficult to manage complexity. However, they allow experimentation with novel elements. When these are successful, and it can be demonstrated that they have large potential, whose realization is, however, blocked by existing architecture, this yields pressure for more radical innovations, with both new elements and new architecture (in radically 'novel combinations').
6 This initiates a stage of experimentation with new technologies and organizational forms, which sooner or later settle down in a new system of dominant designs, as described in the innovation literature.

With this, the cycle is closed, returning to new beginnings. This cycle is proposed as a general 'heuristic of discovery' that applies on all levels, of learning by individuals, communities of practice within organizations, organizations and industries. The term 'heuristic' is intended to indicate that the cycle does not claim to yield a universal, inexorable logic. Obstacles occur in the progress along the cycle, and stages may be skipped, depending on contingencies of technology, market structure and institutions. The 'new contexts for existing practices' may be new markets for existing products, or new applications of existing knowledge, technology or organization. For a more detailed discussion, see Nooteboom (2000a).

At the level of idea formation by individuals the cycle can be quite fast: it can turn around in an hour or a day. Product cycles vary enormously. In financial services and some fashion goods the cycle can be a year; in cars, computers and machine tools two to four years; in major construction projects five to seven years; in pharmaceuticals and telecom infrastructure ten to fifteen years (Quinn 1992). Organizational change requires redistribution of people across tasks or a reconstitution of tasks, goals, motives, perspectives or shared meanings. In networks it requires entry and exit of firms and the building of new network relations. Such developments tend to take a long time, especially if they require a change in the 'deep structure' of organizational culture, such as basic categories of perception, interpretation and evaluation (Schein 1985). As discussed in Chapter 1, these are part of 'organizational focus'. Restructuring of systems of production, supply and distribution also takes a long time.

According to the study of technological discontinuities in the cement industry by Tushman and Anderson (1986) it took twenty-three years to move from the rotary kiln to the Edison long kiln (1896–1909) and sixty years to move to the Dundee kiln with process control. In the airline industry it took twenty-two years to move from the generation of the Boeing 247, Douglas DC-2 and DC-3 (with the DC-3 as the dominant design, in 1937) to the era of the jet aircraft, with the Boeing 707 (1959). Next, it took ten years to the wide-body jets, with the Boeing 747 (1969). In the minicomputer industry it took only two years to move from transistors to integrated circuits (in 1964), and seven years to move to semiconductor memories. The speed of movement to integrated circuits derived from the strong pressure to eliminate the constraints that limited the realization of the potential of semiconductors imposed by the assembly of different components of different materials, as discussed elsewhere. This is a good example of how new elements in a system (adopted in 'reciprocation') can exert pressure towards architectural change.

The cycle connects with 'punctuated equilibrium' theory, as initiated by Eldredge and Gould (1972), to explain the stylized fact that in the development of many species there have been prolonged periods of stasis, punctuated by change that is abrupt in terms of geological time. The explanation of stasis is not yet satisfactory, but some indications are given. It is attributed to external constraints on variety, such as inherent limitations of geometry, physics and chemistry, and to internal factors, such as the elimination of deviants in the population. Punctuation is attributed to 'allopatric speciation':

small populations isolated at the periphery of parental ranges develop into separate species. Allopatric speciation corresponds with the idea, in the cycle of discovery, that often learning requires the switch to a new 'context', in the process of 'generalization', to escape from the home 'niche' and seek new challenges and survival conditions.

The different goals of IORs, listed in Table 2.1, can be connected with different stages in the cycle of discovery. This is specified in Table 2.2.

Learning by internationalization

The product cycle theory of Vernon (1966) suggests that when multinational companies invest in other countries, it is on the basis of standardized technology, organization and management, so that in the host countries we should find no R&D or design, and only simple, standardized production with cheap labour. This is contradicted by recent research. Not only production but design and development also are transferred to host countries, and subsidiaries of MNCs demand, and are given, considerable room for local differentiation of product, production and distribution. Multinationals are said to 'tap into' local complementary competences (Bartlett and Goshal 1989; Glimstedt 1999). Rather than cloning their products and processes the MNCs specialize by location (Storper 1997). Conceivably, the latitude for foreign subsidiaries to adapt products and technologies is not given by design but results from the sheer inability of headquarters to co-ordinate across a multitude of countries. However, empirical research into patent data confirms that increasingly firms conduct R&D abroad, to adjust and develop their products and technologies abroad, tapping into local competences and resources (Cantwell and Piscitello 1999).

The cycle of discovery would explain such phenomena. Like the old industrial life-cycle theory of innovation to which it is related, the product cycle theory of internationalization neglects the importance for discovery, and ongoing innovation, of exploration by differentiation and reciprocation. If multinational corporations are to survive by combining exploration with exploitation they must allow for decentralization and differentiation. As explained in the theory of knowledge, expounded in the previous chapter, they must employ 'external economy of cognitive scope' and indeed 'tap into' complementary competence, including cognitive competence, in the host country. This connects with the fact that access to international markets may contribute to the stage of generalization in the cycle of discovery, as indicated in Table 2.2.

As is explained in the new internationalization literature, this has implications for national policy. One should try to employ incoming foreign direct investment from advanced foreign companies as an occasion for contributing one's local resources and competences to serve the functions of differentiation and

63

Table 2.2 Goals of collaboration in the cycle of discovery

Type of goal	Stage in the cycle of discovery
Efficiency	Mostly consolidation
E1 Economies of scale, scope	Consolidation
E2 Joint support systems	Consolidation
E3 Capacity utilization, economies of time	Consolidation
E4 Spread risk	Novel combinations
E5 Combine or swap products	Consolidation/differentiation
E6 Utilize unequal prices for products and inputs	Consolidation/differentiation
E7 Transport costs	Consolidation/generalisation
Competences	Mostly reciprocation/novel combinations
C1 Complementary competences, skill substitution	Reciprocation
C2 Learning by interaction	Reciprocation
C3 Externalities of location	Various
C4 Flexibility of configuration	Novel combinations
Positioning	Consolidation/generalization
Political conditions:	
P1 Satisfy demands from local government on local content, repatriation of profits, use of expatriates	Generalization
Market access:	
P2 Fast access to new markets of products and inputs	Generalization
P3 Adjustment of products, technology or inputs to local market conditions	Differentiation
P4 Follow the customer	Generalization
P5 Establish a standard in the market	Consolidation
Competition:	
P6 Attack a competitor in his home market	Consolidation
P7 Block a competitor's access to resources	Consolidation
P8 Establish a cartel	Consolidation
P9 Blocking entry or exit	Consolidation

reciprocation, and thereby benefit from mutual complementarity between the foreign and the domestic (Glimstedt 1999). This suggests that, rather than convergence of economic systems across the globe, specialized local conditions, including institutions, may provide a basis for competitive advantage among nations.

Chapter 3

Structure

- ■ Forms
  - ● Structure
  - ● Ties
  - ● Concentration of ownership and control
  - ● Cobwebs
- ■ Choice
  - ● Merger, acquisition or alliance?
  - ● Bad reasons
  - ● Joint ventures
  - ● Network structure
  - ● Licensing
  - ● Structures of buyer–supplier relations
  - ● External corporate venturing
- ■ Concepts and theory
  - ● Third parties
  - ● The revelation problem
- ■ Advanced
  - ● Location

SUMMARY

This chapter presents the forms of organization and networks that are available to achieve goals of collaboration. It analyses features relevant for competence as well as features relevant for governance. First, it proposes a taxonomy of features of network structure and a taxonomy of features of ties within networks. In particular, it 'unpacks' the notion of the strength of ties. Ties can be strong in some features and weak in others. Subsequently, it analyses the choice and design of forms. In particular, it looks at the choice between integration of firms, in a merger or acquisition (MA), and alliances between formally independent firms. It gives reasons that are rational, in the sense of serving the interests of the firm, and reasons that may be rational for managers but counter-productive for firms. It argues that especially from a perspective of learning often MA has been chosen for bad reasons, where alliances would have been better. It discusses equity joint ventures as an intermediate form, and the use of licensing. It pays special attention to structures of buyer–supplier relations, and the emerging form of 'external corporate venturing'. Subsequently, it discusses the essential change that occurs in going from a bilateral relation to relations between three or more players, and the role of 'third parties'. It discusses the notion of the 'revelation problem' in knowledge exchange. In the advanced section, in a link with geography, it discusses the role of location and distance, and the idea of a possible 'death of distance' due to advances in information and communication technology (ICT).

FORMS

The literature has offered a number of dimensions of IORs. A survey is given below. Four types of features are considered here: relating to the identity of participants, to the structure of the network in which they are embedded, and to the type and strength of the ties between them. Each feature has been selected for its relevance, on the basis of theory and empirical studies, for competence and/or governance in IORs. They are identified below, and discussed in later sections.

Note that the network may be an external network, between organizations, but also a network within a (large) organization. Thus, the value that a subsidiary or department of a large firm offers to outside partners may depend on its position in the internal network of the large firm (Kamp 2003).

Identity and characteristics of firms in the network

1　Ownership of the firm;
2　control of the firm;
3　legal form;
4　industries in which it is active.

Ownership, control and legal form determine the autonomy of a firm, and its freedom of action. Industries are indicative of technology, type of knowledge (tacit, codified, speed of change), competition, etc.

Ownership and control matter in view of what might happen to a partner. In particular, if one engages in a close relationship with a partner whom one trusts, one may run the risk of that partner being taken over against his will by an organization one does not trust. That risk depends on ownership and legal structure.

67

Lorange and Roos (1992) give an example of this. It concerned a non-equity partnership between two producers of garden equipment in Norway and Sweden ('Norpartner' and 'Swedpartner'). A Norwegian competitor of the Norpartner firm took over the owner of Swedpartner and ended its alliance with Norpartner, which meanwhile had become so dependent on the alliance that it went bankrupt when the relation was broken. In this way the third party in one stroke eliminated his Norwegian competitor, gained entry into the Swedish market and eliminated a competitor there.

Network structure

1 Number of participants (network size);
2 density/sparseness;
3 connectedness (mutual reachability of participants through direct and indirect ties);
4 degree of centrality (number of direct ties a participant has);
5 betweenness centrality (number of positions a firm takes between others);
6 structural holes (absence of direct ties);
7 isolation (lack of ties to other networks);
8 stability (frequency of exit and entry);
9 structural equivalence (firms having similar patterns of ties);
10 concentration of ownership and control in the network.

These features are all well known from the network literature. For different notions of centrality see Freeman (1978–9). Centrality is, in the first approach, a feature of a participant in the network rather than the overall network. On the network level, it indicates the extent to which some firms have many direct connections and others don't.

Type and strength of ties

1 Scope;
2 investments in the tie:
 (a) size;
 (b) specificity;
 (c) economic life;
3 frequency of interaction;
4 duration;
5 openness of (internal) communication;
6 cognitive proximity;
7 spatial proximity.

68

Scope refers to the nature and content of a tie. A tie may entail a relationship of ownership, authority, control, dependence, membership, family, friendship or a combination of these. It may refer to flows of goods, information, money or people. It may encompass a large or a small share of the total activities of a firm. Investments in a tie have important implications for its cost. As argued in transaction cost economics (TCE), when investments are specific to a tie, one wants the tie to have sufficient duration to recoup the investment. How long that is depends on the economic life of the investment. Openness of communication refers to the extent that players are willing to give information. When cognitive distance is large, players may not understand each other well, and may have to build up mutual absorptive and communicative capacity. Spatial proximity has effects on the cost of flows, mutual understanding and trust. Ties may be strong in one respect and weak in others. For example, a tie may be strong in frequency and openness of interaction, but weak in specific investments and duration. These features of ties have implications for both competence and governance.

Structure

The embeddedness of organizations and relationships in networks matters for a number of reasons. Das and Teng (2002) argue that it is useful to distinguish between the number of players involved within an alliance (internal network) and the wider networks in which multiple alliances may be embedded. Also in a single alliance, whether of two or multiple participants, one must consider the wider network of relationships, with outside ties of partners beyond the alliance. This is illustrated by the case of 'Norpartner' and 'Swedpartner' summarized above.

In the sociological network literature, the key dimensions of competence and governance that are central in this book can be recognized in the terminology of 'information benefits' and 'control benefits' of network structure (Burt 1992). Information benefits are part of the competence side, in particular learning, and control benefits are part of the governance side. On the competence side, partners may offer value not only in their own competences, but also in the access they offer to other, outside resources. On the governance side, the relational risk one runs may arise through network connections, and the risks one creates for others may depend on them. Opportunities for action and instruments for governance depend on network structure and one's position in it.

As indicated earlier, internal networks are also relevant, not only for an internal analysis of a firm, but also for outside relationships. Kamp (2003) studied the effects of the position of car assembly plants in Spain within their multinational parents (Volkswagen and Renault) on the location strategy of their suppliers. The attractiveness of an assembler's position in the parent network can have several dimensions. First, if the assembler is given not only lower added-value activities of standardized production, but also higher-level activities of e.g. production design, perhaps for local adaptation of a product to local conditions of demand or production, this makes it a more attractive partner for suppliers simply because of the higher added value involved. Second, if the plant produces only one model, and particularly if it is the exclusive producer of that model for a wide, international market, it yields opportunities of scale that also benefit suppliers, who are then more inclined to establish dedicated facilities near the assembly plant. Third, if it produces also for export, then suppliers may have the opportunity to 'hitch a ride', in 'piggyback' export, that may later offer an opportunity for further internationalization of operations (in foreign direct investment (FDI)).

Structure is a configuration of relations in an institutional environment. It is both the basis and the result of processes of interaction. This idea derives from the notion of structuration (Giddens 1984; Archer 1995), according to which structure enables and constrains action, and action (re)constructs structure. Thus, networks enable and constrain activities of firms and ties between them, and are constructed by them. Note that structure applies to both inter-firm and intra-firm relations. The following features of structure have been recognized in the sociological literature.

Network *size* is the number of participants. Often, here is no unambiguous boundary to the network. Where one draws it depends on what type and strength of ties one deems important, in the study at hand. Those are considered later. Clearly, the number of participants complicates matters in an alliance (Doz and Hamel 1998; Das and Teng 2002). This is also known from the literature on cartels. Multiple participants increase problems of free riding, shirking, monitoring and collective action. They yield effects of gossip and reputation. They also yield opportunities for coalition formation to restrain opportunism, entry and exit of individual participants.

A second feature of structure is *density*, i.e. the number of direct ties between participants, as a percentage of the maximum possible number. The opposite of density is *sparseness*. With n participants, the maximum number of direct ties is $n(n-1)/2$.

Note that this entails another effect of scale, in addition to those discussed in Chapter 2. The number of ties, and hence the costs involved in managing them, increase with the square of the number of participants. This specifies the point made above that the size of a network complicates matters. The disproportional increase of costs of co-ordination with size has provided an incentive to develop other, less costly forms of co-ordination than direct interaction between everyone involved, such as hierarchies and hub-and-spoke systems.

Density is important for a number of reasons, to be discussed in much more detail later. It has implications for both competence (access to knowledge, diffusion of knowledge) and governance (reputation mechanisms, coalitions).

The third feature, *connectedness*, entails that directly or indirectly every participant can be reached by any other. This has implications for the autonomy of participants, in terms of their ability to shield themselves off from others in the network.

The fourth feature, *centrality* (or more precisely *degree centrality*) entails that there are participants that have many more direct linkages to other participants than those do, and there are participants with few linkages. High centrality has implications for power differences. At the extreme there is a *hub-and-spoke* system, with one central agent surrounded by 'satellites' that are linked only to the central agent, as illustrated in Figure 3.1. Often, one finds such structures in a system of supply to a large original equipment manufacturer (OEM), such as a car assembly plant.

If relations are systemic, in the sense that there are direct dependences between the spokes, in a hub-and-spoke system these are not covered by ties, and then the hub will have to take care of their co-ordination, which can overload the co-ordinative capacity of the hub. This leads to another structure of supply, in a hierarchy or *pyramid* with different tiers, as illustrated in

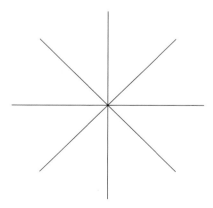

Figure 3.1 *Hub and spoke*

OEM
....

Main suppliers
....

Specialized suppliers
....

Non-specialized suppliers ('jobbers')
....

Figure 3.2 *Supply pyramid*

Figure 3.2. Often, the first-tier suppliers yield not only technical competences, but also organizational ones, in the co-ordination of lower-tier activities. Thereby, the first tier takes a load off the co-ordinating task of the apex of the pyramid. First-tier relations are often more longer-lasting than lower-tier ones. Lower tiers mostly supply less specialized products, and often supply in several pyramids.

Note that the hub-and-spoke form and pyramid form can be combined. A central OEM can be surrounded by supplier systems that each has a pyramid form.

Centrality has implications for power, in terms of access to alternative participants in the network, bargaining power, control of information and gossip, coalition formation, and a policy of 'divide and rule'. This is discussed in more detail in the analysis of governance, in Chapter 4.

The fifth feature, *structural holes* (Burt 1992), refers to gaps in network structure, so that some participants can be reached by some others only by very indirect, roundabout paths. There can be such holes within a group, and there are outside holes between groups. Structural holes arise, in particular, between different groups. As a sixth feature, groups may be inclined to establish *isolation* from outside influences, i.e. maintain many holes between the group and the outside. As will be discussed in more detail later, an important position lies in the bridging of structural holes. Here, there is a second type of centrality, called *betweenness centrality*, as a sixth feature, defined as the concentration of bridging ties.

Important also, as an eighth feature, is the *stability* of group membership. Low stability entails frequent exit, and new entry of 'outsiders'. In particular, stability has implications for opportunities to recoup specific investments, hold-up risk, spill-over risk, mutual understanding, learning and trust.

A ninth feature is *structural equivalence*, that is, two or more members that have ties to more or less the same other members. Structurally equivalent members, having the same pattern of ties in the group, may be rivals in the group. In imitation behaviour, one is more likely to imitate structurally equivalent agents than ones who are dissimilar in their connections and role in the network (Burt 1987).

72

Finally, a tenth feature is *concentration of ownership and control*. Clearly, this has implications for power relations. It will often be associated with degree centrality, but this is not necessarily the case. A player may be central without holding majority ownership or control. For example, a chain store organization has both high centrality and concentration of ownership and control, while a voluntary chain or franchise has high centrality without concentration of ownership, and has some concentration of control.

Ties

In his famous treatise on 'the strength of weak ties', Granovetter (1973) defined the strength of ties as 'a combination of the amount of time, emotional intensity, intimacy (mutual confiding), and reciprocal services'. Here, it is proposed that the 'strength of ties' has seven dimensions. One aspect is the *scope* of a tie, as indicated earlier. It is defined as the share of total activities taken up in the tie. Ties may concern different relations, activities and resources, such as ownership, control, sales, technology, knowledge, etc. Note that now the notion of centrality, discussed before, may be ambiguous. A participant may be central with respect to one type of tie, but not with respect to other types.

A second aspect is intensity in terms of *investment* in the tie, which may be financial and emotional. It has three aspects: size, specificity and economic life. These dimensions are inspired by TCE, and have implications for the duration of ties. Clearly, the division of the total investment in the tie may be asymmetric between the two participants, yielding asymmetric dependence. A third aspect is intensity in terms of the *frequency* of interaction. A fourth aspect is intensity in terms of *openness* of communication. A fifth aspect is *duration* of ties, a sixth is *cognitive proximity* of participants, and an eighth is *spatial proximity*.

For example, a trade association is a type of IOR. Generally it has large size (many participants), low scope (e.g. only joint promotion of political or commercial interests, joint training or information provision), low investment intensity (low subscription fee, no investments), infrequent meetings, long duration (membership), moderate cognitive proximity and low proximity in space.

Openness of communication is reminiscent of what Granovetter called 'mutual confiding' (see above). Strong ties, in the sense of high frequency and intensity, and long duration, yield shared experience, which reduce cognitive distance, and enable the development of empathy and identification (McAllister 1995; Lewicki and Bunker 1996; Hansen 1999). They enhance control and bonding (Coleman 1988).

73

Owing to ICT, proximity in space has become less important. There are claims of the 'death of distance'. This claim is debatable, and will be discussed later. The opportunities from ICT have raised the notion of 'virtual organizations'. That term has been given a wide variety of interpretations. In a narrow interpretation, adopted in this book, it just means an organization where people substitute the use of ICT for direct, face-to-face contact, in virtual meetings. In wider interpretations, the term of 'virtual organizations' appears to cover anything that constitutes a deviation from customary features of organization. For example, the literature has included the following features in the notion of virtuality (see e.g. Child and Faulkner 1999):

1   difference of location (interaction at a spatial distance);
2   high degree of outsourcing;
3   high decentralization or autonomy of organizational units;
4   individualized responsibilities and incentives;
5   highly distributed ownership;
6   unstable structure, with high rates of entry and exit;
7   low duration of ties;
8   non-exclusiveness of membership, in simultaneous membership of multiple networks;
9   use of alliances rather than merger or acquisition;
10 'blurring boundaries' of the firm, with forms of organization 'between market and hierarchy';
11 embeddedness in networks of complementary competences.

In Chapter 1 the concept of organization was characterized in several ways: legal identity to regulate ownership, employment and liability; inseparable economies of scale and scope; forms of co-ordination; incentives and monitoring; motivation; and cognitive focus. If anything that deviates from customary forms of these is included in virtuality, the notion becomes so wide that it becomes indeterminate. The terms used just now are all perfectly adequate to address different, more determinate features. One might preserve the wider notion of a virtual organization as an organizational form that includes all the features listed above: high degree of outsourcing, in networks, with use of complementary competences between decentralized, highly autonomous units, which are responsible for their own profits and survival, are subject to only limited central co-ordination, and have only temporary and non-exclusive allegiance to the organization. But this sounds like a network, or 'industrial district', or a hub-and-spoke arrangement around a large firm, indicated before. Why, then, not use those more precise terms? The term 'virtual organizations' as an encompassing notion adds little more than confusion, and will be avoided in this book.

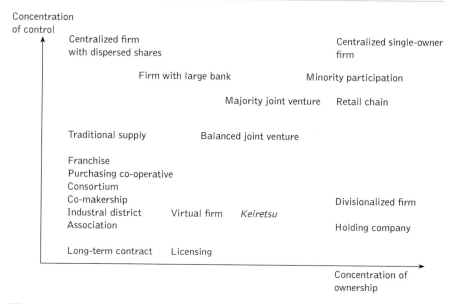

Concentration of control

Centralized firm with dispersed shares

Centralized single-owner firm

Firm with large bank

Minority participation

Majority joint venture

Retail chain

Traditional supply

Balanced joint venture

Franchise
Purchasing co-operative
Consortium
Co-makership

Divisionalized firm

Industral district
Association

Virtual firm

Keiretsu

Holding company

Long-term contract

Licensing

Concentration of ownership

Figure 3.3 *Concentration of ownership and control*

Concentration of ownership and control

A number of authors have distinguished IORs according to concentration of ownership (Contractor and Lorange 1988; Osborn and Baughn 1990; Hagedoorn 1993). Along that scale, IORs range from *ad hoc* spot contracting, through non-equity alliances and joint ventures to full integration in take-overs and acquisitions. Here, and elsewhere in this book, 'joint venture' refers to equity joint ventures, i.e. the setting up of a novel firm under shared ownership and control. Since ownership and control can be separated, as in the separation of shareholders and management in corporations with publicly traded shares, this can be expanded into two dimensions (Nooteboom 1999a). This is illustrated in Figure 3.3.

Contrary to most treatments, Figure 3.3 also includes degrees of integration within the firm. Thus, a merger or acquisition can yield an integrated or dis-integrated company, in terms of both decision making and distribution of ownership. The reason for doing this is that networks of firms with strong ties (such as 'industrial districts') can become very similar to a highly decentralized ('virtual') large firm. Here, a 'virtual firm' would mean a firm with limited central co-ordination of dispersed, decentralized activities and considerable disper-sion of profit in component activities, as discussed above.

A classic case is the fashion firm Benetton. It consists of weak ties between a large number of independent small firms engaged in the production and distribution of fashion clothing, with rapid adjustment to market signals by ICT linkages between the firms. The value of Benetton lies not in any particular competence of design or technology of product or production, but in the brand name and co-ordination of the information network for speedy adjustment to changes in taste (Lorenzini and Baden-Fuller 1993). Is this an industrial district or a virtual firm?

Joint ventures may include multiple parents. Ownership and control may or may not be equally distributed. Non-equity alliances embrace a wide variety of co-operation, with a wide spectrum of organizational concentration. They include franchising; more or less contractual co-operation in research or in product development; joint development of a product between a buyer and supplier (co-makership); joint production, marketing, distribution or sales; licensing; consortia for building projects or for conducting R&D; associations for advertising, quality programmes, certification or political representation; industrial districts; dealerships, service contracts and sales agents. A non-equity alliance can yield different levels of dependence, associated with different heights of exit barriers or switching costs (e.g. due to transaction specific investments, as discussed in transaction cost theory), and this requires different degrees of governance. Licensing yields a more tenuous link through royalty agreements. Co-operatives and franchises centralize some decision rights and distribute rights to profit which are not, however, tradable on a share market, and entail some specific investments, which together yield exit barriers. Consortia also centralize supervision to some extent, which yields some exit barriers, but they generally do not last as long. Associations last longer, and also have some centralized decisions or supervision, but generally concern only a limited part of particip-ants' activities and interests, and exit barriers are generally low. Agreements for management support, training, start-up assistance, maintenance or other services are long-term contracts, approaching market transactions.

Cobwebs

The logic behind the selection of features of ties, presented above, is that, like the features of structure, they are relevant from the perspective of com-petence, governance, or both. This is discussed in more detail later, partly in the analysis of governance, in Chapter 4, and partly in the analysis of the process of IORs, in Chapter 5.

On the competence side, high frequency and sufficient duration, and perhaps also proximity, may be needed to exchange and jointly produce knowledge, especially when it is highly tacit. On the governance side, scope, intensity,

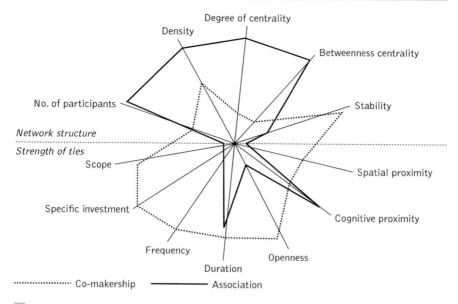

Figure 3.4 Cobwebs of IOR profiles

specificity, frequency and duration have implications for hold-up risk. Frequency, duration and proximity have implications for the build-up or breakdown of trust. Frequency and openness have implications for spill-over.

In other words, the features presented here for structure and ties provide the basis for the later analysis of governance.

The dimensions of relations that allow for a scale of measurement (ordinal or cardinal) can be included in a cobweb diagram, with lines radiating outward from a central point, one for each dimension. A particular IOR can then be plotted along each of those dimensions, yielding a cobweb-like diagram. In this way different IORs can be characterized and compared. This is illustrated in Figure 3.4, for a co-makership relation and for an association.

In principle one would expect high specific investments to go along with long duration, to recoup those investments, and high network stability, for the same reason. In Figure 3.4 the diagram for an association shows that duration can be high when specific investments are low, because usually there are no competing associations, so that there are no alternatives to switch to. In spite of long duration of ties, network stability is low, owing to firms entering or leaving the industry frequently.

CHOICE

This section analyses the choice of form, both normatively, i.e. what is good for the firm, depending on conditions, and descriptively, i.e. what choices are actually made, and why. First, it considers the choice of integration in an organization, in a merger or acquisition (MA), versus an alliance, in which parties remain formally independent (legally and in ownership). Next, it considers the intermediate form of a joint venture. Finally, it considers effects of networks.

Merger, acquisition or alliance?

Note that an MA entails integration in the legal entity of one organization. Within that organization, it may allow for high degrees of decentralization. Table 3.1 summarizes the argument for the alternatives of an MA and an alliance. Overall, the argument for integration, in an MA, is that it yields more control, in particular of hold-up and spill-over risk, and of present and future core competences. For hold-up, the argument comes from TCE. Within a firm, under the grasp of 'administrative fiat', in an employment relation, one can demand more information for control and one can impose more decisions than one could in respect of an independent partner. A similar argument applies to spill-over risk: one can monitor and control better what happens to information. Of course, even within organizations this may not be easy, as a result of asymmetric information, tacit knowledge, and misaligned incentives and motivations. However, under the legal umbrella of a firm, one has more opportunities than between different firms.

As discussed in Chapter 1, an argument for integration may also be that one needs to maintain control of activities or resources that are complementary to core competences, i.e. are needed to utilize them or to appropriate their advantages, or that are needed to retain options for future core competences. The example was given of the chips division of Philips Electronics. Philips might have to hold on to it since it appears to be a platform technology for a range of potential future markets. Another possible argument is that that one may need to retain a certain capability in an outsourced activity to be able to judge its quality. However, it was also argued that there might be opportunities to maintain options for future core competences in alliances. And capability of judging supplier quality may be derived from a joint benchmarking service, in the industry.

The take-over of a young, dynamic, innovative firm may serve to rejuvenate an old firm (Vermeulen and Barkema 2001). In a growing new firm the entrepreneur often has to turn himself around to the role of an administrator, or hire one, to delegate work and institute formal structures and procedures for the co-ordination of more specialized activities in large-scale production. He may not be able or willing to do that, and it may be to the benefit of the firm when it is taken over by a firm with a better managerial capability. However, it may be more likely that the entrepreneurial dynamic of the small firm gets stifled in the bureaucracy of the acquirer, in which case it should stay separate.

Table 3.1 *Reasons for a merger, acquisition or alliance*

	MA (integration)	Alliance (keeping distance)
Efficiency	Inseparable economy of scale in core activities	Economy of scale in non-core activities
	Inseparable economy of scope	Motivating force of independence
		Lower costs and risks of integration
Competence	Maintain appropriability, options for future competence	Maintain focus on core competence
	Spill-over control	Maintain diversity, cognitive distance
	Rejuvenation	Maintain entrepreneurial drive
	Provide management for a growing firm	
Positional advantage	Control hold-up risk	Maintain flexibility
	Control quality brand name	Maintain local identity/brand of partner
	Protect other partners from spill-over	
	Ensure against take-over	
	Keep out competition	
By default	Partner available only in MA	Partner available only in alliance
	Difficulty of evaluating a take-over candidate	Interest only in part of a partner
	Collusion forbidden by competition authorities	MA forbidden by competition authorities
Rule of thumb	*In case of same core competences/same markets*	*In case of complementary competences/markets*

Overall, the argument for an alliance is that it allows partners to maintain more focus of core competence, more flexibility of configuration and more variety of competence for the sake of innovation and learning. The flexibility argument derives from rigidities in rearrangement of activities within organizations. As noted in Chapter 1, this varies across business systems: such rigidity is less in the United States than in continental Europe and Japan. Hence, network structures of firms are more needed in the latter regions.

Also, as recognized in TCE, an independent firm that is responsible for its own survival will be more motivated to perform than an internal department that is assured of its custom. Another great advantage of an alliance is that it entails fewer problems of clashes between different cultures, structures and procedures, in management, decision making, remuneration, labour conditions, reporting procedures and norms of conflict resolution, which often turn out to be the biggest obstacles to a successful MA. Of course such clashes can also occur in alliances, but less integration still entails fewer problems of integration.

There is an argument of scale for both forms. In production, many economies of scale have been reduced, e.g. in computing. However, there is still economy of scale in, for instance, distribution channels, communication networks, network externalities and brand name. For integration, the argument of scale is that one pools volume in activities in which one specializes. For outsourcing, the argument is that for activities that one does not specialize in, an outside, specialized producer can collect more volume, producing for multiple users. That may also offer more opportunities for professional development and career to staff that are specialized in that activity. Note the argument from TCE that if assets are so dedicated that a supplier can produce only for the one user the scale argument for outsourcing disappears.

As discussed earlier, in Chapter 2, there is an argument of economies of scale or scope for integration only if they are inseparable (Williamson 1975). It depends how systemic rather than stand-alone activities are (Langlois and Robertson 1995).

One form of economy of scope is that different activities share the same underlying fixed cost, for example of R&D, management and administration, communication network or brand name. When one of the activities is dropped, the utilization of fixed costs may drop. However, this is not necessarily so. It may be possible to share such overhead with others, as happens, for example, in 'incubators' for small firms, or collaboration in an R&D consortium.

From the perspective of brand image there are arguments for both integration and separation. In an alliance there may be too great a risk that the image or quality of a brand allotted to partners will not be maintained sufficiently scrupulously. On the other hand, it may be better to maintain an independent, outside brand, to preserve its local identity.

The Dutch bank RABO years ago wanted to move into consumer credit, but felt that it would detract from its brand identity, which was associated with savings accounts, and therefore consumer credit was offered by a separate subsidiary with a different name (Lage Landen). However, years later consumer credit had become a normal product, required in the product range of any bank, and RABO incorporated the Lage Landen under its own name.

Staying with the RABO bank, an illustration of reinforcing one's product range by pooling complementary products is the co-operation between RABO, which offered a personal securities investment service through its advisers, and ROBECO, which offered a security investment fund to which consumers could subscribe by phone, without intermediaries. The two were pooled to yield a full line of service.

Finally, there are reasons of default. One is that one would like to take one form but it is not available, because a partner is available only for the other form, or because it is forbidden by the competition authorities.

In the airline business, for example, MA are problematic for reasons of national pride and interest, perhaps strategic military reasons, and the fact that landing rights are nationally allocated.

Another default is that one would like to take over only part of a larger firm, but it is not separately available for take-over without the rest, in which one is not interested because it would dilute core competence. Another is that one cannot judge the value of a take-over candidate and needs some period of collaboration in an alliance to find out. Previously, value could more easily be judged by adding up values of material assets than now, when intangibles such as brand name, reputation, skills and knowledge are often more important, and difficult to value.

Clearly, the choice between MA and alliance is quite complex. If one wants a simpler, general rule of thumb, it is as follows: consider full integration, in an MA, only if the partner engages in the same core activities in the same markets. In all other cases, i.e. when activities and/or markets are different, the rule of thumb suggests an alliance. According to this rule, what one would expect, on the whole, is vertical disintegration and horizontal integration.

In banking, increase of efficiency in an MA can, for example, be achieved by eliminating one of two branch offices (or automatic teller machines) in locations where both banks are represented. Threshold costs in specialized knowledge of specific industries and in setting up ICT networks and databases can be shared. Reserves to cover risks of defaulting customers can be shared and spread. In an MA between banking and insurance there are economies of scope in the utilization of branch offices, ICT networks, advertising, customer relations. In MAs in banking, insurance and accounting an important motive also is the building of a worldwide network of offices from different companies pooling their offices in different continents, in order to yield global service to global customers. However, here one could ask whether the same objectives could not be achieved in an alliance, with the added advantages associated with that.

There are four theoretical arguments for the rule of thumb. First, in horizontal collaboration, with the same activities in the same markets, partners are direct competitors, and it is most difficult to control conflict without integration. The game is more likely to be zero-sum. The temptation to exploit dependence is greatest. There is a threat of direct rather than indirect spill-over. Second, in horizontal collaboration core competence is more similar, so that integration does not dilute it too much. Third, here the cognitive advantages of alliances are less: the diversity in knowledge is already minimal, with small cognitive distance, and thus there is less need to preserve it by staying apart. Fourth, with the same products, technology and markets, differences in culture, structure and procedures are likely to be minimal. Of course, they can still be substantial.

The Dutch steel corporation (Hoogovens) a long time ago undertook a merger with its German colleague. After ten years of struggle it was broken up again, because attempts to integrate the two companies remained unsuccessful. Ten years after that, in Hoogovens there were still two rival camps, of those who had supported the merger, and were reproached that the failure was their fault, and the opponents, who were blamed by the proponents for having sabotaged the merger. More recently, Hoogovens merged with British Steel into Corus. Problems arose due to the fact that, partly because of the strength of the pound, but also due to obsolete installations, the British side was not performing well. To generate funds for restructuring, the British CEO wanted to sell off the Dutch aluminium division. This was contested by Dutch management, and brought to court, which confirmed the Dutch position. Subsequently, the British CEO stepped down.

One important qualification of the rule of thumb is the following. The overlap of activities and markets, which would favour integration, does not concern the situation prior to collaboration, but afterwards. In other words, if collaboration would lead to such overlap, integration may be needed before that overlap arises. In other words, one should look not at current but at intended core competences.

The argument for the rule of thumb is not only theoretical. Bleeke and Ernst (1991) showed empirically that when this rule is applied, the success rate of both MA and alliances rises substantially. If for a given method of measurement the success rate is less than 50 per cent without the rule, success rises to 75 per cent with the rule, for both MA and alliances. However, the rule given above is only a rule of thumb, to which there are exceptions. For more detailed analysis one can use Table 3.1, with the corresponding logic set out above.

Bad reasons

Next to good reasons for MA, alliances and outsourcing, there are also reasons that are bad, in the sense that they are not in the interests of the firms involved. One such reason is the bandwagon effect: one engages in a practice because it is the fashion to do so. When a practice becomes established, the drive for legitimation may yield pressure to adopt it without much critical evaluation. Another reason is a prisoners' dilemma that applies especially to MA: if one does not take over one may be taken over, which may yield a loss of managerial position, so one tries to make the first move, even though it would be best for all to stay apart. Another reason is managerial hubris: managers want to make their mark and appear decisive or macho. This also applies especially to MAs: they are quicker, more visible and dramatic than collaboration between independent firms. There is also the often illusory presumption that a take-over is easier than an alliance. Subsequently, however, the MA often fails owing to problems of integration and has to be disentangled again. Even speed is a dubious argument. It may on the surface seem that an MA is in place faster than an alliance, for which one must negotiate longer and set up an elaborate system of 'bilateral governance'. However, the speed of an MA is misleading: the decision may be made quickly, but the subsequent process of integration is often much slower and more problematic than is assumed. An alliance is often better even if in the longer run a takeover is the best option, to allow for the process of trust development, discussed before. Also, it yields the option to retract when failure emerges, without too much loss of investment.

Bad reasons of bandwagon effects, managerial hubris or macho behaviour and career profile may also thwart alliances. However, here the damage is more limited, and it is easier to retrench when failure emerges.

Joint ventures

An equity joint venture is an intermediate case between full integration and staying apart. Clearly, it entails considerable cost of setting up a joint, new firm. Apart from direct set-up costs, it entails some integration of staff from the parent companies. Thus, it entails similar problems of integration as in an MA, though on a more limited scale. Also, people may be uncertain about divided loyalties between the joint venture and the parent company.

However, it yields advantages of control without full integration of all activities of the parents. Thereby, it allows more focus on core competences and limits integration problems. It can separate off and protect a new, entrepreneurial activity from established bureaucracy. By separating new ventures from the parents one can also better control spill-over problems for existing partners. If collaboration regards an activity that remains incorporated in a large, diversified firm, with other activities that may be seen as potentially competitive to a partner, or which maintains connections with his competitors, the spill-over risk to the partner is higher than when the activity is shielded off in a joint venture, under partial control by the partner. The new venture may also offer new opportunities for financing. Finally, when it is difficult to judge the value of a potential take-over candidate, as discussed above, a joint venture might offer an intermediate step, to assess value better. Earlier, in Chapter 2, an example was given of a joint venture in 'white goods' (refrigerators, cookers, etc.) between Whirlpool and Philips, for Whirlpool to assess its value prior to takeover.

A well-known issue in the literature on joint ventures is whether ownership and control should be distributed equally, among the parents, or concentrated in a clear majority shareholder (Killing 1983; Anderson and Gatignon 1986; Geringer and Hebert 1989; Bleeke and Ernst 1991). The argument for the latter is that it yields more decisiveness. The argument for the former is that a minority participant may suffer from a 'Calimero syndrome': with less influence and high dependence, he may not be motivated to do his best and may be overly suspicious of becoming the victim of opportunism, which blocks the building of trust. However, there is a well known solution to this problem. It is to separate ownership and management, with symmetric ownership and a rotating majority in decision making. At any time this yields a clear initiative in management for one side, whose actions are monitored by a balanced supervisory board. Whoever has the management prerogative is disciplined by his knowledge that he will be subject to evaluation by the partner, and that the prerogative will be switched in future. Perhaps it is also a possibility to hire a third, independent party as a manager.

Network structure

As discussed before, one should look not only at direct linkages, but also at indirect ones, in linkages that partners have with others. There are also important roles for 'third parties', especially for the governance of relations, as will be discussed in Chapter 4. A theoretical analysis of the position of such third parties, or go-betweens, or boundary spanners, is given later in the present chapter. Here, the focus is on innovative properties of network structure. Chapter 4 analyses implications of network structure for governance.

The literature exhibits a confusion of different types of networks, such as industrial districts, clusters and regional innovation systems. The differences between these three are not always clear. They all have an aspect of local or regional embeddedness, and they may all include public institutional arrangements (universities, governing bodies, education and training, information centres, etc.). A distinguishing feature of industrial districts is that the firms they incorporate are mostly relatively small and formally (legally) independent.

Network structures in general, and industrial districts in particular, yield attractive properties of *flexible specialization* (Piore and Sabel 1983, 1984): network structures of partially co-operating and partially competing small firms in research and development, production, distribution and supporting services make optimal use of the motivating force of the market and flexible combinations of products, production units, knowledge, depending on market conditions.

More specifically, there are three arguments for such network structures. The first is to maintain the autonomy of participants, each with its own set of activities and connections, to maintain cognitive distance. The second is the argument of strategic flexibility: the novel combinations of innovation are achieved by variable configurations of participants in the network. There is no guarantee of inclusion. Participants are included or excluded according to the viability of configurations. There is a certain romanticism surrounding industrial districts, but it is to be noted that their main strength lies in harsh exclusion according to expedience. What is allowed between organizations would not be allowed within them. The third argument is that participants can specialize in a stage of innovation. Some units concentrate on exploitation and others on exploration, and activities are shifted between the units as they move through the cycle of development. It can be an attractive position to act as orchestrator of activities in such a network. It is a constellation of high potential 'dynamic' efficiency, especially in the exploration that accompanies radical innovation (Nooteboom 1998).

Illustrations in practice are the development of microelectronics in 'Silicon Valley' and machine, textile and shoe industries in northern Italy (Piore and Sabel 1983). High decentralization of authority and responsibility in large firms (a 'virtual' firm?) may be seen as their answer to this.

The argument connects with the advantages of alliances over MA discussed before. Granovetter (1973) proposed that new information is found in weak rather than strong ties (where strength is defined as 'a combination of the amount of time, emotional intensity, intimacy (mutual confiding), and reciprocal services'). Granovetter associated these with a dense structure. In view of the frequent and intense interaction between many actors, much of the information circulating in the system is redundant. Hence the notion of the strength of weak ties, in sparse (non-dense) networks. An example he used was the discovery of new employment opportunities, through acquaintances with which one has only sporadic contacts. Burt (1992) made a clearer conceptual separation between the strength and the density of ties. It is the dense structure, apart from the strength of ties, which yields redundancy, when the aim is access to new knowledge. Novelty is to be obtained especially from bridging structural holes, i.e. gaps in connections between actors. In dense networks one needs to expend many resources on the maintenance of ties (even if they are weak), while for access to sources of knowledge many direct relations are redundant, since a source can be accessed indirectly, through intermediate linkages. These considerations refer to the competence side of relations.

The argument of Granovetter and Burt can be contradicted. This done in the Chapter 5. It will be proposed that, counter to the claim of Granovetter and Burt, for radical innovation, in networks for exploration, dense structure may be needed, for both competence and governance, with ties that are strong in the dimensions of frequency, scope, openness, and possibly spatial proximity, and of limited strength in the dimensions of commitment of resources, duration and cognitive proximity. The argument yields a further illustration of the need to distinguish different dimensions of the strength of ties.

Licensing

Licensing is also a form of collaboration (included in Figure 3.3). Table 3.2 gives a survey of reasons for and against licensing. When licensed, an unintended outcome of unpredictable R&D, whose exploitation would not fit in one's intended markets, production or organization, at least yields some revenue. And there is not much harm in giving it to a competitor if it does not compete with one's own products, either because it is not a substitute or because the licence is given for countries where one does not distribute one's own products. Another reason for a licence is that an innovation cannot be protected in any other way, and could be imitated.

Especially for small firms, protection by patents is problematic. First, there are high entry and set-up costs. Patenting is a lengthy and complicated procedure that presents a threshold, especially the first time round. Second, small firms may lack credibility of legal action on patent infringement, in view of, again, the high set-up costs, with outside legal specialists, and the risks involved.

A third advantage is that one would otherwise not have access to the relevant market. Yet another is that the licensee would be an attractive partner for learning: he would do other things with the licence that one could not do oneself.

Table 3.2 *Arguments for and against licensing*

For	Against
For the licensor	
Assets	
Local volume is not worth own investment	Profit goes mostly to licensee
The product cannot be protected against copying	Lack of control of quality brand name, sales effort
Competence	
The activity lies outside core competence	
Perspective for learning from licensee	
Positional advantage	
Entry into market is blocked or entails too many risks or investments	Lack of control; danger of creating a competitor
For the licensee	
No R&D expense and risk	Arrow's paradox of information for assessing value
Profit from knowledge, expertise, contacts of licensor	Contractual limits on operations
	Risk of obsolescence
	Ongoing royalty payments

A disadvantage of licensing is of course reduced revenue. Another is that by granting the licence, one might create a competitor, either because he infringes or sidesteps the agreement not to supply on one's own market, or because the patent yields experience and insight in one's technology, marketing or organization. In other words: a licence might be a vehicle of wider spill-over.

Structures of buyer–supplier relations

In the 1980s, Western nations were confronted with a Japanese challenge in the organization of supply (Dore 1983, 1989; Womack *et al*. 1990; Cusumano and Fujimoto 1991; Helper 1991; Helper and Levine 1992; Dyer and Ouchi 1993; Lamming 1993). One aspect of this was the phenomenon of several tiers of supply, in the 'supply pyramid', illustrated in Figure 3.2. The principle here is that the buyer concentrates on direct relations with the highest echelon of a limited number of 'main suppliers', who have to satisfy special demands, e.g. concerning the supply of entire subsystems, in which elements from lower tiers are integrated, with the addition of services of co-ordination, vendor selection, monitoring of quality, development. On the second tier are firms that offer special products and technical competences, and on the lowest tier are suppliers without special competences, who are often used for capacity sourcing, or for the supply of standardized goods, materials or services. Fluctuations in demand are often devolved to the lowest tier. Volume flexibility on that level is often based on less job security for workers.

Special demands are made on main suppliers, entailing specific investments, but in return they are awarded a longer-term contract and technology transfer and other support from the buyer. The focus of attention on main suppliers in the course of the past decennia has shifted from attention to mere price and quality of the supplied product to additional demands on technological capability, flexibility and innovative capacity. Especially striking, in contrast with earlier buyer–supplier relations in Western countries, was that buyers had only one main supplier (for each type of activity), at least for the duration of the life cycle of the particular model of the product involved (Kamath and Liker 1994). And while in Europe and the United States buyers were used to dictating design and price, regardless of whether the supplier could achieve a sufficient profit, in Japan it was reversed, in the practice of 'price-minus costing': the buyer takes as his point of departure a sufficient profit margin for the supplier, and then sees it as a shared responsibility, with pooling of resources, to design and develop the product so that an acceptable cost to the buyer is achieved.

Lower down the pyramid, firms will tend to have multiple customers. This makes sense in the analysis from preceding chapters. If one has a single customer, with dedicated investments, one must have compensatory power in the relation on the basis of unique products or competences. If one supplies undifferentiated staple goods, one should have multiple customers.

In practice the pyramid principle is not adhered to rigidly, but the figure serves to indicate that there are levels with different functions, demands and conditions. There are firms that supply directly, on the first tier, but also indirectly through other main suppliers. Indirect supply through main suppliers is not a feature only of small firms, and need not be tied to lack of influence or power. Especially second-tier specialists can be powerful owing to scarce competences.

In the car industry there are main suppliers who offer system supply for the interior, e.g. seats. They in turn outsource the material for the upholstery to specialized producers. The supply of electronic instruments for the dashboard (by large firms such as Bosch, Siemens, Philips) illustrates how a firm can supply indirectly through a main supplier, and yet be involved in joint development with the ultimate buyer.

In more detail, the following characteristics determine the position that a firm can take in the pyramid:

1 technical competence to integrate component technologies, including the logistics involved;
2 organizational competence to co-ordinate several participants;
3 direct supply;
4 specialization in some (technological) area;
5 international presence, to supply 'just in time' at different locations;
6 flexibility, in volume, availability of people, competences;
7 competence in team work inside the firm, with the customer, and with lower-level suppliers;
8 innovative competence;
9 multiple customers, as a source of learning;
10 support in service: design, training, maintenance, repair.

For a typical main supplier, on the first tier, the desired characteristics are, in particular: 1, 2, 3, 6, 7, 8, 10 and perhaps also 5. A technical specialist, on the second tier, will typically need: 4, 5, 8, 9, 10. But other combinations may occur. These dimensions of value are built into the analysis, in the dimensions of value that partners can have for each other, in Chapter 4.

In Europe and the United States there has been a certain development towards 'Japanese practice', with attention not only to price and quality but also to technological and innovative competence. There also, there is concentration on fewer main suppliers and some semblance of pyramids emerges.

For example, in the car industry the number of direct suppliers is systematically reduced. Table 3.3 gives some figures for the car industry in 1988. It shows that, at the time, in Europe and the United States the reduction of first-tier suppliers had not yet progressed as far as in Japan. However, Table 3.4 shows that since then the development has proceeded in the United States. Kamp (2003: 106) showed a similar development for the European company Renault, where the number of direct suppliers declined from 1800 in 1984, to 720 in 1990, to 507 in 2002. Volkswagen has a policy of maintaining a relatively large number of direct suppliers, but it has declined there as well, from 30,000 in 1983 to 4,532 in 2001 (Kamp 2003: 81).

The reduction of the number of direct suppliers, on the first tier, is a general phenomenon: the pyramid is getting 'steeper'. The reason is simple: often the '20–80 rule' applies: 80 per cent of volume is supplied by 20 per cent of the suppliers. The remaining 20 per cent of volume is supplied by 80 per cent of the suppliers, and one would rather shift the relatively costly task of managing these relations. If the end product is based on diverse, non-related 'families' of technology (Lamming 1993: 185), as in the case of cars, then it is also impossible for

89

Table 3.3 Number of direct suppliers in the car industry in Japan, North America and Europe

Producer	No. of direct suppliers (domestic)	No. of cars produced (million)
Japan		
Toyota	340	4.0
Nissan	310	2.2
Honda	310	1.3
North America		
General Motors	2500	5.9
Ford	1800	4.0
Chrysler	2000	2.2
Europe		
Fiat	900	1.9
Renault	1050	1.7
PSA	900	2.0
VW/Audi	1580	1.9
Daimler-Benz	1650	0.7
Rover	850	0.52
BMW	1420	0.44
Volvo	590	0.33
Saab	485	0.15
Jaguar	540	0.05
Porsche	600	0.03

Source: Lamming (1993: 172).

Note: All figures apply to 1988, except 1987 for BMW.

Table 3.4 Reduction of number of direct suppliers in the American car industry

Manufacturer	1980	1985	1990
Ford	3200	2600	1300
General Motors	4000	3500	1800
Chrysler	1600	1300–1400	700–800

Source: Hoffman and Kaplinsky, *Driving Force Auto Components and Global Restructuring* (1990), quoted in Ministry of Economic Affairs (1991).

the buyer to have sufficiently deep competence to be able to judge supply to its lowest level of detail in all families. This also specifies a limit to the reduction of the number of direct suppliers: for each technology family at least one supplier.

Lamming (1993: 185) reported that in the middle of the 1980s, Peugeot identified 257 families, Fiat 250 and Renault 150. On the basis of two suppliers for each, one arrives at the numbers of direct suppliers indicated for the Japanese industry in Table 3.3.

The orientation towards vertical co-operation in buyer–supplier relations, not only for efficiency but also, and increasingly first of all, for improvement and innovation of products is exhibited in a survey by McKinsey in 1988, as summarized in Table 3.5. It gives a self-report from firms, which does not necessarily give a reliable picture of actual activities. It is likely that since 1988 the focus on product improvement and innovation has increased.

The table indicates that improvement and innovation of products and processes are considered more important than control of costs, and that for this purpose one considers especially vertical co-operation, while for cost control one needs others less. These results are in full agreement with the analyses in

Table 3.5 *Sources of improvement (%)*

% of firms that judges activity as one of the two most important	How does one intend to realize improvement?						
	Alone	In co-operation			With support		
		Horizontal	Vertical	Both	External (Semi) gvt.		Research institute
Development of new products or processes: 85	13	13	49	7	11	4	31
Improvement of present products or processes: 79	25	14	45	5	9	1	16
Better control of costs of products/processes: 23	39	9	12	3	21	0	12
Better control of costs of product-process development: 10	25	25	13	0	33	0	4

Source: McKinsey (1988).

previous chapters: the learning theory in Chapter 1, goals of alliances in Chapter 2, and dimensions of partner value in the present chapter. It was noted that co-operation is needed especially in innovation and learning, particularly under conditions of rapid change of technology and markets. Vertical co-operation is easier to control than horizontal alliances between competitors, and there is less risk of direct spill-over, since partners are not themselves competitors.

External corporate venturing

A special form of IOR is external corporate venturing. Here, a parent firm allows an individual or team from its organization to start up an external venture on their own. From earlier analysis, this can be understood as follows. First, from the perspective of combining exploitation and exploration, this allows exploration in a new unit that has too unorthodox ideas to fit in existing ways of doing things without destroying the integrity of the system needed for exploitation. As discussed before, this is a problem to the extent that this system is 'systemic', with complex and tight linkages between elements of the system. By externalizing the venture, one sets it aside from the established order. The venture may be facilitated in several ways. One is to provide venture capital. A second is to provide a return guarantee when the venture matures or when it fails. This approach has several additional advantages. First, it allows one to maintain a relation with staff who would otherwise have left the organization with some frustration, without ever wanting to return. Often, these are not the worst kind of staff. Second, it allows one to hedge bets concerning future core competences. If the venture opens up new options, one may reabsorb it to build new core competence. Third, more insidiously, if the venture turns out to yield a competing product that cannibalizes existing products, one may put it on hold, if one has a controlling stake in the venture, or if one can make a sufficiently attractive counter-offer to the entrepreneur.

CONCEPTS AND THEORY

This section discusses special effects in networks with respect to 'third parties', and a problem in bidding for information (the 'revelation problem').

Third parties

Simmel (1950) argued that a fundamental shift occurs in going from dyadic to triadic relations (Krackhardt 1999). In dyadic relations no coalitions can occur, and no majority can outvote an individual. In a triad any member by himself has less bargaining power than in a dyad. The threat of exit carries less weight, since the two remaining partners would still have each other. In a triad, conflict is more readily solved. When any two players enter conflict, the third can act as a moderator or 'go-between'.

One stream of literature on networks suggests that players who span structural holes can gain advantage (Burt 1992). If individuals or communities A and B are connected only by C, then C can take advantage of his bridging position by accessing resources that others cannot access, and by playing off A and B against each other (in *divide and rule*). As a result, the third party is maximally powerful and minimally constrained in his actions. This yields Burt's (1992) notion of *tertius gaudens.* Krackhardt pointed out that this principle goes back to Simmel (1950).

However, Krackhardt shows that Simmel also indicated that under some conditions the third party is maximally instead of minimally constrained. This occurs when he bridges two different cliques, with dense and strong internal ties, who entertain different values and norms, while both can observe his actions. The third party then has to satisfy the rules or norms of both cliques (the intersection of norm sets), and thereby he is constrained in his actions. The key factor that determines whether the bridging party is minimally or maximally constrained is the degree to which his actions are public, or at least known to both A and B. If not, then the situation described by Burt obtains, and he is minimally constrained. If his actions are public, he is maximally constrained. Membership of multiple cliques then yields a position of potential power, but also constrains the use of it. This often applies to managers or boundary spanners who bridge different departments or organizations. As indicated above, in the discussion of joint ventures, it can apply to a manager who still has allegiance to the parent who remains his long-term employer.

This yields an unfortunately undemocratic argument against openness of deliberations between different interest groups, until negotiation has yielded an outcome that can be 'sold' to all constituencies.

The revelation problem

In this book, exchange of knowledge and information is important, hence a summary of a paradox identified by Arrow, called 'the revelation problem'. In order to assess what one is prepared to pay for information it needs to be revealed, but after that one no longer wants to pay. This applies, among other things, to licences. The problem is not insoluble. One at least partial solution is to pay only a small fixed amount up front, which does not exceed the minimum a priori plausible value, and contract to pay a percentage of revenues or profits derived from it as its value proves that minimum. Another at least partial solution is to have the value of the information or licence assessed by a third party who is mutually trusted both in his competence to evaluate its value and in his commitment to fair dealing. Thus an impartial assessment of value can be given to the licensee without the latter actually obtaining the information.

ADVANCED

This section looks into the issue of 'death of distance'. In the maintenance of relations, do distance and location still matter, or have they become irrelevant, or will they do so, owing to new opportunities from ICT?

Location

Of course, for physical products, which have volume and weight, transport and hence distance matter as much as they did before. That is why suppliers may need to offer facilities (in production or distribution) not too far from their industrial customers, to ensure 'just-in-time' delivery. However, concerning communicative relations it has been proposed that in view of opportunities from ICT, location and distance will no longer matter ('death of distance'). Most geographers appear to disagree with this. What are the arguments why location and distance still matter?

Before turning to spatial, geographical, distance, let us consider cognitive distance. Inter-firm relations, networks, clusters and regional innovation systems can get bogged down in inertia and lack of exploration when cognitive distance gets too short, i.e. when there is too much overlap of cognitive frameworks. Here, social capital degenerates into social liability (Gabbay and Leenders 1999). This can happen when relations become too exclusive and durable. Then cognitive distance will reduce: units will come to perceive and think alike.

In view of this, in order to maintain innovative potential, regional innovation systems (RIS) must have linkages not only within but also outside the region. As proposed by Oinas and Malecki (2000), we should think not so much in terms of knowledge at a location, but of movements of knowledge across space, within and between regions, in what they call 'spatial systems of innovation'. The argument mirrors the discussion of the firm as a focusing device, in Chapter 1. An RIS also may require some focus, for efficient exploitation, but this entails a risk of myopia, and to compensate for this an RIS needs external linkages at greater cognitive distance.

In the context of knowledge exchange, let us now consider spatial distance. When knowledge is tacit, spatial distance matters more than when knowledge is documented, to the extent that for the transfer of tacit knowledge one needs close, face-to-face interaction. However, it may be that increasingly such interaction can be provided also at a distance, with multimedia and virtual interaction.

Will distance ever become totally irrelevant; will there be 'death of distance'? Will there be no limit to virtuality of relations?

One hears stories of rooms with video walls, on which life-size images of participants in a virtual meeting are projected, so that, for example, one sees their images enlarge as they move closer to the wall in their own location. Later, with holography, it may be possible to project three-dimensional 'spooks' of people into a room. If the argument for co-location is that tacit knowledge can be exchanged only in real-time, mixed media interaction, this may eliminate that argument.

However, in communication at a distance, the question is not only how knowledge could be transferred, but also how one knows what knowledge to exchange, and with whom. In exploration of new knowledge, chance encounters play a role, and for this one needs more or less frequent and unstructured interaction of people meeting each other pell-mell in a context of roughly shared interest (like scientists at a conference, or entrepreneurs at a fair, or firms in an industrial district). While this seems to require at least occasional physical proximity, so that spatial distance matters, perhaps the Internet begins to provide such a facility at a distance, in chat communities.

A further reason why distance may still matter is that exchange of knowledge also requires trust, which may be enhanced by frequent face-to-face meetings, not only in business but also in social settings. Thus, one might infer someone's trustworthiness from his behaviour towards a waiter, during dinner. Later, in Chapter 4, it will be shown that reputation mechanisms are important for governance, and one may have to be locally embedded to tap into them. However, reputation mechanisms may also arise on the Internet.

Chapter 4

Governance

- Risk analysis
  - Governance
  - Relational risk
  - An audit of hold-up risk
  - Network effects
- Instruments
  - Risk control
  - Strategic orientations
  - Instruments
  - Contingencies
- Concepts and theory
  - Trust
  - Go-betweens
  - Hostages
- Advanced
  - Detailed risk audit
    - Value
    - Switching costs
    - Room for opportunism
    - Intent towards opportunism
    - Overall system
  - Detailed choice
    - Conditions
    - Problems of governance
    - Examples
  - Empirical tests

SUMMARY

While goals represent the positive side of IORs, governance is concerned with the negative side, i.e. with relational risks. This chapter analyses the conditions for those risks, and instruments for governing them.

96

RISK ANALYSIS

Governance

The notion of 'governance' includes the notion of 'control', but is a wider concept. 'Control' has a connotation of rational design, mastery and one-sided influence of one actor on another. Rational design, however, is bounded by (radical) uncertainty. Unforeseen contingencies and unintended effects of control are bound to arise. As a result, ex-ante design of control does not suffice, and adjustments are needed ex-post, in improvisation or 'muddling through'. Relations enter into a dynamic of interaction that is difficult to predict, particularly when multiple players are involved, and often one must shift from the 'substantive' rationality of choosing the best of foreseeable outcomes to the 'procedural rationality' of following heuristics that are likely to take one in roughly the right direction, setting conditions in which relations are likely to work. Here, 'control' would be far too strong a word. Also, relationships are generally most fruitful when there is not the one-sided influence suggested by the term 'control', but bilateral or multilateral influence, in mutual give and take. In view of the general counterproductiveness of one-sided influence, at the start of this book a principal–agent framework was rejected. Rather than trying to impose conditions on the alliance partner that will force him in a direction one desires, it may be better to step into his shoes and see what would make it attractive for him to move in that direction, or what might contribute to his intrinsic motivation to do so. However, elements of control will seldom be fully absent.

Earlier, in Chapter 1, it was indicated that governance is one of the purposes of organizational culture, in creating a shared 'focus' of purpose, meaning (interpretation), standards and values of behaviour. This yields a generalized cognitive and normative platform for adaptation, in face of the unpredictability of conditions and outcomes.

Of course, relations are entertained for the value that they add. As in any investment, value and risk should be traded off against each other. Especially relevant here is the resource/competence view taken in this book, as discussed in Chapter 1. It entails that firms seek and achieve more or less firm-specific resources that enable them to differentiate their products from those of competitors, and thereby achieve a higher profit than under pure price competition between perfect substitutes. To achieve profits, such resources should remain firm-specific for a while. That raises risks of hold-up and spill-over, indicated in Chapter 1.

For the analysis of risks, and for the design of IORs to cope with them, use will be made of transaction cost economics (TCE), extended with the resource/competence view and considerations of innovation and learning, and with allowance for trust next to opportunism, as discussed in Chapter 1.

97

The scheme to be developed here is as general as possible, so that it can be applied to many different kinds of relation: vertical relations between suppliers and buyers, horizontal alliances between (potential) competitors, relations between managers and owners of firms, and even relations in the realm of public administration, although the latter will not be elaborated in this book. Much of the analysis could even be used for such personal relations as friendship and marriage, but that also will not be elaborated here.

Relational risk

In the economic literature there is a distinction between risk and (radical) uncertainty, going back to Knight (1921). There, risk entails that the set of choice options for action and/or possible outcomes of actions is closed and known, so that one can have a probability distribution on those possibilities. If there is no prior knowledge about probabilities, the procedure is to assume equal probability for all possibilities, in a rectangular probability density function on the range of possibilities. Radical uncertainty, by contrast, entails that the set of options or outcomes is open, i.e. indeterminate. They are not known prior to choice and action, but are created or manifested as a result of actions. In this book, the term 'relational risk' includes uncertainty: what may go wrong in a relation may not be, and in fact often is not, knowable in advance. As a result, while we can speak of expectations, we cannot speak of probabilities, because under radical uncertainty the axioms of probability theory are not satisfied.

Chapter 1 identified four types of relational risk: loss of resources, hold-up risk, spill-over risk and psychological/social risk. Psychological risk arises on the level of individuals, and will not be discussed here, where the focus lies on inter-organizational relations. It will come back in Chapter 5, in the discussion of the process of relationship development. Social risk, which includes the risk of loss of reputation, prestige or legitimation, does also apply to organizations.

In Chapter 1 it was noted that in IORs organizational actors can become dependent on others, who may then make opportunistic use of that to expropriate advantage. In particular, one may become dependent because there are no adequate alternatives for present IORs, because partners yield a unique resource of competence or market access that is hard to replace in other relations. Another cause of dependence lies in switching costs, which may, in particular, be due to relation-specific investments. One may also be vulnerable to the loss of hostages, often in the form of sensitive information, held by partners. If specific investments are required, one would like to ascertain, prior to making the investment, whether the relationship will last sufficiently long, with sufficiently frequent interaction, to recoup that investment.

In fact, hold-up risk, due to specific investments, can take two forms:

1 Partner Y wants to break the relation, against the letter or intent of agreements, and X pays a price in the form of costs of switching to a different partner (or doing without).
2 Partner Y wants to exploit the dependence of X to extract a greater share of the surplus or added value generated by the relation (better price, better quality, etc.).

Chapter 1 gave a definition and an example of specific investments. Here, they are analysed more systematically. Transaction cost economics recognized the following types:

1 location specificity;
2 specific physical assets (installations, instruments, tools);
3 specific brand name, reputation;
4 human asset specificity (training, knowledge);
5 dedicated capacity.

An example of location specificity is when a supplier locates his production facility on the 'doorstep' of a customer, to assure 'just-in-time' delivery, perhaps, while alternative customers are nowhere in the neighbourhood.

Dedicated capacity entails that one creates additional capacity, for a specific customer, which will not be utilized when that customer drops out.

Note that the other forms of specificity depend on the flexibility of technology and knowledge. If technology/knowledge is flexible and generic, so that it can produce many customer-specific product forms with one investment, e.g. in programmable machinery, then specificity of investment is limited.

Recall the example of the die for stamping some component of a physical product into shape, as a paradigmatic example of a specific investment, given in Chapter 1. Such a mould has two parts: a 'male' part pressing into a 'female' part. For a range of products made of plastic, a new technology blows the material into the female part with air pressure. Thus, it can do without the male part, roughly halving the specificity of investment. Another example is the following. Thermo-hardened material for the pressing of plastic shapes can increasingly be replaced by thermoplastic materials. One advantage is that the material can be reused for new pressings. Another is that thermoplasts require less pressure, allowing less robust and thereby cheaper dies. Both contribute to a lower degree of specific investments.

Yet another possibility is to shift the 'decoupling point' in production, where a generic flow of production is split into separate flows for specific products, further downstream in the production process. In the extreme case, different products consist of different assemblies of standard components.

Nooteboom (1999a) added two additional types of specific investment:

1 To cross cognitive distance (discussed in Chapter 1), i.e. to build mutual absorptive capacity, one has to make investments that may be specific to a relationship.
2 If there is no prior trust in a relationship, it may have to be built up, and this also may be highly relation-specific. This will be discussed later in this chapter.

The first of these two includes the trouble a firm often has in finding out what the 'buy group' is within a large industrial customer. Who influences the buy decision, what are their roles in the buying organization, how much power and support do they have, and how much professional understanding? What should one talk about with whom, and how? This is often a problem, in particular, for small suppliers facing large buyers. Chapter 2 also discussed the problems of knowledge transfer when the knowledge of the receiver is highly tacit, as occurs, typically, in the smaller firm.

The second type of relational risk, identified in Chapter 1, is that of spill-over. This entails that knowledge that is crucial to one's competitive position, as part of core competence, is copied for competition.

In the past many firms have been overly concerned with spill-over risk. First of all, one should realize that to get knowledge one must offer knowledge. The question is not how much knowledge one loses, but what the net balance is of giving and receiving knowledge. Second, when knowledge is tacit it spills over less easily than when it is documented. However, even then it can spill over, for example when the staff or the division in which the knowledge is embedded are poached, or when staff are eager to spill their knowledge to outside colleagues out of professional vanity. Furthermore, the question is not whether information reaches a competitor but whether he will also be able to turn it into effective competition. For this he needs to understand it, and his absorptive capacity may not enable that. There may be 'causal ambiguity' (Lippman and Rumelt 1982). Next, he will need to implement it effectively in his organization. And finally, if by that time the knowledge has shifted, one does not care. Nevertheless, taking all this into account, there may be a real spill-over risk.

100

In addition to hold-up and spill-over risk there may be a risk of an accidental loss of resources. This is due to disasters or lack of competence rather than the opportunistic intentions of a partner, such as a partner going broke, accidents or novel potential partners appearing on the scene.

An example of vulnerability to disaster is given by Reitman (1997). A supplier to Toyota was hit by a fire. Toyota had only a few hours' supply in stock. Toyota's local companies and suppliers pooled resources and together rebuilt the plant in a few days.

An audit of hold-up risk[1]

A general scheme for a risk audit, i.e. an analysis of the extent and causes of relational risk, is specified in Figure 4.1. The unit of analysis here is a dyadic relation. The analysis focuses on hold-up risk. In the management of relations it is crucial to take into account the effects that one's actions have on the position of the partner, his reactions and the effects of that on one's own position. That is why in the consideration of X one should also consider the position of his partner Y. The causality is symmetrical for X and Y, but here the analysis is

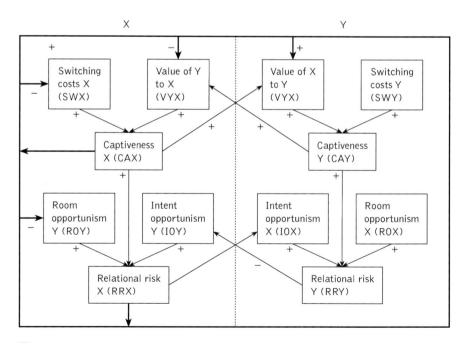

Figure 4.1 *Relational risk audit*

conducted from the perspective of X. The scheme in Figure 4.1 is explained in two rounds: first the variables will be defined, and then the lines connecting them.

The reason for X to engage in a relation with Y lies in the relative value that Y offers, i.e. his contribution to the joint surplus or added value that the relation generates, in comparison with the next best alternative for X (VYX). There are two ways in which relative value can become negative. One is that the value itself, regardless of alternatives, becomes negative: the partner detracts value rather than adding value. This covers the problems of competition and spill-over in a relation: that is, when the partner takes away value rather than adding it. The second possibility is that the value of the partner itself is positive (he adds value), but the value of an alternative partner would be greater. Then X would prefer another relation. Neither possibility by itself implies that X will break up and switch to another relation. That depends on switching costs and on the room that he has, in view of contractual obligations. X might also decide to improve the relation so that he no longer *wants* to exit. He can do this, for example, by getting a competing partner to co-operate rather than compete, or to help a partner whose value is deteriorating compared to alternatives to get back to scratch. Relative value is maximal when there is no alternative; when Y is the only source for some resource that X needs. Usually there will be some more or less close and imperfect substitute, and the ultimate fallback position is that one tries to do it in one's own firm.

As discussed, especially specific investments yield switching costs. However, switching costs could also include the value of hostages that one has supplied to the partner, which can be destroyed or expropriated. The *captiveness* of X (CAX) is defined as the sum of switching costs (SWX) and the relative value of Y (VYX): CAX = SWX + VYX. With a greater relative value of the partner one has more to lose when the relation breaks down. It will be more difficult to find a partner of equal value, and meanwhile one incurs a loss of sales, a loss of quality or high replacement costs. The sum of relative value and switching costs determines the motive for X to continue the relation, and determines his dependence on it, or 'captiveness' as it is called here. If it is positive, but the relative value of the partner is negative, one is continuing the relation only because of switching costs. Then one can try to increase the value of the partner to make the relation worthwhile or reduce switching costs to get out. If an alternative comes along that is so much better than Y that captiveness becomes negative, this means that the alternative is so much more attractive that switching is worth its cost.

When X's captiveness is high, the partner Y may be tempted to 'hold up': to exert pressure for an increase of his share in the surplus or added value of the relation. Whether he tries that depends on two things: the *opportunities for opportunism* (room for opportunistic conduct) (ROY) and his *intentions towards opportunism* (intent to utilize opportunities for opportunism) (IOY).

Within organizations, the opportunities for opportunism are determined by the tightness of hierarchical supervision. Between organizations, they are determined by the tightness of contractual regulations and of the monitoring of their compliance. Contracts are tight, i.e. yield little room for opportunism, to the extent that relevant contingencies can be specified, there is effective monitoring of compliance, and the detail with which conditions have been specified in the contract. There are obstacles to all of these. When there is uncertainty of external conditions, not all contingencies cannot be foreseen. Monitoring of compliance may be difficult to the extent that neither outputs nor inputs of efforts can be reliably observed, taking into account that information is 'asymmetric' between X and Y. Detailed specification of a contract is costly in time and money, and even legal language cannot yield semantic closure (completely unambiguous terms under all possible conditions of execution).

Y's intent towards utilizing opportunities for opportunism depends on material *incentives for opportunism*, including his own dependence on the relation. In other words: intent depends on bargaining position; on the uniqueness of values that partners offer each other, and on switching costs. Intent towards opportunism also depends on *inclination towards opportunism*, beyond self-interest. Here, we enter the realm of trust, to be discussed later.

As noted before, hold-up risk has two forms: loss of resources because a partner exits from the relation, and his threat of exit to expropriate advantage. These risks have two dimensions: the penalty for X if it occurs (PEX), i.e. the price that X pays, and the probability that it will occur (PRX). If relational risk (RRX) is defined as expected loss, then we have: $RRX = PEX \times PRX$. The maximum penalty equals captiveness, i.e. the sum of partner's relative value and switching costs: $PEX = CAX = VYX + SWX$. That is the maximum to which X can be held up: if it were larger, it would be better for X to accept exit than to give in to the threat. The probability of loss is determined by the room for opportunism and the intent to utilize it, and more specifically by their product: $PRX = ROY \times IOY$. Thus we obtain:

$$RRX = PEX \times PRX = (VYX + SWX) \times ROY \times IOY \qquad (4.1)$$

In Figure 4.1, causality is indicated by single lines. Most of them are clear from the above discussion, but some require comment. There is a line running between the switching costs of the two partners, with the minus sign of a negative relation. This is intended to indicate that ownership of transaction-specific assets can be redistributed, increasing switching costs for one partner and decreasing them for the other, so that higher switching costs for one entail lower switching costs for the other. Note also that there are lines running from

103

the captiveness of a player to the value he offers to his partner. This reflects the fact that a more captive partner offers a better perspective for returns not only now but also in the future.

In the 'advanced' section (p. 119), the basic variables from Figure 4.1 are analysed in their underlying determinants. For example: value can have many dimensions, and inclinations towards opportunism can have several sources.

Network effects

Specific investments may also pertain to networks rather than individual, dyadic relations. Building network knowledge, identity, understanding, reputation, trust and collective culture will largely be network-specific. Thus, one may be locked into networks, as a result of switching costs in the loss of specific investments, and suffer hold-up from individual networks members or coalitions among them.

Spill-over risk results mostly from indirect connections: sensitive information may spill over through a direct link with a partner who is in turn linked with a competitor. Risk of a partner being taken over by a competitor depends on his linkages with competitors. Loss of reputation or legitimation also are network effects. These risks increase with the density and connectedness of the network, and they are mitigated by structural holes. However, dense structure also facilitates reputation mechanisms and coalition formation for controlling relational risk (Coleman 1988). Risks increase with some dimensions of the strength of ties: scope, frequency and openness of communication. On the other hand, openness and frequency, and long duration of ties may help to monitor spill-over and to build trust, mitigating risk.

INSTRUMENTS

Risk control

Bold lines in Figure 4.1 indicate a control loop, to change the relation by changing the values of its variables. The origin of a double line indicates what triggers control.

This is associated with Hirschman's (1970) distinction between 'exit' and 'voice'. If one is dissatisfied with something one can walk out (exit), but one can also try to improve the relation by deliberation (voice).

Control action is triggered mainly by relational risk, when it is considered to be too high, in the size of possible loss (captiveness), the probability that such loss will occur or expected loss as the product of the two. On basis of the scheme one can analyse systematically what can be done to govern the relation. One can try to influence the basic variables, as follows:

V change the relative value of the partner (VP), or the value that one offers to the partner oneself (VS);

S change own switching costs (SS) or those of the partner (SP);

R change own room for opportunistic conduct (RS) or that of the partner (RP);

N change own intent towards opportunistic behaviour (IS) or the partner's (IP).

This demonstrates the difference between classical transaction cost economics, as developed by Williamson, and the extended theory used here. While TCE limits itself to S, R and the self-interested part of N, this book includes trust beyond self-interest, and pays more attention to the values that partners offer each other. Control actions can be taken in an aggressive, adversarial or in a more co-operative fashion, depending on whether one takes the interest of the partner into account. Control can be aimed at strengthening or loosening the relationship. This taxonomy of control actions will be developed in more detail later.

Note that each of the variables can in principle be affected on the side of the partner (P) or on the side of oneself (S). A crucial issue of governance is the ability not only to focus on the variables that determine one's own risks of dependence, but also to step into the shoes of the partner and consider the situation from his perspective. Thus, an option is to reduce one's own risk of opportunism by increasing the partner's dependence, by increasing one's unique value to him. This is a particularly constructive mode of governance because it reduces risk by increasing value. This is more constructive than refraining from specific investments, which reduces value, in order to reduce the risk of dependence by reducing switching costs. It is also more productive than safeguarding risks by means of detailed contracts, which limit flexibility and innovation and tend to create mistrust. Another example is that one may deliberately limit one's alternative options, by giving exclusiveness to a given partner, thus increasing one's own dependence, as compensation for the partner's binding himself to the relation, by engaging in specific investments, and thereby encourage him to do so (cf. Bakos and Brynjolfsson 1993). Yet, as is detailed in the 'advanced' section of this chapter, practice shows that firms do not see such options, simply because they are not used to looking at the relation from their partner's perspective. It can be very fruitful to protect oneself by helping the partner, and to help oneself by protecting the partner.

105

Table 4.1 *Typology of strategy*

	Binding	*Loosening*
Adversarial	Decrease room conduct partner	Increase own room for conduct
	Increase switching costs partner	Develop own alternatives
		Decrease own switching costs,
	Tie down	*Offload*
Co-operative	Reduce mutual inclinations to opportunism	Reduce switching costs both sides
	(Build mutual trust)	Develop alternatives both sides
	Increase mutual value	
	Reduce room for opp. both sides	
	Improvement	*Setting free*

Note: A co-operative strategy also is: yield; i.e. accept an aggressive strategy of the partner (tie down, offload).

Strategic orientations

Table 4.1 specifies a general typology of strategic orientations – adversarial versus co-operative; binding versus loosening – which increase or reduce ties between the partners. In the strategy of *tying down* one binds the partner aggressively by limiting his room for conduct, increasing the closeness of monitoring, taking more hostages. In *improvement*, one binds a partner co-operatively by increasing mutual value, reinforcing bonds of emotions, norms, values and habits, and limiting one's own room for opportunism. In *offloading* one aggressively increases one's own freedom at the expense of the partner, by increasing one's own room for action, dodging monitoring, expropriating value from the partner, developing alternative relations and shifting the burden and the responsibility for the relation to the partner, by increasing his burden of transaction-specific investments, and exacting more guarantees and penalties for lack of performance and disloyalty. In *setting free* one opens up one's options in a way that allows the same for the partner, by helping him to engage in other relations, or to prepare such alternatives, and by reducing switching costs on both sides. In *yielding* one submits to an aggressive action by the partner.

Instruments

After expansion of the central variables, in Figure 4.1, of value, switching costs, opportunities, incentives and inclinations for opportunism, into underlying determinants, a detailed set of instruments is derived for the governance of

Table 4.2 *Instruments of governance and their drawbacks*

Instrument	Drawback

Risk avoidance
  No specific investments
  No knowledge transfer
	Lower added value, with less product differentiation (in case of dedicated technology)
	No learning

Integration MA	Less flexibility, variety, motivation Problems of integration (see Chapter 3)

Number of partners
  Maintain alternatives
  Demand exclusiveness
	Mutiple set-up costs, spill-over risk for partners
	Limitation of variety for learning

Contracts	Problematic under uncertainty, can be expensive Straitjacket in innovation, can generate distrust

Self-interest
  Mutual dependence
  Hostages
  Reputation
	Opportunistic: requires monitoring and is sensitive to change of capabilities, conditions and entry of new players

Trust	Needs building up if not already present Has limits, how reliable? Relation between individual and organization
Go-betweens	May not be available, how reliable?
Network position	Needs time to build, side effects

hold-up risk. This is done in the 'advanced' section (p. 119). Table 4.2 gives a less detailed survey of instruments, which includes instruments not only for hold-up risk, but also for spill-over risk. Every instrument also has its drawbacks, which are also specified in the table.

The first instrument entails a cop-out. In view of relational risk, hold-up is avoided by not engaging in dedicated investments, and spill-over is avoided by not giving away any sensitive knowledge. The opportunity cost of this is that one may miss opportunities to achieve high added value in the production of specialities by investing in collaboration and learning with partners. The second instrument is integration in a merger or acquisition (MA), with the advantages and drawbacks discussed earlier, in Chapter 3.

Below the line, in Table 4.2, there are instruments for alliances between formally autonomous organizations, where one accepts risks of dependence due to specific investments and of spill-over, and seeks to control them by other means than full integration in one organization.

One option is to maintain multiple partners, in order not to become dependent on any one of them, and to demand exclusiveness from any partner, to prevent spill-over. However, maintaining relations with alternative partners entails a multiplication of costs in dedicated investments and the governance needed to control the risks involved. Exclusiveness entails that in the specific activity involved one forbids the partner to engage in relations with one's competitors. The first problem with this is that the demand of exclusiveness forbids the partner what one allows oneself: partnerships with the partner's competitors. By having those relations one increases the spill-over risk for partners. As a result, none of them may be willing to give sensitive information, which degrades their value as sources of complementary competence and learning. Furthermore, the demand for exclusiveness blocks the variety of the partner's sources of learning, which reduces his value as a partner in learning, at a cognitive distance that is maintained by his interaction with outside contacts. Hence one should consider whether spill-over is really a significant risk, as discussed before. If it is not, all parties can gain from maintaining multiple partners, perhaps for maintaining bargaining position, but especially for maintaining variety of sources of learning and flexibility of configurations.

A second instrument is a contract, in an attempt to close off 'opportunities for opportunism', by contracts. The problem with this instrument is fourfold. First, it can be expensive to set up. Second, it can be ineffective for lack of possibilities to monitor compliance, due to asymmetric information. Even if one can properly assess the execution of agreements, especially small principals may not be in a position to credibly threaten litigation, due to the economies of scale involved. A scale effect arises when the risk, effort and cost of litigation are large relative to the damage involved. Third, contracts have limited feasibility because of uncertainty concerning future contingencies that affect contract execution. This applies especially when the purpose of collaboration is innovation. Finally, detailed contracts for the purpose of closing off opportunities for opportunism express distrust, which can raise reciprocal suspicion and distrust, with the risk of ending up in a vicious circle of regulation and distrust that limits the scope for exploration of novelty and obstructs the build-up of trust as an alternative approach to governance.

Another approach is to aim at the self-interest of the partner and limit incentives to utilize any opportunities for opportunism left by incomplete contracts. These instruments have been mostly developed in TCE. Self-interest may arise from mutual dependence, in several ways. One is that the partner participates more or less equally in the ownership and hence the risk of dedicated assets.

In a study of suppliers in the car industry, Semlinger (1991) found conditions that in his view, at the time, contradicted TCE. Suppliers of car parts had to invest in the highly transaction-specific dies for stamping the parts into shape. According to Semlinger's interpretation of TCE, the prescription would be that the buyer should either give guarantees of custom for as much or as long as needed to recoup the investments, or take full ownership of the dies. Neither occurred. The buyers did offer to take ownership of the dies, but the suppliers refused. Does this contradict TCE? The suppliers refused because they did not want to relinquish decision rights on the dies, because it would eliminate their value for the customer, and hence all dependence of the customer, and the customer could then at any time transfer the die to a different supplier. But this still leaves the possibility of shared ownership, with the supplier retaining sufficient decision rights to prevent that.

A second approach to self-interest is to use one's own dedicated investments to build and offer a unique, valuable competence to the partner. Thus, the effect of dedicated investments can go in different directions: it makes one dependent owing to switching costs, but it can also make the partner dependent by offering him high and unique value. This instrument can yield an upward spiral of value, where partners engage in a competition to be of unique value to each other.

Dependence also arises from a hostage, as also suggested by TCE. One form of hostage is minority participation, where one can sell one's shares to someone who is eager to undertake a hostile take-over of the partner. A more prevalent form is sensitive information. Here, the notion of hostage connects with the notion of spill-over. One may threaten to pass on sensitive knowledge to a partner's competitor. Reputation also is a matter of self-interest: one behaves well in order not to sacrifice potentially profitable relations with others in the future (Weigelt and Camerer 1988).

The limitation of instruments aimed at self-interest is that they are not based on intrinsic motivation, and require monitoring, which may be difficult, especially in innovation. Furthermore, the balance of mutual dependence is sensitive to technological change and to the entry of new players that might offer more attractive partnerships. Hostages may die or may not be returned in spite of compliance with the agreement. Reputation mechanisms may not be in place, or may work imperfectly (Hill 1990; Lazaric and Lorenz 1998). They require that a defector cannot escape or dodge a breakdown of reputation, e.g. by selling the business or switching to another industry or another country. It requires complaints of bad behaviour to be checked for their truth and to be communicated to potential future partners of the culprit.

Beyond self-interest, one may also appeal to more intrinsic motives that determine 'inclinations towards opportunism'. This leads to the notion of trust, discussed on p. 111. Another possibility is to employ the services of a third party or 'go-between'. That also is discussed on p. 116.

Contingencies

One will generally select some combination of mutually compatible and supporting instruments from the toolbox of governance, and the use of a single instrument will be rare. There is no single and universal best recipe for governing IORs. The choice and effectiveness of instruments depend on conditions: the goals of collaboration, characteristics of the participants, technology, markets and the institutional environment.

For example, there is no sense in contracts when the appropriate legal institutions are not in place (lack of appropriate laws), or are not effective (the police or judiciary are corrupt), or when compliance cannot be monitored (for lack of accounting procedures).

When technology is flexible, so that one can produce a range of different specific products with one set-up, the specificity of investments and hence the problem of hold-up are limited. Possibilities of spill-over are constrained when knowledge is tacit, and do not matter when technology changes fast. Reputation mechanisms don't work when there are ample exit opportunities for defectors. Trust is difficult in a distrustful environment, where cheating rather than loyalty is the norm.

Innovation has its special conditions. Exchange of knowledge is crucial, with corresponding risks of spill-over. Especially in innovation, the competences and intentions of strangers are difficult to judge. Relevant reputation has not yet been built up. Uncertainty is large, limiting the possibility of specifying the contingencies of a contract. Specific investments are needed to set up mutual understanding. There is significant hold-up risk. Detailed contracts would limit the variety and scope for the unpredictable actions and initiatives that innovation requires. Under these conditions, trust is most needed to limit relational risk. An additional problem with contracts is that they may obstruct the building of trust. This does not mean that there are or should be no contracts at all. Indeed, there will almost always be some form of contract. However, they should not be too detailed with the purpose of controlling hold-up risk.

Especially in innovation, a productive combination of instruments is mutual dependence complemented by trust, on the basis of an emerging experience in competent and loyal collaboration. Trust is needed besides mutual dependence, because the latter is sensitive to changing conditions. Trust is more difficult under asymmetric dependence because the more dependent side may be overly suspicious (Klein Woolthuis 1999), in the 'Calimero syndrome' mentioned before. In all this, go-betweens can help. Their roles will be specified in the next section. Without them the building of trust may be too slow.

In the literature, contracts and trust are seen primarily as substitutes. Less trust requires more contracts, and detailed contracts can obstruct the building of trust. However, this view is too simplistic. Trust and control can also be complements (Das and Teng 1998, 2001; Klein Woolthuis 1999; Klein Woolthuis et al. 2002). There may be a need for an extensive contract, not so much to foreclose opportunities for opportunism, but to serve as a record of agreements in a situation where co-ordination is technically complex. A simple contract may provide the basis for building trust, rather than being a substitute for it. One may need to build up trust before engaging in the costs and risks of setting up a contract. These risks may include a spill-over risk: in the course of negotiation much information gets divulged for partners to assess each other. Finally, a contract may be psychological and serve to flag trust, and signing a contract may constitute a ritual of agreement.

Perhaps the most important point is that relationships should be seen as processes rather than entities that are instituted and left to themselves. Conditions may change. A frequent problem is that a relationship starts with a balance of dependence, but in time the attractiveness of one of the partners slips, due to slower learning, appropriation of his knowledge by the other partner, institutional, technological or commercial change. This is discussed in more detail in Chapter 5.

Choice of instruments for governance may be constrained. Options depend on the structure of the networks one is in, and on one's position in them. Coleman (1988) proposed that a dense structure with strong ties enables the build-up of reputation, the formation of coalitions, and social capital, in the form of trust and social norms. This helps governance, but also constrains actions.

Strong ties, in the sense of high frequency and intensity, and long duration, yield shared experience, which reduce cognitive distance, and enable the development of empathy and identification (McAllister 1995; Lewicki and Bunker 1996; Hansen 1999). These help governance, but can weaken competence building, in the elimination of cognitive distance needed for learning. Dense networks with strong ties can also yield inefficiencies due to redundant ties, and rigidities due to lock-in into the network, with exit prevented by coalitions of network members. This theme will be picked up again in Chapter 5.

CONCEPTS AND THEORY

Trust

Trust is a slippery and complex notion, and cannot be dealt with in detail in this book. For an extensive discussion, see Nooteboom (2002). Here, only some salient points will be summarized, concerning the object of trust (things one can have trust in), and its foundations.

One may have trust in things (e.g. one's car), the laws of nature, supernatural powers, institutions, people and organizations. One can have trust in institutions (*institutional trust*), and one can have trust in people on the basis of institutions (*institutions-based trust*). Trust in individual or corporate agents is called *behavioural* trust. Such trust has several aspects. One is *competence trust*, in the partner's ability to perform according to expectations. Another is *intentional trust*, in the partner's intention to perform according to the best of his ability (*dedication*), and to refrain from opportunistic behaviour (*benevolence*). This distinction has also been called a distinction between 'passive' and 'active' opportunism. The first is lack of dedication, in shirking or free riding. The second is expropriation of advantage by cheating, lying, stealing, and the like. A third aspect of trust relates to the availability of resources to perform according to expectations. A fourth is trust in robustness under external shocks. A fifth is trust in honesty (telling the truth). If expectations are not met, this may be due to lack of competence, lack of intention (opportunism), lack of means, or outside conditions that affect the results of efforts. This distinction is important, because when trust is broken the proper response depends on the cause. To breach of competence one may respond by trying to improve it, or to provide assistance. To breach of intentional trust one may improve incentives (in the case of lack of dedication) or issue warnings or threats (in the case of opportunism). In the case of unforeseen external disasters, one may seek to make agreements less sensitive to them, or take out a joint insurance. The problem of course is that it may not be clear which is the case.

Organizations can be the object of trust, in all the aspects indicated above, including competence and intentions. We can trust an organization to behave responsibly regarding its stakeholders and the environment. Of course an organization itself does not have an intention, but it has interests and can try to regulate the intentions of its workers to serve those interests. One's trust in an individual may be based on one's trust in the organization he belongs to. Trust in an organization can be based on trust in the people in it. It can be affected by corporate communication, which aims to project a certain image. But ultimately the proof lies in the performance of its people. Particularly important for the perceptions that underlie trust in an organization are the public conduct of the firm's leadership and of people in roles that connect the firm with customers or outside partners. These are the 'boundary spanners and gatekeepers' such as purchasers, marketers, negotiators, and staff exchanged or combined in joint teams with partner firms. In both the foundation of organizational trust on trust in people and the foundation of personal trust on trust in an organization, we need to carefully take into account the position and role of those people in the organization (Ring and van de Ven 1994). Are their competences and intentions supported and backed up by the organization? Are the interests and the culture of the organization properly endorsed and implemented by the people?

According to many definitions of trust, it entails acceptance of relational risk, in the expectation that no harm will be done. One submits to vulnerability to the actions of others (Deutsch 1973). Most people would agree that one cannot speak of 'real' trust when the expectation is based on instruments of coercion by hierarchy or contract, or only on incentives of self-interest, discussed before. 'Real' trust is then defined as the expectation that no harm will be done, even though the partner has both the opportunity and the incentive for opportunism (Bradach and Eccles 1984; Chiles and McMackin 1996; Nooteboom 1999a).

Another important point is that trustworthiness will almost always have its limits. Williamson (1993) was surely correct to say that blind, unconditional trust is generally unwise. Even the sincerest wish to be loyal may break down under temptation or pressure. One cannot expect even one's best friend to remain loyal even under the direst pressures of survival, such as torture, and it would even be unethical to demand that. Thus, trust is subject to tolerance levels: one trusts within limits of observed conditions and actions. Within those limits, one does not continually question competences and loyalties, and one is not continually on the lookout for opportunities for opportunism, for the partner and for oneself. When the limits are exceeded, one starts to be aware of potential opportunism, and to consider exit. In voice, such concerns are communicated, in an effort to jointly resolve them. Nevertheless, voice is constrained by the possibility of exit, as Hirschman recognized. However, though this may seem paradoxical, one can exit also with the use of voice. This will be investigated in the discussion on the development of IORs, in Chapter 5.

On the *macro level*, beyond specific relations, the basis for trust, in institution-based trust, may lie in established, socially inculcated norms and values. They include pressures of allegiance to groups one belongs to, and norms inculcated by socialization into those groups. Underlying values are part of culture in the anthropological sense. This may apply to countries or professions, but cultural norms and values also apply to organizations, with their specialized cultures in a wider institutional environment. Norms and values of behaviour tend to be internalized, to a greater or lesser extent, by people, as part of tacit knowledge, assimilated in socialization and habituation.

How can one determine how trustworthy a partner is? To some extent it may be inferred from social characteristics such as membership of a family or association, in 'characteristics based trust' (Zucker 1986). Of course, one can never be sure ex-ante to what extent a stranger without reputation has actually internalized such norms and values. Here, Williamson (1993) was right in saying that under such conditions of behavioural uncertainty one must take the possibility of opportunism into account. However, that does not automatically imply that one should always go for control by deterrence, in opportunity and incentive control, even if they are feasible and effective.

On the *micro level* of specific relationships, there is a principle of reciprocity (Gouldner 1960), discussed widely in the sociological and anthropological literature on the giving of gifts. Reciprocity may be seen as an intermediate form between self-interest and altruism. It has been characterized as short-term altruism for long-term self-interest (Putnam 2000: 134). In economic exchange, there is a principle of strict 'quid pro quo', where returns in exchange are either immediate or contractually guaranteed, with a specification of future conditions

113

and procedures. In the social giving of gifts, reciprocity is not immediate, not guaranteed, not specified, and cannot be demanded. Such demand would invalidate its social function, which is to bond a relationship. Immediate reciprocation would even be a signal that the recipient declines to engage in a relationship. Nevertheless, the gift establishes an informal, non-strict obligation to reciprocate, in due time and measure. It is important to maintain reciprocation as a free choice, and avoid any impression of manipulation, compulsion or gift giving as a purchase of obligation. In view of this, the giver is expected to soften the obligation, by belittling his gift when he is thanked ('you are welcome', 'my pleasure', 'pas de quoi', 'de nada'). In social reciprocity, giving must remain spontaneous, surprising and imperfectly predictable. Nevertheless, gift giving, with this type of reciprocity, often does serve our self-interest. It fosters good reputation, gratitude and return gifts. As Vandevelde (2000: 15) formulated it: 'The logic of the gift thus can be reduced neither to disinterestedness or altruism, nor to strict, calculative egotism. Something of both motivations inheres, or even better: the logic of the gift is situated beyond the opposition between egotism and altruism.' Gift giving can be used for manipulation, imposing a claim for something in return. However, though perhaps unusual, gifts or sacrifices *can* be completely disinterested or altruistic, without an expectation or even wish of reciprocity. Then they fall squarely under altruism. A form of extreme altruism is friendly reciprocation to a hostile action ('turn the other cheek'; cf. Vandevelde 2000).

If trust is not in place prior to collaboration, it has to be built up in the relation, in 'process-based trust'. One cannot buy and install trust, but one can create the conditions for it to develop, in 'trust-sensitive management' (Sydow 2000: 54). As a relationship develops, partners begin to know each other better, and to develop empathy, and can better assess the extent and limits of trustworthiness ('knowledge-based trust'). Convergence of cognitive frameworks may arise, which can lead to mutual identification ('identification-based trust') (McAllister 1995; Lewicki and Bunker 1996). Partners understand and can identify with each other's goals, weaknesses and mistakes, and are able to engage in the give-and-take of voice. This does not entail that they always agree. There may be sharp disagreements, but those are combined with a willingness to express and discuss them more or less openly, in 'voice', offering mutual benefit of the doubt. As a result, when conflicts are jointly resolved they will deepen trust rather than breaking it.

Lewicki and Bunker claimed that when trust is not in place at the beginning, one has to start with control, and later switch to trust based on empathy and the growth of identification. However, as noted before, control in the form of detailed contracts to close off opportunities for opportunism can yield an escalation of mutual distrust that precludes the building of trust. Alternatively, one could start a relationship with small steps of low-level mutual dependence, and

114

increase commitment as trust in competence and commitment grows (Shapiro 1987). One limitation of this is that one may not have the time to build trust in this way. The process of trust building may be speeded up by the use of intermediaries. This is discussed below.

Mutual openness is also central to trust. Note that it is both the basis and the outcome of trust. It is associated with the notion of voice. It is also needed to pool complementary assets and competences.

In buyer–supplier relationships, for example, one needs to achieve the openness that is needed in co-makership and early supplier involvement, both for utilizing such opportunities of complementarity and to build and maintain trust. However, it is difficult to achieve openness when the focus is on bargaining for price, to secure sufficient profit. One may need to hide information on costs and competence to maintain bargaining position. Therefore, partners must grant each other profit, in 'price-minus costing': production cost is set at price minus a profit margin for the supplier. One argument for this is that there is lack of continuity in a partner who may go broke for lack of profit. Another is to 'earn' the partner's openness. What may be lost in price may be more than regained in quality and speed. This is particularly so when contracts cannot be closed, and a partner regains profit in unforeseen, uncontracted work. An example of this is the building industry. Bargaining focuses on minimum price, which yields closure of information, which inhibits opportunities to collaborate for optimal quality, speed and fit in time, place and technical interfaces. Insiders claim that up to 25 per cent of final cost is due to such mismatches. And then the builder recoups profit in unforeseen work, so that minimum price is not actually achieved.

This open-book contracting and price-minus costing is one of the lessons the West has learned from the Japanese, particularly in the car industry (Helper 1990; Cusumano and Fujimoto 1991; Dyer and Ouchi 1993; Lamming 1993; Kamath and Liker 1994; Dyer 1996; de Jong and Nooteboom 2001). However, Western buyers did not copy the all too durable and exclusive buyer–supplier relations that were customary in the Japanese vertical structures of keiretsu. As discussed before, some durability is needed to recoup dedicated investments, and exclusiveness may be needed to control spill-over, but too durable and exclusive relations yield rigidities. The development of keiretsu is discussed in Chapter 5.

As already indicated, openness is essential to the building of trust (Zand 1972). A rich flow of information is needed for the 'let's work things out' approach of the voice strategy (Maguire et al. 2001). As noted before, things may go wrong in a relation because of outside accidents, mistakes, lack of competence or opportunism, but in practice they are difficult to identify. For example, an opportunist will claim mishaps or mistakes as the cause of disappointing results. That is why openness also about one's mistakes is crucial, to prevent their being interpreted as opportunism.

Firms have learned this lesson, concerning problems with products. It is better to come out immediately when a problem with a product occurs than try to hide it. Then it is credible that there was a mistake, not carelessness or opportunism. It gives users maximum opportunity to prevent or reduce damage and gives the producer maximum opportunity to make amends.

Routine-based trust, proposed by Nooteboom (1999a), entails that when a relation has been satisfactory for a while, awareness of opportunities of opportunism, for oneself and for the partner, is relegated to 'subsidiary awareness' (Polanyi 1962). One takes the relation for granted and does not continually think about opportunities to gain extra advantage. As Herbert Simon has taught us long ago, routinized behaviour is rational, in the adaptive sense, in view of bounded rationality, since it allows us to focus our limited capacity for attention and rational evaluation on matters that are new and have priority. Routines are rational also in the sense that they are based on proven success in past behaviour. On the other hand, their lack of awareness creates the problem that they may no longer be adequate when conditions change. However, when results or perceived events exceed certain tolerance levels, routines are often summoned back from subsidiary into focal awareness (Polanyi 1962), to be subjected to calculatively rational scrutiny. However, routines may subside so deeply into tacit knowledge as to become incorrigible.

Go-betweens

There are a host of different types of intermediaries whose task it is to help judge performance and to provide intermediation or arbitration in conflicts. Shapiro (1987) called these intermediaries 'guardians of trust', Zucker (1986) saw them as part of 'institution-based trust', and Fukuyama (1995) used the term 'intermediate communities'. Many of these serve to develop and police technical or professional standards, with certification systems. There are also roles for go-betweens as consultants in the management of IORs (Nooteboom 1999a).

One role of these, recognized in TCE, is that of arbitration or mediation in 'trilateral governance'. When there is relational risk, but transactions are insufficiently substantial or frequent to warrant the cost of developing intricate forms of 'bilateral' governance, with instruments described above, it may be efficient to establish only simple agreements and submit to arbitration or mediation.

A second role is to assess the value of information before it is traded, to solve Arrow's 'revelation problem': if one wants to sell information, the partner will want to assess its value by looking into it, but then he already has the information and might no longer pay for it. This problem can be solved in several ways. As discussed in Chapter 3, one is the use of licences, with a limited payment up front, and later payment in proportion to the emerging yields of the information. Another is to let a go-between assess the value of the information for the potential buyer.

A third role for a go-between is to create mutual understanding, helping to cross cognitive distance. A fourth role is to monitor information flow as a guard against spill-over. The reason for this role is that if partner A does the monitoring himself, in the firm of partner B, then this scrutiny inside B's firm may increase the spill-over from B to A. A fifth role is to act as a guardian of hostages. Without that, there may be a danger that the hostage keeper does not return the hostage even if the partner sticks to the agreement. The third party has an interest in maintaining symmetric trust and acceptance by both protagonists.

A sixth, and perhaps most crucial, role is to act as an intermediary in the building of trust. Trust relations are often entered with partners who are trusted partners of someone you trust (Sydow 2000). If X trusts Y and Y trusts Z, then X may rationally give trust in Z a chance. X needs to feel that Y is able to judge well and has no intention to lie about his judgement. This can speed up the building of trust between strangers, which might otherwise take too long. This is particularly important in view of the dynamics of the build-up and breakdown of trust. It was noted above that new relationships might have to start small, with low stakes that are raised as trust builds up. This may be needed especially when extended contracts are not feasible or desirable, as is the case particularly in innovation. As indicated, the disadvantage of such a procedure is its slowness. A go-between may provide help for a more speedy development. Intermediation in the first small and tentative steps of co-operation, to ensure that they are successful, can be very important in the building of a trust relation. The intermediary can perform valuable services in protecting trust when it is still fragile: to eliminate misunderstanding and allay suspicions when errors or mishaps are mistaken as signals of opportunism.

A seventh role, related to the sixth, is to help in the timely and least destructive disentanglement of relations. To eliminate misunderstanding, to prevent acrimonious and mutually damaging battles of divorce, a go-between can offer valuable services, to help in 'a voice type of exit'. This is discussed in Chapter 5.

An eighth role is to support a reputation mechanism. For a reputation mechanism to work, infringement of agreements must be observable, its report must be credible, and it must reach potential future partners of the culprit. The go-between can help in all respects.

117

Hostages

A true hostage satisfies the condition that it has intrinsic value for the giver but not for the keeper, to ensure that when the time has come, and the giver has honoured his commitments, the keeper will not be tempted to retain the hostage and will not hesitate to return it.

In this context there is the following riddle: when in the past a king had to supply a hostage to guarantee a treaty with another king, and had the choice between giving an attractive and an unattractive daughter, whom he loved equally, whom should he give? The standard answer is: the unattractive one, because that better satisfies the condition of asymmetric value. The attractive daughter could more easily assume value for the hostage keeper, who might then be tempted never to return her. But what if the first king did not really intend to honour the treaty? Then he can better give the more attractive daughter, because she would be less likely to be harmed. But the second king might see through this, and become suspicious when the attractive daughter is offered. Unless, of course, the first king can create the false impression, without being found out, that he does not love his unattractive daughter. Then the second king might demand the attractive daughter, for fear that the unattractive one would not keep the first king from betrayal. Then the second king would fall into the first king's trap.

In relations between firms, people can play the role of hostage, for example in the intermarriage between family businesses, or in the exchange of staff between the partners. But also information, knowledge or technology can play the role. Earlier the problem of spill-over was discussed, but here we see that sensitive information, under threat of spill-over, can be put at risk on purpose, as a device for establishing commitment to a relation. Cross-participation between firms can also be interpreted as an exchange of hostages. In the Japanese system, for example, cross-participation by exchange of shares is motivated not by the height or diversification of profits, but by the stabilization of relations; by the prevention of adversarial action. This use of cross-participation as a hostage was admitted in a document in 1992 from the Japanese Agency for Economic Planning (Scher 1996: 17).

When some years ago the Dutch minister of economic affairs accompanied the co-operation between Volvo and Mitsubishi in a new joint venture NEDCAR (the former Dutch car producer DAF), he kept under his care what he called a 'shoe box' with the design of a new model of the Volvo to be produced in Holland (which is now on the roads). This served as a hostage, to make sure that Volvo would not shift the higher value-added activity of design and development to Sweden. The example also illustrates that a hostage may die a natural death. Currently, the new models of Volvo are on the road.

ADVANCED

Detailed risk audit

The basic scheme for the risk audit, in Table 4.1, contained only the basic variables of (relative) value, switching costs, opportunities for opportunism, and incentives and inclinations towards opportunism. There are many underlying variables, which are detailed below.

Value

The purpose of a relation is the value of the partner. This is especially important from the resource/competence perspective taken in this book. Value includes, in particular, firm-specific resources that one needs in order to complement one's own limited, path-dependent, myopic competences. As indicated before, value here is relative to the next best alternative, including the possibility of doing without any partner, and doing it oneself. The dimensions of value are, of course, related to the goals of IORs specified in Chapter 2. They are specified in Figure 4.2, with the now familiar grouping of resources into assets, competences and positional advantages.

Most of the components of value can take on a negative value, which signifies that rather than complementing one's own resources the partner detracts from them. For example, the partner's contribution to technological capability may have a net negative value because more knowledge belonging to one's core competence value spills over to the partner than one receives from him. It may spill over to a competitor through the partner, or the partner himself may use it to engage in competing activities. Internationalization ('internat') is negative

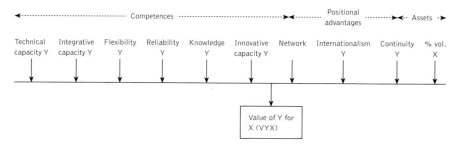

Figure 4.2 *Value of Y to X*

when the partner detracts from one's international presence by competing abroad. One may accept negative values in some components if they are sufficiently compensated by positive value elsewhere.

An illustration is given by the account of the long-lasting and successful Japanese joint venture between Xerox and Fuji given by Lorange and Roos (1992). It started out as a classic product–market entry alliance, with Xerox providing the product and Fuji providing entry in the difficult Japanese market. After a while, technology spilled over to Fuji, and it developed a capability for its own design and production of copiers. At Xerox this was seen as a loss; as negative value due to spill-over of technology, the building of a new competitor and a threat to home-country employment. But this was amply compensated by the fact that Fuji developed a low-end product that was complementary to Xerox's range of products, and helped to stop competitive entry to the market by IBM.

Below, each of the different components of value is discussed.

Value of course depends on the extent of the partner's involvement: the percentage of one's activities in which the partner is involved, indicated by the variable '% vol. X'. This is related to the dimension of 'scope' in the strength of ties, discussed in Chapter 3. This can refer to several things. The relevant measure may be the share of transactions with this partner in the total value added in X's activity under consideration. For example: if X is a supplier to Y, it is the percentage of sales in the product going to this customer; if X is a customer of Y, it is the share of Y's supply in X's total purchase expense of the input under consideration; if X and Y engage in a joint venture it might be the percentage of one's share in added value or profit of the joint venture in the firm's total added value or profit; if the alliance is an R&D consortium it is the share of one's contribution in one's total R&D commitment in the area under consideration. Under change of technology and markets, the value of the partner depends on a range of competences: his technological capability, which includes the level of quality, speed and costs. It also includes not just the level but also the reliability of quality, time and costs. It may also include the partner's 'integrative ability': the ability to integrate contributions from others. This applies especially to 'first-tier' suppliers. Also, flexibility is important, in production volume, personnel, time, organization, and goals of co-operation. Of increasing importance is the value of the partner as a source of knowledge, concerning technology, markets and innovative capability. This is related to the notion of 'external economy of cognitive scope', discussed in Chapter 1.

Positional advantages are international presence, to serve the partner in different markets. Another is network position, in connections with other players or sources beyond the focal relation. Note that such ulterior relations can also pose a threat to partners, e.g. of spill-over. That is discussed below.

Network position has a number of aspects. One is indirect access, through the partner, to resources beyond, which may include materials, components, apparatus (machinery, instruments), labour, reputation, legitimation, permits, licenses, distribution channels. An apparently risky or even loss-generating alliance may be warranted if it yields access to an otherwise inaccessible resource, e.g. a market.

This covers alliances where one side offers the other entry into a market. It explains the fact that sometimes suppliers accept unfavourable conditions to become a 'preferred' supplier to a prestigious customer, in order to gain access to other customers on the basis of prestige derived from it. It also explains why buyers sometimes prefer foreign suppliers for their willingness to accept unfavourable conditions in order to gain a foothold in the country of the new customer.

The consequences of breaking a relationship are greater to the extent that it cuts one off from access to important resources. A well-known example is that of a 'main supplier', who provides access to various sources that he co-ordinates. This saves costs for his customer but also makes him more dependent. The partner's network position can also entail a threat. Customer A can yield indirect access, through him, to another customer B, to whom one also supplies directly. If one gets into problems with B, he may exert pressure on his supplier A to also withdraw his custom, so that one loses not only the sales to A but also the sales to B (Berger *et al.* 1995). Another problem can be the risk of spill-over to competitors, through the partner, particularly if the knowledge involved is documented. One may try to prevent that through patents, but often such protection is not cost-efficient, or is even undesirable on the grounds that public information in the patent is enough to yield an undesirable spill-over, because it gives sufficient information to set competitors on the track of substitution or imitation by some 'work-around' that dodges patent restrictions. An important question is whether spill-over can be monitored, so that partners who leak information to a competitor can be punished.

In the car industry and many other industries, knowledge is embodied in a publicly available product, and then spill-over can be traced. The use of knowledge is 'published', as it were (Lamming 1993: 197). One can disassemble a competitor's product to see whether use has been made of firm-specific competence supplied to a partner. One can then blame the partner for not keeping to agreements of secrecy or exclusiveness.

121

Internationalization of the partner is closely related to network position, but merits separate attention. It can be extremely important that the partner can supply his services for markets at different locations. Local presence may be crucial to enable 'just-in-time' supply or to yield the same service to different locations or subsidiaries of a customer, for the sake of economy of scale.

The latter is the case for accountancy firms: efficiency and controllability increase if the same accountant can perform his services in all locations of some multinational customer. This, together with economies of scale in setting up and widely utilizing information networks, has been an important reason for collaboration between accountancy firms with offices in different parts of the world.

Finally, value, as well as costs of governance, depends on how long the relation is expected to last. For value this was already indicated: a longer duration increases the present value of future benefits in relation to the specific investments needed for the relation. The effect on costs of governance is based on the notion of the 'shadow of the future' (Telser 1980; Axelrod 1984; Heide and Miner 1992). One is less inclined towards opportunism to the extent that the relation and its benefits are expected to last indefinitely, because then the benefits of opportunism, which would be followed by a breakdown of the relation, become less in relation to the cumulative value of the relation over years to come.

Recall that the risk of breakdown of a relation is not only due to opportunism. It can arise from accidental failure of the partner, other calamities or the fact that the partner is taken over by someone who has no interest in continuing the relation, e.g. because he is a competitor. An illustration of this is the case of a non-equity alliance between two producers in garden equipment in Sweden and Norway ('Swedpartner' and 'Norpartner', Lorange and Roos 1992), discussed in Chapter 3. A third party, which competed with one partner, took over the owner of the other partner, and thereby caused the demise of the first partner.

To a greater or lesser extent, firm size has an effect on these dimensions of value. Small firms usually have fewer products in fewer markets, and therefore often less international presence, for example. For reasons discussed in Chapter 1, there are effects of scale in transaction costs. Small firms often cannot afford the infrastructure for quality assurance systems, R&D, electronic data interchange (EDI) or distribution. Integrative capability is often limited in smaller firms. Owing to a lesser spread of risks, small firms are also more vulnerable to bankruptcy, and can be taken over more easily, and thus present a risk of discontinuity of the relation.

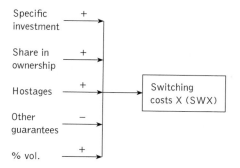

Figure 4.3 *Switching costs for X*

Switching costs

The factors that determine the level of switching costs are specified in Figure 4.3. Switching costs due to specific investments are determined by the total of such investments in the relation, multiplied by one's share in their ownership. Note that if specific investments are one-sided, their ownership can be redistributed: the partner can participate in ownership and thereby participate in the corresponding risks, which tends to lessen his incentives to opportunism. Before, an example was given in the sharing of the investment in a die-stamp in the car industry.

Recall that specific investments by X can cause switching costs for Y even if ownership is not shared. If the relation breaks, the partner will at least temporarily suffer a loss before he finds an alternative partner who is able to engage in similar investments, and before such investments are in place. Note, however, that this is already included in the relative value that is offered to the partner, as part of total 'captiveness'. Note also that this does not automatically imply that dependence is symmetrical. In general, loss due to loss of specific investments made is greater than loss due to discontinuity for the partner.

Other switching costs are the provision of hostages and the supply of other guarantees.

If X and Y exchange hostages, and the mechanism works well, then if X reneges on agreements, he will lose his hostage and Y will not lose his. In that sense the level of switching costs is conditional on who reneges. Guarantees can take several forms. One is a minimum duration or a minimum volume of transactions, so that specific investments may be recouped. Or the buyer can guarantee that in case of premature exit he will refund all or part of what is left of the specific asset, after depreciation. Another form of guarantee is price indexing, so that the risk of price increases of materials, components or labour is shared, or benchmarking as a guarantee that increases of quality or productivity will be in line with average or best practice in the relevant industry. The supply of guarantees often requires counter-guarantees against misuse. This may entail, for example, agreements to monitoring, by the giver of the guarantee, or some third party who supplies arbitration, to verify that the conditions for effecting the guarantee are satisfied. For example: to check whether the investment is indeed so specific that it cannot and is not used for other partners. Note that there is a special effect of hostages. Both hostages and guarantees can be given and received, and net switching costs depend on the balance: hence the plus or minus sign attached to them in Figure 4.3.

A special form of guarantee is the possibility that if withdrawal by one side jeopardizes the continuity and hence the employment of the partner, one will be held up on that, by being made responsible for the loss of employment. One is pressed to compromise by social obligation. That would add to switching costs. This cost of switching would depend on the percentage of the *partner's* total production that the partnership covers. Hence the box in Figure 4.3: share in volume Y.

This yields a reason especially for big firms in alliances with small firms to demand that the small firm does not become too dependent. It has been given as a reason for the oil industry not to contract small firms in e.g. supply to the offshore industry.

The reason why in Japan large firms are less hesitant to contract small firms for 100 per cent of their sales may be that in this way they are not held responsible for employment in the small firm, or the burden of responsibility is shared in a larger group of firms (*keiretsu*), or they have a greater commitment and better means to prevent the small firm's failure, on the basis of a greater involvement in its operation and development and a sharing of resources.

As noted before, switching costs due to specific investments can be reduced by reducing the transaction specificity of the investments, i.e. by making technology more flexible, so that a single general-purpose installation can be adjusted, at low cost, to produce a variety of specific products for different customers.

Thus a programmable machine, e.g. for metalworking (such as a computer numerically controlled workbench) can yield more opportunities for different product forms, handled by a single operator, than when for different forms different skills are needed, to be supplied by different craftsmen.

Finally, it should be noted that investments made to reduce the probability of opportunistic action, such as building relation-specific trust, to be discussed

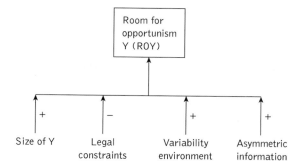

Figure 4.4 *Opportunities for opportunism, Y*

in the next section, is itself a specific investment and can thus further add to switching costs. Thus such an investment has opposing effects on relational risk, and the question is whether the positive effect on probability of opportunistic action exceeds the negative effect on switching costs.

Room for opportunism

The factors that determine opportunities for opportunism are indicated in Figure 4.4. This comes straight from transaction cost economics. According to TCE, opportunities for opportunism depend on the legal tightness of agreements, which depends on the predictability of contingencies, in view of the uncertainty or variability of the environment, and contractual detail of legal constraints, and on ability to monitor compliance with agreements, which depends on asymmetry of information. The reliability and cost of such 'legal governance' depend on institutions in the form of 'legal infrastructure': the quality of laws and their administration. This includes incorruptibility of the legislature and police.

Transaction cost economics does not take into account that a formal, legal approach can ruin 'atmosphere' and enhance perceptions of and inclinations towards opportunism, and can goad partners into a vicious circle of regulation that can stifle the relation. That connection between opportunities for opportunism and inclinations towards opportunism is not indicated in Figure 4.1, but it should be kept in mind.

Firm size affects room for opportunism, as a result of the effects of scale in transaction costs discussed in Chapter 1. A larger firm tends to have a wider reach, with a wider market, more customers and suppliers, more specialists inside and around the firm, a higher level of training, and more political influence. Thus one can expect a large firm to have more room for opportunism and less vulnerability to opportunism in a single relation. On the other hand, a large firm is more visible and may have to be more careful in protecting its reputation.

125

Firm size also has effects on the availability of information. Because in small firms there is less need for formal information, because operations can be supervised by direct inspection and there is less specialization of work and hence less need for co-ordination, and its cost is higher, due to the set-up costs of information systems, small firms tend to have less documented information, which makes them less accessible to evaluation and monitoring. That also makes it more difficult to give them guarantees to cover the risks of specific investments, because of the difficulty of monitoring counter-guarantees to ensure proper conformance to the conditions for those guarantees.

Intent towards opportunism

Opportunism entails that someone dodges the letter or intent of agreements to his advantage and at the expense of the partner. This can take the form of breaking the relation or exploiting the partner's dependence on the relation (hold-up), up to the maximum of the partner's captiveness, i.e. sum of relative value offered to him and his switching costs. The probability of opportunism is determined by the mathematical product of opportunities for opportunism and intent towards opportunism. In TCE, intent is based only on self-interest, including the degree to which the partner is himself dependent on the relation, and considerations of reputation. In the extension of the theory, with trust next to opportunism, it also depends on what is here called 'inclination towards opportunism' which consists of 'real' trustworthiness, or trustworthiness 'in the strong sense', as discussed before. This is summarized in Figure 4.5.

Y's self-interest depends on the benefit he might acquire by opportunism, in a greater share of joint surplus or added value or the switch to a more attractive partner. That depends on his own dependence, or more precisely relational risk (RRY). As illustrated also in Figure 4.1, his intent is affected not just by captiveness (CAY), which is the price he will pay if the relation breaks, but also by the probability of opportunistic conduct by his partner. That indicates the possibility of retaliatory action by the partner. Opportunistic conduct can be penalized by contractual sanctions, loss of hostages or counter-actions by the partner to appropriate added value. It also depends on the possible effects of reputation mechanisms. However, intent is also dependent on trustworthiness, along the lines discussed earlier. This may be based on ethics, empathy, identification, friendship, kinship or routinization. The effects of those are mediated by emotions, character and heuristics of inference and decision making, discussed in Chapter 1. They depend on the duration of the relation, and the bonds or shared ethic or habits based on it.

Figure 4.5 illustrates that trustworthiness and self-interest are not separate, but influence each other. The weight of self-interest depends on strength of character to resist 'weakness of will' in short-term temptation, for the sake of

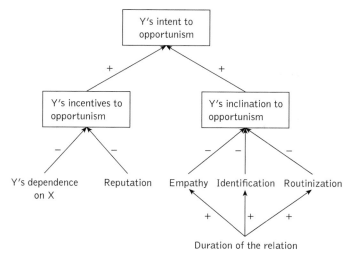

Figure 4.5 *Intent towards opportunism, Y*

long-term interest. And as discussed before, trustworthiness is limited by lack of resistance to 'golden opportunities' and pressures of survival. The latter also depend on the degree of competitive pressure in the industry.

Overall system

Since X's relational risk depends on Y's advantage in opportunism, and that depends on Y's relational risk, the causality of the system becomes recursive. Thus an iterative process of mutual adjustment arises, until the relation falls apart or some equilibrium is reached, perhaps like a 'Nash equilibrium' in game theory: given the current actions of partners, the other partner sees no need to change his action. But there may be different possible equilibria, which may or may not be reached, depending on where one starts and what strategic orientations are chosen. If an equilibrium is reached, this takes time, and it may be that no equilibrium is reached, owing to unending cycles of adjustment or because meanwhile conditions and pay-offs have changed. If an equilibrium is reached, it may be upset by external conditions, such as the appearance on the stage of a more attractive partner for one of the players, and the process of adjustment starts again. This process of adjustment will be analysed in more detail later. It makes governance complex and often unpredictable and imperfectly manageable. That is one of the reasons why ambitions of 'controlling' a relationship should be modest, and preference was given to the wider term 'governance'.

127

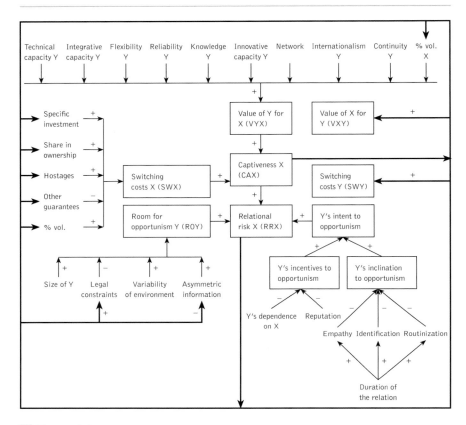

Figure 4.6 *Integrated risk analysis*

   The results are now combined in a more detailed scheme for the analysis, diagnosis and design of alliances, in Figure 4.6. This yields the basis for a more detailed inference of instruments for the governance of hold-up risk. Not all logically possible options are specified, but only salient and frequently manifested ones, in Table 4.3. In Table 4.3, not all factors from Figure 4.6 have been assigned instruments. Not all determinants of room for opportunism, for example, can be influenced: for example legal institutions. This may require political action on the basis of coalitions (e.g. in employers' associations). Norms and values of conduct also cannot easily be changed in the short term. Limitation of uncertainty and the variability of conditions is also difficult and when possible would require collective action. One has little direct control of the partner's size. It is, however, possible to achieve joint power by pooling resources with others, as in consortia or associations.

   Note that the different instruments of strategy are not independent and can reinforce or neutralize each other. Formal, legal measures can have a negative

Table 4.3 *Detailed instruments*

Influence on value

VPH   Increase the (relative) value of the partner. In case value is low due to competition, try and turn competition into co-operation. In case relative value is low due to more attractive alternatives, increase value by investing in partner's resources. This may entail specific investments, which also increase switching costs. The purpose may be to revitalize a relationship that needs to be continued because of high switching costs

VPL   Lower partner value by destroying his resources, or by shifting volume to alternative partners

VPSL   Reduce both the partner's value and one's own value to the partner by expropriating his resources

VSH   Increase own relative value for the partner. Generally this will entail specific investments, which also increase switching costs. The goal may be to make the partner more dependent and thereby ensure his loyalty and reduce relational risk

VSL   Lower own value by stopping to invest in it or by creating or finding alternatives for the partner

Influence on switching costs

SSL   Lower own switching costs by stopping specific investments

SSLPH   Lower own switching costs and simultaneously increase those of the partner by selling part of one's share in specific investments, or by demanding more guarantees for continued partnership or refunds for specific investments when the relation is broken prematurely

SSHPL   The reverse: accept higher share of specific investments, or give more guarantees

SPH   Increase the partner's switching costs by demanding a hostage

SSH   Increase own switching costs by posting a hostage

SSPL   Lower switching costs for both sides by switching to a more flexible technology or by developing common standards for contracts, procedures and techniques

Influence on room for opportunism

RPL1   Restrict room for the partner, by tighter legal or other formal constraints, with corresponding sanctions

RPL2   The same, by closer monitoring of the partner's activities and performance

RSL1   Accept constraints on one's own room for action

RSL2   The same, by accepting closer monitoring

RSH1   Increase one's own room by loosening constraints

RSH2   The same, by shielding off monitoring

Influence on intent towards opportunism

IPSL   Bonding: investments in the relation to enable or enhance the development of institutional ties such as norms or values of conduct, or emotional ties, or habituation. In other words: invest in 'atmosphere'

ISH   Signal greater inclination towards opportunism by a show of indifference, lack of interest, antipathy or loss of norms, so that the partner perceives a heightened risk of opportunism

129

effect on 'atmosphere'. A vicious circle of distrust can develop, in which partners engage in an accumulation of constraints on actions. Adversarial action can invite retaliation. The co-operative strategy of increasing the partner's dependence by means of more transaction-specific investments can increase the price of dependence. But investment in a reputation of reliability can also benefit alternative relations, and thereby reduce switching costs.

Thus, in choosing a package of instruments one should consider their consistency, not to undo in one area what one is trying to do in another. The complication is that the optimal package depends on conditions, and on the responses of the partner.

One step further in the analysis is to trace what the effects of the actions are on the basic variables in Figure 4.1: value, switching costs, room and intent towards opportunism for X and Y, and the implications for their inclination to continue or discontinue the relation, and for their relational risk. The results are specified in Table 4.4, by means of pluses and minuses to indicate the direction of change. The table only indicates first-order effects. Of course,

Table 4.4 Effects of instruments

Action by X	Effects on variables in Table 4.3											
	VYX	SWX	CAX	ROX	IOX	RRX	VXY	SWY	CAY	ROY	IOY	RRY
VPH	+		+			+						
VSH							+		+			+
VPL	−		−			−						
VSL							−		−			−
VPSL	−		−			−	−		−			−
SPH								+	+			+
SSL		−	−			−	−		−			−
SSPL		−	−			−	−		−			−
SSLPH		−	−			−	+	+				+
SSHPL	+	+				+	−		−			−
RPH						+				+		
RSPL				−		−				−		−
RSL1/2				−								−
RPL1/2							−			−		
RSH1/2		+										+
IPSL				−	−						−	−
ISH					+							+

owing to the recursiveness of the scheme, there are secondary and further effects, due to the reactions of the partner, one's own reactions to that, etc.

Detailed choice

Like instruments of governance, the contingencies for their use can also be treated in more detail.

Conditions

More detailed conditions concerning market and technology are specified in Table 4.5. Conditions of market and technology are mutually related. To give a few examples: radical innovation and incipient innovation yield uncertainty; in incipient innovation knowledge tends to be tacit, which creates dynamic transaction costs (costs of transferring or sharing knowledge); under radical innovation the benefits of experience become limited.

Institutional conditions depend on nations or regions. Some of them are specified in Table 4.6. Underdeveloped institutions yield high transaction costs. But high transaction costs can also result from contractual attitudes: a highly legalistic attitude, for example (as in the United States), or prolonged processes of consensus creation (Japan, Netherlands). The first is associated with a system of exit: when dissatisfied, walk out and sell up. The second is associated with voice: when dissatisfied, deliberate in an attempt to save the relation. The first makes for low-trust, short-term relations with limited depth and intensity, high costs of legal litigation (Fukuyama 1995) but yields few obstacles to the dynamics

Table 4.5 *Detailed conditions of market and technology*

- Degree of uncertainty: complexity (number of items and their relations), variability, radical uncertainty (openness of contingencies), observability of outputs and inputs of efforts from contributors, and their preferences
- Degree of innovation: zero, incremental, radical ('creative destruction')
- Stage of innovation: incipient, breakthrough, stabilization, decline
- Type of knowledge and technology: tacit, documented, standardized; systemic, stand-alone
- Appropriability; share of fixed costs
- Effects of scale, scope, experience
- Differentiability of products
- Intensity of competition, in relation to concentration and degree of mono/oligopoly, price elasticity, entry barriers

Table 4.6 *Institutional conditions*

- When the legal infrastructure (laws, law enforcement) is poor, legal governance may be very expensive or infeasible
- When contractual attitudes are highly legalistic, costs of legal governance may be excessive
- When contractual attitudes are relational or personal, and the moral order is familial, clan-based, elitistic or religious sectarian, entry barriers are high
- Problems arise when voice-based and exit-based contractual attitudes meet

of radical innovation. The second makes for high-trust, long-term and intensive relations that enhance incremental innovation and diffusion of innovations, but the strength of ties in networks of firms may form an obstacle to radical innovation. However, this is not necessarily the case. In contrast with some stability of relations, high volatility may yield lack of specific investments in them, resulting in low added value (Nooteboom 2000b).

When different partners are used to different institutions, and particularly when they are not aware of these differences, styles of governance may clash.

In a society without clear laws and regulations, or with corrupt, arbitrary or incompetent execution of laws, the importance of personal networks increases, and they are expensive to set up. Then, entrepreneurship would need to include relational competences, for the development of personal networks of contacts to gain access to resources and to manage them.

Birley *et al.* (1991) found that in Italy entrepreneurs spend significantly more time on the set-up and maintenance of networks of personal contacts than in Sweden, Northern Ireland or the United States.

Anthony Pagden (1988) gave an analysis of the breakdown of trust in the kingdom of Naples in the seventeenth and eighteenth centuries, when it belonged to the Habsburg empire of the Spanish king Carlos and later Philip II. The Spaniards opted for a cheap way to hold the country down from a distance, by breaking down the social structure and culture of trust. In the Netherlands they had learned that sheer military repression is costly and does not suffice, and that for control from a distance the institutions of a society must be broken down, in a strategy of *divide and rule*. The nobility were divided by creating a new, upstart nobility that owed their position to the Spanish masters. These were given the task of collecting exorbitant taxes, of which they could keep a large share for themselves provided that it was spent on idle, economically useless and politically harmless games such as duelling and the defence of personal honour. This destroyed trust in the nobility as the defenders and personification of order and reliability. The characteristic of personal, knightly honour, in contrast to honour in the sense of loyalty to the state, is that it relates to self-respect rather than a sense of community or state: 'the man of honour is his own law giver'. This contributed to the breakdown of the state. Trust in the state is based on public information on conduct, standards and procedures, so this was abolished. The critical role of the intelligentsia was destroyed by means of mystification and a relaxation of academic standards. Universities were obliged to continue the teaching of Aristotelian logic 'because it never accounted for anything'. Excessive attention to religious ceremony was required. Academic requirements for the legal degree were lowered, and the degree was also awarded as a token of honour to the upper class, which contributed to the undermining of the legal system. Arbitrary and unpredictable exceptions to legal rules were granted. Through the oversupply of incompetent lawyers their price was lowered, yielding an excess of worthless and inconclusive litigation. The populace were distracted by frequent public feasts. Social ties were replaced by mutual suspicion, and people were thrown back on themselves or close family. Trade became a game of mutual cheating. Exchange was reduced to immediate quid pro quo, without credit or investment. Gambetta (1988) showed how this breakdown of institutions as a basis for trust in the kingdom of Naples, which included Sicily, allowed the mafia to insinuate itself, to steal into the holes created by institutional breakdown, and install their perverse order to fill the vacuum. The first evidence of the mafia as an established order is from 1838. The mafia is connected with Sicily, but something similar developed in Naples: the Camorra.

Problems of governance

Product differentiation and intensive co-operation in knowledge exploitation and exploration are important goals, but they yield problems that need to be solved. The gravity of these problems depends on the conditions, such as institutions and their effect on transaction costs. The problems of governance are summarized in Table 4.7. P5 reflects the fact that costs of governance depend on uncertainty. P6 reflects that apart from direct out-of-pocket costs there are opportunity costs: by regulating what is to be done one excludes not only undesirable but also desirable alternatives. Also, an excessively control-oriented approach to governance may confirm or create suspicion and thereby ruin the basis for a build-up of trust and loyalty as an alternative basis for co-operation. Note that a modest amount of regulation will not destroy the basis of trust and may indeed establish a basis for it.

P7 (effects of competitive conditions) is illustrated below in Table 4.7.

Table 4.7 *Problems of governance*

P1 If products are differentiated and production technology is inflexible, outsourcing entails specific investments, which yields exit barriers (which may yield a hold-up problem)

P2 To the extent that knowledge is tacit, which is particularly the case in R&D and in small firms, its transfer or linkage requires close observation and interaction or the transfer of teams of staff. If required contributions from collaborators cannot be specified, contractual arrangement becomes difficult. Communication requires close interaction and transaction specific investment in mutual understanding, which yields exit barriers

P3 When there is (radical) uncertainty of conditions, or when neither outputs of efforts nor inputs of efforts and preferences of contributors are measurable, no ex-ante regulation in contingent contracts is possible (Grandori 1997)

P4 There are other means of governance than governance by contract, as discussed in Chapter 4. But they entail costs of set-up, running and maintenance

P5 To the extent that markets are turbulent, with many exits and entries on markets, and there is rapid innovation, the loss of flexibility is most serious, there is a chance that a more attractive partner appears on the scene, and this increases risks of dependence and puts a strain on loyalty in existing relations

P6 To the extent that ex-ante regulation is feasible, then apart from direct costs there may be opportunity costs of restricting the flexibility of collaboration

P7 To the extent that competition is more intense, there is greater pressure to utilize opportunities for opportunism, in switching to a new, more attractive partner, or using that opportunity for leverage in bargaining

P8 To the extent that technology is systemic but not yet standardized, and there is no innovation or innovation is incremental (rather than radical), close co-ordination of component technologies is required

Some time ago, the author of this book approached the company that exploits the Dutch gas reserves, to discuss their supplier relations. From experience in the highly competitive car industry, we were explaining our approach to the issue in terms of benefits but also risks of dependence in specific investments due to possible opportunism. In the car industry we had been criticized for talk of 'trust and loyalty in lasting relations of co-makership'. Under the conditions of slump and excess capacity that prevailed at the time, there was cut-throat competition, and suppliers were squeezed for the last penny. The people at the gas exploration and production company were puzzled at our talk of the risk of opportunistic exploitation of dependence due to specific investments. They had very amicable, enduring and loyal give-and-take relations with their suppliers. Of course: they had a monopoly and were under no pressure to do otherwise.

P8 goes back to the earlier discussion of systemic as opposed to stand-alone technologies, such as materials (Willinger and Zuscovitch 1988) or telecommunication systems, which require integration across interfaces between components of the system, and in early stages of technology, when standards for such linkages have not yet been developed, this requires close co-ordination. Furthermore, under incremental innovation close co-ordination is needed to keep innovation in the different parts in tune (Teece 1988; Langlois and Robertson 1995). However, the latter argument loses force when innovation is so radical as to exert 'creative destruction' on existing systems of component technologies.

Examples

Some examples of a more detailed analysis are now supplied, to yield solutions of problems for more specific combinations of goals and conditions. Even those still constitute generic cases. Intermediate cases require even more detailed evaluation. The purpose is not to give solutions for all conceivable situations, but rather the contrary: to show that often generic rules are simplistic, and more specific solutions should be made to measure, given specific goals and conditions.

CASE 1

Goals	The goal is to utilize complementary resources or to achieve market entry, with partners who are not competitors (so that there is no need to integrate in order to control competition).
Conditions	Technology is systemic and innovation is absent or incremental (not radical), so that co-ordination is crucial, there is no problem of spill-over (either because the goal is not to innovate, or because appropriability is secure); there are no significant problems of dependence due to exit barriers from specific investments, knowledge is not so tacit as to exclude specification of required products, there is no uncertainty or excessive complexity or variability, and outputs of effort or inputs and preferences are measurable, so that contingent contracting is feasible, and there are no other obstacles to contracting.
Then:	
S1	Choose a disintegrated structure with contingent contracts (Grandori 1997). Example: a building consortium.
but	When complexity and unpredictability become excessive, and complete contracts become infeasible, *then*:
S2	Some centralization of decisions and monitoring becomes necessary (Grandori 1997). Example: consortium for building a refinery, with project management by one of the participants.

135

but   If there are no competent partners, and/or contingent contracts cannot be specified (uncertainty or unmeasurability of outputs and inputs and preferences of contributors; tacit knowledge; problems of legal infrastructure and contractual attitudes), *then*:

S3   Engage in full integration. For example: in Russia at the moment sometimes outside collaboration cannot reliably be set up.

Note, however, that even when the conditions of S1 are satisfied, contracts will never be complete. Furthermore, any co-operation entails a greater or lesser degree of socialization, in a community of practice (Brown and Duguid 1991), which constitutes a relation-specific investment, which yields an exit barrier to some extent. Thus, when collaboration is successful, a preference will arise for continued collaboration.

Next, the problem of spill-over is analysed more systematically and in more detail.

CASE 2
Goals   Learning, utilize complementary resources.
Conditions   Knowledge is highly documented and the speed of development is not high.
Then:
S4   More integration yields better control of spill-over, *but*:
S5   Under conditions of radical speed of change, outside partners are needed to yield the requisite variety of knowledge, and this entails no problem of spill-over to the extent that the knowledge involved is either tacit or subject to radical change.

CASE 3
Goals   Learning, utilize complementary resources for novel combinations.
Conditions   Incipient, radical innovation and high speed of change, uncertainty.
Then:
S6   Industrial districts, virtual firms.

The argument is as follows. In radical innovation systemic connections between component technologies break down, so that co-ordination across interfaces is not relevant, either for production or for incremental innovation or diffusion. Varied sources of learning and variability of association are crucial. Under conditions of radical speed of change, outside partners are needed to yield the requisite variety of knowledge, and this entails no problem of spill-over to the extent that the knowledge involved is either tacit or subject to radical speed of change.

136

CASE 4

Goals	Differentiated products, learning, utilize complementary resources, market entry.
Conditions	Exit barriers due to specific assets, as a result of the goals, in production or development; contractual problems.

Then:

S7   More integration to the extent that exit barriers are higher, monitoring requires close supervision, conditions for contracts are difficult, knowledge is tacit, the risk of creating a new competitor is higher, the threat to existing partners and behavioural uncertainty (P5) are higher.

S8   When in a vertical buyer–supplier non-equity alliance the supplier unilaterally has to incur specific assets for the benefit of the buyer, the buyer should participate in its ownership.

Empirical tests

The practical value of the tools for analysis, diagnosis and design of alliances should be tested in practice. An often heard complaint concerning theories of IORs is that they are difficult to operationalize and test in empirical research. Variables such as asset specificity, transaction costs, learning, innovation and trust are difficult or perhaps impossible to measure, or so the complaint goes. But there are methods to treat such variables as *latent* ones, which can be seen as being *spanned* or *indicated* by items that can be measured, where relevant in terms of judgement by people, on a five or seven-point Likert scale. The methodology is derived in part from psychographics. The indicators can then be combined into a joint variable. As Erin Andersen, a researcher who applied TCE in marketing, put it graphically: 'with many small', 'weak sticks one can build a strong bridge'. In this way one can subject hypotheses to 'hard', quantitative empirical tests on the basis of 'soft', qualitative indicators.

No attempt is made here to give a comprehensive review of the many empirical studies in the field. Just a few are selected in which the author of this book was involved. In the empirical studies described below, most indicators were five-point Likert scales. They were chosen on the basis of their hypothesized relation to latent variables that resulted from the theoretical analysis. Confirmatory factor analysis was used to test the measurement hypotheses. Cronbach's alpha was used to determine overall construct reliability, with the cut-off point at the usual value of 0.7. Factor loadings were used to determine whether each item contributed significantly to the joint factor, with the cut-off point at the usual value of 0.3. When an item had a lower loading, it was dropped, and the analysis was repeated for the remaining items until a scale with reliable loadings emerged. The items were then added to yield a measure of the latent variable.

137

In the first study, Berger *et al.* (1995) tested part of the basic causal scheme of governance of Figure 4.1 on the basis of a postal survey, prepared and later complemented with interviews, among eighty suppliers to Océ van der Grinten, a Dutch producer of copying machines (annual sales about US$1.5 billion, about 12,000 employees). The response was 84 per cent. The focus of the research was on the hypothesized effect of a number of variables on the perceived dependence of suppliers on the buyer. That perceived dependence was measured in two ways: independently from the perceived dependence of the buyer ('gross dependence'), and the degree to which the supplier perceived himself to be more dependent on the buyer than vice versa ('net dependence').

Not all hypothesized effects could be tested in this way. For example: the effect of shared ownership of specific assets was so predominant that it applied to all suppliers to approximately the same extent, and therefore did not exhibit the variation needed for testing effects. Yet this gives confirmation in showing that the problem of specific investments is indeed covered at least to some extent by shared ownership, as predicted.

The data allowed testing of the effects indicated in Table 4.8. The table also shows whether the predicted effect on perceived dependence was positive or negative, and how far the effect was statistically significant. The measurement of the variables and the results are discussed below.

The variable 'specificity of assets' is measured as the sum of different types of specificity, entirely in line with TCE: location specificity (measured by one

Table 4.8 Tests of effects on dependence perceived by suppliers

Test	Net perceived dependence	Gross perceived dependence
Dependence buyer		−
Length of supply	−	−
Trust in buyer's loyalty	−	− **
Competence trust in buyer		−
Specificity of assets	+ ***	+ ***
Extensiveness contract	−	−
Knowledge exchange	−	− **
Sales size supplier	− **	−
Supply to buyer as % of total sales	+	+ ***
Indirect supply	+ **	+ *
Bundling of supply	−	−

Source: Berger *et al.* (1995).

Notes: * Significance > 90%. ** Significance > 95%. *** Significance > 99%.

138

indicator), physical asset specificity (two indicators), dedicated capacity (four indicators) and knowledge specificity (two indicators). 'Extensiveness of contract' is measured as a sum of indicators regarding supply conditions, technical specifications and security stocks. Trust in loyalty (lack of opportunism) is construed on the basis of six indicators. The remaining variables are more easily measured, and are all based on a single indicator (direct measurement). When the theoretical effect, hypothesized on the basis of the analyses of preceding chapters, is indeed found this is indicated with one asterisk (*) when the statistical reliability was more than 90 per cent, two asterisks if it was more than 95 per cent, and three asterisks if it was more than 99 per cent.

The disconfirmation of hypotheses can be as interesting as confirmation, or even more. It is interesting to find that the extensiveness of contracts had no significant effect on perceived dependence, and this confirms earlier studies (Macauley 1963). This confirms the suspicion that extensive contracts, in formal, legal governance can have only limited value. A closed contract is impossible anyway; it can limit the flexibility of operations and can even have a negative effect, in confirming and stimulating mutual suspicion. Of course this does not imply that there should be no contracts at all, only that they should not be too extensive.

The strongest result is the positive effect of the transaction-specificity of assets, which confirms a central thesis of TCE. Of great theoretical importance is the effect of trust in the partner's loyalty, because that is one of the two main extensions of TCE. It does have the expected negative effect on gross perceived dependence, but not on net dependence. This could make sense: net dependence would depend on the balance of loyalty. If partner's loyalty is reciprocated by own good faith, then the effect on net dependence (the degree to which supplier is more dependent on buyer than vice versa) is not to be expected: partner's dependence is as much reduced as one's own is. The expected effects of the share of supply on total sales (positive) and of total sales as a measure of the effect of the size of the supplier (negative) were also confirmed. The confirmation of the negative effect of information transfer from the buyer to the supplier is interesting. The theory of this was that thereby the buyer makes himself more vulnerable, by weakening his bargaining position and by the risk of spill-over to competitors (information as hostage), which reassures the supplier with respect to his own perceived dependence. Interesting also is the confirmation that supply to other suppliers of the same buyer ('indirect supply') increases supplier dependence. But the expected effect that a bundling of supply, as main supplier, would decrease dependence is not confirmed.

Summing up: effects from both TCE and its extensions are confirmed, and this indicates that the framework developed in previous chapters is indeed fruitful. One of the shortcomings of the study is that it concerns only one buyer, so that effects due to the buyer cannot be investigated. This is eliminated in the second study.

In the second study, Nooteboom *et al.* (1997) conducted a survey of ten companies supplying components and sub-assemblies to producers of electrical/ electronic apparatus, with ten customer relations for each of the ten companies. The firms were visited by a member of the research team at the beginning of 1994. The visits took an average of three and a half hours. During the visit, data pertaining to the relationships with ten of the firm's most important customers were collected. The questionnaire was based on one that was developed and tested in the previous study (Berger *et al.* 1995). Items that had proved to be of little value were omitted; some new items were added. The questionnaires were completed by a respondent who was either the general manager or the sales manager of the firm, with the researcher clarifying questions when necessary. This min- imized the risk of misunderstanding the questions and also guaranteed that there was no non-response, and hence no missing data. To maintain comparability between relationships, the questionnaires were completed horizontally, i.e. a question was answered for all ten relationships before moving on to the next ques- tion. In this way, data were obtained with regard to ninety-seven relationships.

Two dimensions of trust were hypothesized: habitualization and institu- tionalization. By the latter was meant the emergence of common norms to regulate behaviour within a relationship. The indicator variables (five-point Likert scales) are specified below. Cronbach's alpha for the constructs is also given.

1 HAB: habitualization (Cronbach $\alpha = 0.75$):
   (a) Because we have been doing business so long with this customer, all kinds of procedures have become self-evident.
   (b) Because we have been doing business for so long with this customer, we can understand each other well and quickly.
   (c) In our contacts with this customer we have never had the feeling of being misled.
2 INST: institutionalization ($\alpha = 0.73$):
   (a) In this relation, both sides are expected not to make demands that can seriously damage the interests of the other.
   (b) In this relation the strongest side is expected not to pursue its interests at all costs.
3 HI: habitualization/institutionalization ($\alpha = 0.77$) = habitualization + institutionalization + item:
   (a) In this relation informal agreements have the same significance as formal contracts.

The last item is kept apart from HAB and INST because it could with equal theoretical and empirical justification be added to either of them; in both cases

Cronbach's alpha increases with ten percentage points. The resulting variables were included in an econometric model to explain perceived relational risk, with two dimensions: the probability that the relation will go wrong, and the penalty involved if it does. These were operationalized as follows:

1 SLE: size of loss ego ($\alpha = 0.90$):
   (a) Actually, we cannot afford a break with this customer.
   (b) If the relation with this customer breaks down, it will take us much effort to fill the gap in turnover.
2 PLE: probability of loss ego:
   (a) The risk in this relation is sufficiently covered by contractual and non-contractual means.

The trust variables competed for explanation next to other non trust-related explanatory variables, as illustrated in Figure 4.1. Again, we look at X (here the supplier). Factors that contribute to the (relative) value of the partner (VYX) and to X's switching costs (SWX) should determine captiveness (CAX, i.e. size of loss should the relation break down (see formula 4.1 and the surrounding text (p. 103)). Factors that limit the room for opportunism for the partner (such as contractual, legal governance and monitoring, ROY) and factors that limit incentives to the extent that the partner is himself dependent (RRY) (due to shared ownership of specific assets, guarantees, own interest in the relation, due to the value of the focal partner VXY) and inclination towards opportunism (on the basis of the trust-related variables habitualization and institutionalization, HI) should determine the probability of loss.

One of the explanatory variables was the 'continuity' of the relation (CON), which was expected to have a positive effect on the value of the partner (in view of the perspective of co-operation in the future, see Figure 4.1), and hence on size of loss, as well as on loyalty (due to habit formation, growth of familiarity and trust) and hence on probability of loss.

The above analysis stressed the recursiveness of the system: dependence of one side depends on dependence of the other side, because to the extent that someone is dependent he is less likely to exploit the dependence of his partner. That is why the value that the supplier thinks he has for the buyer was also included, with the hypothesis that it would have a negative effect on the perceived probability that things would go wrong owing to the partner's opportunistic conduct.

Control variables were added to control for firm-specific attributes such as firm size (measured by annual sales, SX) and risk or uncertainty avoidance (UA). The latter was expected to have a positive effect on perceived probability of loss: risk-averse firms take a dimmer view of the risks of dependence. The operationalization and measurement of the variables (ASE, VA, ROY, VXY and UA) are specified in the appendix. The empirical results are specified in Table 4.9.

141

Table 4.9 Tests of effects of trust

Test	Size of loss (SLE)	Probability of loss (PLE)
Value partner (VA)		
% share turnover (%S)	☺ 0.52 (0.000)***	☺ 0.02 (0.78)
Remaining value (RVA)	☹ 0.07 (0.42)	☺ −0.05 (0.60)
Switching costs (SW)	☺ 0.17 (0.031)**	☺ 0.11 (0.21)
Restricted opportunism partner (RO)	☺ 0.07 (0.36)	☺ −0.34 (0.003)***
Trust (HI)	☺ −0.03 (0.75)	☺ −0.22 (0.033)**
Own value for partner (VE)	☺ +0.01 (0.87)	☹ −0.05 (0.58)
Continuity (CON)	☺ 0.306 (0.000)***	☺ −0.249 (0.019)**
Uncertainty avoidance (UA)	☺ 0.05 (0.48)	☹ −0.201 (0.022)**
Firm size (SE)	☹ 0.01 (0.94)	☺ 0.08 (0.43)
Adjusted R^2	0.52	0.32

Notes: * Significance > 90%. ** Significance > 95%. *** Significance > 99%. In brackets: significance level (T). Confirmed hypotheses are indicated with ☺; lack of confirmation is indicated with ☹.

The results show that indeed trust has a significant effect on perceived probability of incurring a loss due to opportunism, next to the effects of other variables that one would expect from transaction cost economics. One disconfirmation of hypotheses was that instead of the expected positive effect of uncertainty avoidance on probability of loss there was a negative effect. But this can be interpreted very well: risk-averse suppliers make sure they have low-risk partners. The second disconfirmation was that a high perceived value offered to the partner did not have the expected negative effect on the perceived probability of loss. Our interpretation of this is that firms are not sophisticated enough in their assessment of the situation: they did not take into account the motivations of the partner; did not ask the question what they would do if they were in his shoes.

There is independent evidence of this lack of sophistication. It was also observed in a study of a European producer of telecommunication services. The firm (X) was one-sidedly dependent on a single American supplier (Y) of hard and software for communication, which was unique in its products, service and innovation. Out of fear from this, X considered employing a second source. But that would mean incurring huge costs of duplication of systems, because the products from the different suppliers were not mutually compatible in the complex systemic coherence of apparatus and software. Nevertheless, X attached so much weight to the dangers of dependence that it was on the point of accepting these costs. The question was not asked what interest Y would have in taking advantage of X's dependence. It turned out that X had so much value for Y, in offering privileged access to a large chunk of the fast-growing European market, that Y would have been mad to jeopardize that. X's unique value to Y was sufficient compensation for X's dependence.

Chapter 5

Process

- ■ Stages of relations
  - ● Beginning
  - ● Management
  - ● Adaptation
  - ● The end
- ■ Networks for exploration and exploitation
  - ● Networks for exploration
    - ● The competence side
    - ● The governance side
  - ● Networks for exploitation
  - ● Contingencies
  - ● Conclusion
  - ● Empirical evidence
    - ● Multimedia
    - ● Biotechnology
  - ● Development of clusters
  - ● Development of multinational corporations
  - ● *Keiretsu*
- ■ Advanced
  - ● Opening game
  - ● Closing game
  - ● Generic strategies of outsourcing

SUMMARY

This chapter considers the dynamics of inter-organizational relationships (IORs) and networks. This was neglected in much earlier research, of both inter-firm alliances and networks. IORs are not simply designed and implemented once and for all. They arise with some design, but also as a function of circumstances, then they adapt, and at some point they end. The dynamics of IORs and networks raise an important challenge, for both managers and scholars. Comparisons of business systems have tended to focus on two extremes. On one side the literature pictures a system, often associated with the English-speaking world, which is characterized by high flexibility, in easy buy-and-sell of (parts of) firms and easy hire-and-fire of personnel. This is supposed to be good for radical innovation (exploration). This is reflected also in the thesis of the 'strength of weak ties'. On the other side there is supposed to be a system that is associated with the European 'Rhineland' countries (Albert 1993), and, in a similar but also different way with Japan, which is characterized by more stable inter- and intra-firm relations. This is supposed to be good for quality production but to obstruct radical innovation. However, the real challenge lies in finding a balance of stability and flexibility. Some stability is needed to recoup the specific investments needed for quality, but also, as argued in this book, for exploration. However, this should not yield undue rigidities in relations that last too long and become too exclusive (Nooteboom 2000b). This is reflected in the criticism and modification of the thesis of the strength of weak ties, set out in this book.

In the development of a relation, there may be a shift from exploration to exploitation, or vice versa. The mix of instruments for governance may change. Trust may be built up and may break down. Relations can last too long, and trust can become too strong, yielding myopia and creating rigidities, with obstacles to learning and innovation. Organizations can be subject to different stages of development, in their structure, or in their technologies or markets, which require different approaches to their IORs. Organizations may learn how to better design and govern relations. This chapter analyses these process aspects of IORs. First, it discusses the stages of an IOR, with a beginning, adaptation, and an end. Subsequently it analyses networks for exploration and for exploitation, and relations and shifts between the two. It summarizes empirical evidence, derived from Gilsing (2003), for multimedia and biotech-pharma industries. It discusses the development of clusters, multinational corporations (MNCs), and changes in the well known Japanese *keiretsu*. The 'advanced' section of this chapter (p. 179) gives a more formal analysis of the end and of the beginning of IORs, with a simple use of game theory. It closes with a presentation of 'generic forms' of buyer–supplier relations.

STAGES OF RELATIONS

This section goes through the different stages in which relationships develop, and the implications for the management of relations.

Beginning

The beginning of a relation is often not simple, because one cannot be sure what it will yield, yet relation-specific investments and knowledge sharing are needed to build mutual value and get the relation going, and those may yield risks of hold-up and spill-over. In marriage the blindness of infatuation helps, which is blind to risk and yields only rosy visions of the unique value of the partner. In business relations blind friendship or kinship may help to set relations going, but are not generally advisable.

The 'advanced' section of this chapter gives a formal analysis of the beginning of a collaborative relationship, with the aid of game theory. The analysis shows how collaboration, in building mutual value, may arise. In this section, a richer, more verbal analysis is given.

In the initial negotiation stage, there is manoeuvring for position, profit, power and flexibility. If there is no basis of prior trust, in previous collaboration or in reputation, it has to be built up. As noted in the discussion on trust, in Chapter 4, it has been proposed that under those conditions the relation can start only on the basis of calculative self-interest (McAllister 1995; Lewicki and Bunker 1996). This entails attempts to cover all risks by formal control. As discussed in Chapter 4, this includes control of opportunities or room for opportunism, by contract or hierarchy, or control of incentives for opportunism, by means of unique partner value, switching costs, hostages or reputation. Too much formal control, especially by constraining room for action, demonstrates suspicion, and is likely to be met with reciprocal suspicion. There are two problems with this. First, it may lead to a vicious circle of constraints on action that limit the innovative potential of the relation. Second, in view of the social-psychological heuristics of 'availability, representativeness, and anchoring and adjustment', discussed in Chapter 1, a suspicious stance at the beginning may become the psychological 'anchor', or norm, of the relation, which sets expectations, from which only incremental changes are made, and which is difficult to turn round once it is established. Deutsch (1973) suggested that there is circular causation between characteristics of participants and the results of interaction. He offered his 'crude law of social relations': 'The characteristic processes and effects elicited by a given type of social relationship (co-operative or competitive) tend also to elicit that type of social relationship.' If this is true, then one must be very careful how to start a relationship, because it may be difficult to get out of the initial mode of interaction.

This applies also to relations within organizations. In a study of 'trust and trouble' in organizations, Six (2001) found how important it is to create mutual trust with regard to new, incoming staff.

Earlier, mention was made of the 'Calimero syndrome'. An actor who is small and weak, relative to his partners, can be overly suspicious, expecting power play at every turn. This sets the frame of mind in which events are interpreted when things go wrong in relations, as they always will. Rather than allowing for accidents, mistakes or failures of competence, and extending the benefit of the doubt, one jumps to the conclusion that since the partner has more power, he is probably taking opportunistic advantage of it. New staff may feel such insecurity. To make them feel confident, it helps to pay attention to their socialization upon entry, and to grasp every opportunity to compliment them when they do well. This helps on two sides. It makes the newcomer more confident, alleviating any Calimero effect. It may also help incumbent staff to overcome their natural inclination to suspicion of newcomers. Note that this connects with the earlier discussion, in Chapter 1, of an organization as a focusing device, and the role in that of organizational culture, to align perceptions and expectations.

After inadvertently creating an atmosphere of mistrust, in the early bargaining process, the bargainers from the top of the firms throw the problem in the lap of the poor implementation manager, who is confronted with a huge obstacle that can jeopardize the relation before it has properly started. The problem may be aggravated by the 'macho' behaviour of some managers, discussed in Chapter 4, who want to project a 'top dog' image, 'calling the tune', with a view to their future careers.

These phenomena of difficult beginnings yield lessons for the development of collaboration. First, it might be wise to let the bargaining be led by people who no longer have a stake in building a macho profile, e.g. because they are already near the end of their careers. Second, those responsible for implementation should be included in the bargaining process, or bargainers should also be made responsible for implementation. Perhaps there is a role here for a go-between (see Chapter 4), to guide negotiations prior to collaboration.

An alternative approach is to take more time, and develop a relation in small steps, to allow for socialization, the development of empathy and perhaps even some identification, and to achieve quick results, to build initial trust, so that the relation can be developed without the risks and constraints of calculative control (Shapiro 1987).

A few years ago, KLM had a failed alliance with Alitalia. There was an objective problem over the position and perspectives of Malpensa airport as a 'hub' near Milan. However, there were also problems of culture, with different attitudes about how a relation of collaboration should begin. The Italians were oriented to prior socialization, in the approach of small steps. The Dutch were impatient, and wanted to go ahead fast and do the deal. In addition, apparently there was a problem of 'macho behaviour'. Reportedly, the Dutch CEO wanted to project an image of a go-getter, perhaps for his future career prospects. Also, KLM had been involved in earlier alliance failures, and may have been in a hurry to catch up with developments in the industry. The Italians, on the other hand, were led by a senior manager at the end of his career, who had no need for profile-building behaviour.[1] The development of the alliance halted amid suspicion and frustration, and was broken up by the exit of the Dutch. Later, the Italians lodged a claim for compensation. It was agreed that the conflict would be arbitrated in Holland, but according to Italian law. The outcome was that an enormous fine was imposed on KLM, for not acting in good faith according to the principles of Italian law, by abruptly exiting from the relationship, without due effort to reach agreement.

Another pitfall in the beginning is to be too closed, divulging as little information as possible, on the intuition that any information might be taken advantage of by the partner. In particular, people will hesitate to be open concerning their weaknesses and corresponding fears of opportunities for partner opportunism. Recall also the problem of psychological and social risk, discussed before. There are two problems with this. One is that it robs the partner of opportunities to alleviate such fears.

An important question is how one sees negotiation. One way is to concede as few points as possible, as a matter of principle: an aim in itself. Another way is to look for ways to allay the fears of the partner, and to serve his interests, at minimum cost to oneself, and help the partner to reciprocate in the same vein. That, surely, is the gist of Hirschman's notion of 'voice'. The first view also goes against the principle, proposed by Zand (1972), that openness is needed for the building of trust. In fact, the two arguments are probably the same: one needs to be open to problems on both sides, and accept some control by the partner in order to have some control oneself.

In a student's master's project, the author of this book became involved with a supplier of chemicals (Merck) to Philips's semiconductor plant in Nijmegen, the Netherlands. The supplier's investments were as specific as they can get. It had dedicated installations inside the Philips production hall, integrated into the production system. There was a tendency to hide risks and fears of dependence, on both sides. The chemicals supplier did not want to expose his vulnerability, and Philips did not want to recognize them either, for fear of then having to make concessions. However, the result was that the supplier held back developments that would have been to mutual advantage. Both sides were surprised, and relieved, to find that when perceived risks were brought out into the open, they could be discussed, and ways were found mutually to alleviate them, in give-and-take, with little cost. This resulted in increased trust. Recall from the discussion of trust, in Chapter 4, that trust does not entail or require absence of conflict. Nothing may strengthen trust as much as the joint and satisfactory resolution of conflict.

148

This does not imply that one should exercise openness without limits. In fact, excess of openness also constitutes a pitfall. For one thing, there may be a risk of spill-over. Staff involved in deliberations may, from professional zeal or vanity, prematurely divulge commercially sensitive information (close to core competence), before it is clear what one will get in return, how problematic or not the spill-over problem would be, and whether the relationship will develop and succeed, to make the risks and sacrifices worth while. One may be justified in maintaining hidden agendas or secrets that are too sensitive. People may do that even in the most private of relationships. The motive may be strategic. However, recall that one of the risks of relations also is psychological and social risk, of losing self-esteem or social legitimacy. However, the point here is that one should not close off as a matter of principle, minimizing information, but should be as open as possible for fruitful and creative bargaining.

Management

According to the 'trust process', discussed in Chapter 4, after a relation begins and develops success, trust and trustworthiness may develop on the basis of, first, empathy, and possibly, next, identification and routinization. But how does one assess emerging trustworthiness, or the lack of it? According to transaction cost economics it is impossible to do so reliably. The sociological literature, by contrast, gives instructions on how to infer intentional trust-worthiness from observed behaviour (Deutsch 1973). Did the partner act not only according to the letter but also according to the spirit of the agreement? Did he give timely warning of unforeseen changes or problems? Was he open about relevant contingencies, and truthful about his dealings with others that might constitute a threat to one? Did he defect to more attractive alternatives at the earliest opportunity? How much voice rather than exit did he exhibit? This is elaborated below.

When X observes a supportive action by Y, how does he judge what lies behind it? The following sequence of questions can help (adapted from Deutsch 1973):

1 Was the outcome intended by Y, or was it an unintended result of his action?
2 Did the action entail significant risk to Y?
3 Was Y aware of risk, and was it not neglected out of impulsiveness?
4 Did Y attach a *positive* value to this risk, out of masochism, sensation or (self-) image (overconfidence)?
5 Did Y have a choice, or was the action dictated by compulsion or conformity?

149

6 Was it out of confidence in the system rather than a positive evaluation of the situation?
7 Was it out of enlightened self-interest?
8 Was it out of enjoyment of trust relations?
9 Was it out of ethics, empathy, identification, friend- or kinship, routinization?

Deutsch noted that, as can be seen from the above, power could have an adverse effect on trust. If one is very powerful, there is justified suspicion that people subjected to one's power are trustworthy only because they are dependent or have no choice. In case of absolute power, the hypothesis that this is the case can never be rejected. This is how dictators become paranoid.

A problem with mistrust is that it feeds upon itself even more than trust does. (Mis)trust by X tends to engender (mis)trust on the part of Y, which justifies and deepens X's (mis)trust. But while trust can be falsified because it leads to reliance on others which can be disappointed, and then adapted, mistrust cannot, because it blocks trusting action that might disprove it.

There is also an argument from evolutionary psychology, discussed in Chapter 1. Evolution may have favoured the development of an intuition for reciprocity, and a psychological 'cheater detection mechanism'. We may have instinctive intuitions of opportunism.

In collaboration between organizations, there will be go-betweens, or 'boundary spanners'. They are in a sensitive position. As discussed in Chapter 3, a boundary spanner, crossing a 'structural hole', may personally profit by playing the sides off against each other (the principle of *tertius gaudens* discussed by Simmel and Burt). He may indeed form a risk for the organizations that act as his principals. They are therefore likely to exert some monitoring of his conduct. This may lead to constraints on his actions from both sides. The go-between may be subject to different sets of values, norms and expectations that are difficult to reconcile. He may be suspected of consorting 'with the enemy' (creating hold-up situations), giving away company secrets (spill-over) or revealing skeletons from the cupboard (hostages). Therefore, it is crucial that boundary spanners have support in their home organizations, from sufficiently senior 'champions'. The analysis relates to the discussion, in Chapter 4, of the relation between personal and organizational trust. Both will be needed: trust in the competences and intentions of boundary spanners, and trust in their backup in their parent organizations.

Next to problems of intentional trust, there are also problems of competence, in the 'crossing of cognitive distance'. It is the job of boundary spanners to translate between company jargons and to build mutual absorptive capacity. This may take time, especially when the knowledge involved is highly tacit. Before being able to take part in outside 'communities of practice' he may have first to participate in 'legitimate peripheral participation' (Lave and Wenger 1991), before trust in competence and intentions can be given. Differences appear, not only in procedures, but also in often highly tacit underlying norms and values that are part of organizational culture (interpreted here in terms of fundamental underlying values, cf. Schein 1985). If such distance between partner organizations is large, any boundary spanner, coming from either side, will have great trouble in establishing the bridge to cross cognitive distance.

All this puts boundary spanners in a difficult position. It may be better to employ a more neutral and experienced outside go-between (see Chapter 4), who is less entangled in partisan interests, personal loyalties, career prospects and psychological and social risk.

A well-known question concerning the governance of joint ventures (JVs) is whether ownership and control should be symmetrical or concentrated in a clear majority shareholder (Killing 1983; Anderson and Gatignon 1986; Geringer and Hebert 1989; Bleeke and Ernst 1991). The argument for the latter is that it yields more decisiveness. Balanced ownership and control may delay decisions. The argument for the former is that a minority participant may suffer from the 'Calimero syndrome': with less influence and high dependence, he may not be motivated to do his best and may be overly suspicious of becoming the victim of opportunism, which blocks the building of trust. A solution may be to separate ownership and control, with symmetrical ownership and a rotating majority in decision making, which at any time yields a clear initiative in management for one side, whose actions are monitored by a balanced supervisory board.

Adaptation

How to govern a relationship in its different stages of development? What problems may arise, and what can one do to prevent or mitigate them? One problem may be that a partner gets taken over by a competitor.

An example is discussed by Faulkner (1995): the alliance between Honda and Rover for the development and production of cars in the United Kingdom. This was a non-equity alliance. For Rover it yielded access to efficient Japanese production methods and for Honda a bypass of European import restrictions and access to experience with European tastes of styling. A threat arose for Honda when Rover was taken over by BMW.

A lesson to be learned from such cases is that in the design and governance of an alliance one should consider not only one's partner's interests, but also the possibility that the partner may be taken over, and the interests of potential new

151

owners. Another illustrative case was given in Chapter 4, with a Norwegian company ('Norpartner') whose Swedish partner was taken over by the Norwegian partner's main competitor. This might yield an argument for substantial equity participation (as already indicated it Table 3.1). A problem may also be the reverse: one's partner takes over one's competitor, whereby the partner becomes a competitor.

An example of an alliance getting into trouble because one side takes over a company that forms a competitive threat to the other side is discussed by Lorange and Roos (1992). This is the case of the joint venture for the production and distribution of sanitary products in the United Kingdom between Swedish Mölnlycke and British Scott. Scott's sales network provided entry to the British market for Mölnlycke, who yielded complementary products, thus increasing the utilization of the network (economy of scope) and also offered Scott access to advanced technology. All went well for eleven years, until Mölnlycke acquired French Peaudouce in order to expand its market to other countries. But Peaudouce also had a sales organization in the United Kingdom, thus creating a potential problem for Scott. It weakened Scott's relative value in the alliance, and thereby increased the risk of opportunism by Mölnlycke.

The analysis of governance, in Chapter 4, indicated that often a productive form of governance is to establish symmetrical, mutual dependence. Mutual dependence may be built by specific investments: they create dependence on the side of the party who makes the investment, but may also build exclusive value for his partner, who thereby becomes dependent. A problem with this approach is that often after a while the balance of dependence is broken.

A class of cases is that of product–market entry alliances between an American company that supplies design or technology and a Japanese company that supplies access to the Japanese market. After a while, the Japanese company has copied the technology and competences, but is itself still needed for market access. This often leads to a disentangling of the alliance or one side buying the other out. Alliances may from the start have been designed for a limited duration. It may be used to have a joint standard accepted in the market, or as an exploratory stage for an MA, to assess value and the viability of integrating cultures.

A specific example in this class is that of the long-lasting and successful Japanese joint venture Between Xerox and Fuji given by Lorange and Roos (1992). It started out as a classic product–market entry alliance, with Xerox providing the product and Fuji providing entry in the difficult Japanese market. After a while, technology spilled over to Fuji, which developed a capability for its own design and production of copiers. At Xerox this was seen as a loss; as negative value due to spill-over of technology, the building of a new competitor and a threat to home-country employment. But this was amply compensated by the fact that Fuji developed a low-end product that was complementary to Xerox's range of products, and helped to stop competitive entry to the market by IBM.

Adaptation is needed to take into account changed goals and shifting conditions of markets and technology.

In their study of forty-nine alliances Bleeke and Ernst (1991: 131) found that of the alliances that were able to adapt their perspective 79 per cent were successful, against 33 per cent for alliances whose aim and scope remained the same.

Imbalance of value and dependence can arise in several ways. In the above example, value of one partner was appropriated by the other. It may also be that one partner will fail to renew his value, for lack of learning, or that his value declines because of (competence-destroying) shifts in technology or markets. It may also be that value, which is value relative to the next best alternative, declines owing to the emergence of a new player who is more attractive.

In view of the possibility of emerging imbalances of dependence, it becomes important to complement this strategy with trust, to ensure that when such imbalances begin to occur, there is sufficient openness, in voice, to signal that and to engage in deliberations on how to redress the balance of value, and in what time frame.

In the discussion of exploitation and exploration, in Chapter 2, it was noted that exploration often requires loose, flexible structures, while exploitation requires more integrated, tight structures, especially when the technology is 'systemic'. IORs for exploration, including industrial districts, may start loosely, and then become more tightly integrated when exploration shifts into exploitation. Here, the ties between organizations may become too strong and durable, creating rigidities and obstacles to learning and innovation. That danger is particularly large if relations are not only more durable than needed to recoup specific investments that were desirable to create mutual added value, but are also exclusive, possibly by design, to avoid spill-over. Then mutual identification and routinization may reduce cognitive distance too much, creating 'group think'.

Another problem may lie in network structure and network position. If the network becomes denser, with more division of labour, with ties that are strong on one or more of their dimensions (scope, intensity, specificity, frequency, duration, openness, proximity, see Chapter 3), then this may also create rigidities. Exit may be constrained by coalitions of members of the network. If ties are strong ties in terms of high, specific investments, the reason may be to protect those investments. If ties were strong in terms of high mutual openness, the reason may be to prevent spill-over or loss of hostages.

A straightforward idea is to design collaboration, at the beginning, with a view to options for later adaptation, and options for exit. The theory of repeated games provides an argument against specifying the end of a relation. Then collaboration would unravel, as follows. When the end approaches, people will no longer take care, in mutual give-and-take, to preserve a basis for continuation, for future advantage. Then, there will be a race for who is the first to stop collaborating, and the result is that no one collaborates from the start, or so the theory claims. However, while keeping the relation open-ended, one can agree on procedures of voice, for signalling and solving problems.

The end

Voice entails that when the value of the partner drops, one does not immediately go for exit, but voices one's concern and tries to redress the balance of value, in collaboration. However, when this fails, and fails repeatedly, the point may be reached where the relation needs to be broken off. How is this to be done? This may be as important as, and perhaps more difficult than the beginning of a relationship. This situation is analysed formally, with the aid of game theory, in the 'advanced' section of this chapter (p. 179).

Informally, the analysis is as follows. Suppose one side, X, wants to exit, for lack of value from his existing partner Y, while Y still needs X. X has two choices of action. One is to prepare his exit as secretly as he can. He prepares his new relationship, lowers his switching costs by making no more specific investments, stops giving hostages, and retracts existing ones, by no longer stationing staff at the partner's location, buying back minority shares that Y may have, and holding back on sensitive information. Then, when he is prepared, he drops the bomb on Y and exits as quickly as he can. This is really exit: an exit form of exit. There is an alternative, in a 'voice mode of exit'. This entails that X announces his intentions well ahead of time, and announces that he will help Y to disengage from the relationship with as little damage as possible. X and Y jointly stop specific investments, return hostages, stop giving sensitive information, and X helps Y find the best replacement partner possible. He may also give compensation for his exit.

Which action should X choose, if he is purely calculative? The advantage of the first option is that Y hardly gets time to stop X from exiting. However, Y is likely to feel held up, cheated, wronged. If there is great uncertainty of technology and markets, one disadvantage is that X may yet need Y in the future. Furthermore, having had no opportunity to prepare for the disaster, Y may face such losses that there is nothing to be lost in an aggressive reaction. He may take legal action, destroy whatever hostages he may still have, divulge sensitive information, or attempt to destroy X's reputation. Here, recall the discussion of a loss versus gain frame, in 'prospect theory', discussed in Chapter 1. X faces a gain frame, Y a loss frame. According to the theory, Y might take much more drastic and risky action to prevent his loss than X would to get his gain. Y might take legal action even in the virtual certainty of losing, he might resort to slander to damage X's reputation.

Y's reaction is more likely to be extreme when in the past the relationship was characterized by voice and mutual trust. As noted before, trust entails openness, and here there was none in the exit.

A similar predicament may arise in the selling of a firm. When does one announce it to the workers? If one announces it suddenly, just prior to the hand-over, this can cause a shock that destroys confidence and motivation. However, with an early announcement, there may be a risk that especially the best staff get time to leave for a job elsewhere, which would detract from the firm's value, and hence its take-over price. On the other hand, since it is in the interest of the buyer to maintain the motivation of personnel, unless he does not intend to maintain the firm in its present set-up, he might go along with an early announcement, accompanied with assurances and guarantees to staff concerning their future work.

As indicated before, another obstacle to exit can arise from embeddedness in a network. Exit may be seen as a threat not only to direct partners but also to their partners, and they may form a coalition to restrain any 'defector'. This may frustrate the voice mode of exit discussed above. One may have to prepare one's exit in secret in order to be able to escape at all.

NETWORKS FOR EXPLORATION AND EXPLOITATION[2]

Next to change in individual relations, there are also questions concerning processes of change in networks, or network dynamics. How do network structure and ties change? In particular, how do they change if one goes from exploration to exploitation? As discussed in Chapter 3, Granovetter and Burt argued that exploratory networks should have a sparse structure, with weak ties. This section develops a counter-argument. It also contributes to discussions of the dynamics of industrial districts and clusters, and the role that MNCs may play. Finally, it gives an analysis of the change in the vertical structures of the Japanese *keiretsu*.

Networks for exploration

The competence side

In the theory of discovery proposed by Nooteboom (2000), which was summarized earlier in this book (Chapter 2), a basic proposition is that for exploration one would expect disintegrated or loose structures, to allow the flexibility, variety and cognitive distance needed for exploration. This seems similar to the thesis of 'strength of weak ties'. However, this needs to be analysed in more detail. Below, networks for exploration are first analysed from a competence perspective, and then from a governance perspective.

In networks for exploration, there is uncertainty concerning future dominant designs, in both technology and organization, and hence also concerning the configuration of future networks for exploitation. In other words, network configuration cannot be driven by static efficiency of exploitation. Here, the focus is on gathering, combining and generating technical knowledge in different configurations, from a variety of sources, and experimentation with prototypes. One needs access to a variety of other actors who might offer complementary knowledge, but one does not know clearly what elements of knowledge will turn out to be relevant when a dominant design develops. Also one does not know what actors will survive by that time. In the argument of Granovetter and Burt for the strength of weak ties, implicit assumptions are that it is known:

1 what knowledge will be relevant (Hagedoorn and Duysters 2002);
2 who has what knowledge, including knowledge of sources of knowledge;
3 who will survive to offer direct or indirect access to knowledge.

These aspects of knowledge in networks bear some resemblance to the distinctions made by Burt (1992) between different kinds of 'information benefits': access (who knows what), timing (when do they know) and referrals (who gets to participate in opportunities). Access is related to point 1 above, and timing to point 2.

The issue now is that in exploration one does not yet have knowledge of types 1, 2 and 3. There are three types of uncertainty: about what is relevant knowledge (knowledge uncertainty), about who has what knowledge (source uncertainty) and about who will be a member of the network, in what position (structural uncertainty). This yields four arguments for network density in exploration, from the competence perspective. Later, arguments will be added from the governance perspective.

First, one has to hedge relational and structural bets, by maintaining direct linkages even if they may later turn out to be redundant. Second, one does not yet know what ties will turn out to be redundant, since one does not know what the configuration of relevant elements of knowledge will be. If at this stage one cuts the connection with an agent, to limit redundancy, on the argument that one could also access that knowledge indirectly, through an intermediary actor with whom one does preserve a direct link, then one runs the risk that this intermediary may drop out, so that indirect access is broken.

Third, structurally redundant linkages might also be needed to reliably assess and understand knowledge accessed in another relation. This is the case especially when knowledge is newly emerging and highly tacit, as is typically the case in exploration. Suppose that A can access B only through C. Part of the thesis of the strength of weak ties is that this has an advantage in preventing information overload. C can help A by clarifying and selecting knowledge from B. That is certainly a relevant consideration. However, then B's knowledge is interpreted, and thereby possibly distorted, in C's absorptive capacity. Then A may need direct access to B to avoid the filtering and distortion of knowledge acquired through C. This is especially relevant in exploration, in view of knowledge uncertainty. Under that uncertainty, on what basis would C know what A needs to know? Also, if A remains linked to both B and C, even if there is also a link between B and C, this may help A to understand C by discussing with B what he understands from C. In other words, one may need to pool absorptive capacity to absorb knowledge from a third source. A dense network structure enables firms to triangulate among multiple sources and thus better assess the meaning, value and reliability of the obtained information. Here, firms can use existing strong ties, where mutual understanding has already been built up, to evaluate knowledge from new, weak ties. In other words, we might expect a dense structure of strong and weak ties.

Fourth, the disadvantages of redundancy may be limited, in exploration. The argument against redundancy was that the maintenance of redundant relations entails excess costs. There are two aspects here: number of ties and cost per tie. Note that the number of possible ties increases quadratically with the number of participants in the network. Thus, one may have to limit network size. However, that need depends on the cost per tie, which depends on the size only of specific investments required, since other investments can be used in multiple relationships. Apparently, a more explicit and detailed trade-off between the costs and benefits of redundancy is needed. That requires a consideration of the size of investments, their specificity, and their economic life. Furthermore, in exploration static efficiency from the elimination of redundant relations is less of an issue, since competition focuses on the dynamic efficiency of connecting complementary competences in the fast development of prototypes.

On the other hand, there are indeed also possible arguments against a dense structure, apart from the cost of redundancy. One is an increased risk of spill-over: if one has a tie with a partner who also has ties with one's competitors, the probability of spill-over increases. That will be analysed in the later discussion of

157

the governance side of relations. Another possible argument against dense structure is that one may be constrained, by reputation mechanisms or coalition formation, to exit from the network, and this may limit the variety needed for exploration. Another possible adverse effect of density is that one is more constrained in coming up with novel ideas that do not fit the cognitive foci, including norm sets, of connected others. In other words, one may be tied down in the 'group think' of a clique. This also may constrain exploration. These two points will be taken up later.

Now the analysis turns to the strength of ties, from a competence perspective. As discussed, high cognitive proximity would reduce learning, so that ties should not be strong in that sense. To allow for the flexibility needed for experimenting with novel combinations, ties should not be too durable. A second argument against durability is that it would reduce cognitive distance too much, in mutual convergence in cognition (identification). On the other hand, in view of the time pressures of innovation, in a race to markets, frequency of interaction is high. In view of frequency of interaction and tacitness of knowledge, ties may also need to be strong in terms of spatial proximity. Later, from the perspective of governance, spatial proximity may also be needed to build trust, partly by tapping into local gossip and localized reputation mechanisms. As indicated, in exploration there is uncertainty concerning the relevance, sources, meaning and reliability of information. There is also limited relevant, established experience concerning matters of organization, potential customers, potential suppliers, skills, staff, etc. As a result, ties encompass a variety of issues. In other words, ties are strong in the sense of having a wide scope.

The governance side

Now the analysis turns to the governance side of exploration networks, in the management of relational risks of dependence, in hold-up and spill-over risk. Dependence due to specific investments depends on the size, specificity and economic life of investments. In exploration, much knowledge is new and tacit, and hence difficult to absorb. As a result, one needs some specific investment to develop mutual understanding, to cross cognitive distance (Nooteboom 1999a). This connects with the insight from the network literature that strong ties may be needed for the 'exchange of complex knowledge'. Here, we specify the notion of 'knowledge complexity' as follows: wide scope, tacitness of knowledge and cognitive distance. Later, in a discussion of instruments of governance, it will be argued that especially in exploration there is a need for building relation-specific trust. That also entails a specific investment. However, in exploration it is difficult to judge which investments will be specific and which will not be. One cannot yet judge to what extent an investment will be useful in other relations. If knowledge is uncertain, its specificity is also uncertain. Some investments developed in one relation may well turn out to be useful in other relations, and one does not know in what relations. As a result, since the specificity of investments is difficult to judge, it may not be relevant for the decision to make them. Furthermore, in exploration the size of specific investments is limited, compared with those needed for exploitation. Specific investments are needed in building mutual understanding and trust, and they may be needed in instruments or experimental set-ups. However, unlike networks for exploitation, in exploration the focus is not on large and relation-specific investments in production facilities, distribution channels and brand name, with a long economic life, but on experimental set-ups for the fast development and adaptation of prototypes, which are often relatively small in size and may be so flexible as to hardly involve relation-specificity.

In the case of specific investments, either the duration of the relation or the frequency of interaction has to be sufficiently high to recoup the investments. Economic life of specific investments is relevant for the duration of the relation in which they would have to be recouped. As indicated before, ties with long duration have two adverse effects for exploration, from the perspective of competence. One is that they limit the flexibility and speed of experimenting with Schumpeterian novel combinations. A second is that they lead to reduced cognitive distance, with too much identification, yielding excessive trust and loyalty, and possibly blindness to opportunities in other relationships. Thus, whatever specific investments are needed, and can be identified as such, have to be recouped in frequent interaction rather than in long duration of ties. Under the volatility of exploration, with fast change of knowledge, investment in mutual understanding has a short life, so that only a short duration of the relation is relevant to employ and recoup the investment involved.

Now the analysis turns to dependence in the form of spill-over. In exploration, the pooling of knowledge in a dense network, with frequent interaction and openness of communication, yield a great potential spill-over. Yet, there are four reasons why this may not yield a significant risk.

First, in exploration competition is hardly an issue yet. Second, with great uncertainty about what dominant design will emerge, and to what products it will lead, in what markets, and structural uncertainty about who will in future still be a player, it is very difficult to assess who will in future turn out to be a competitor. Therefore, restricting relations for fear of spill-over would soon entail no relations at all. Third, to be a player at all in the exploration process may entail that one's knowledge spills over anyway, regardless of how open one is to others, and then one might as well be open and use openness to gain knowledge and build trust. Fourth, as noted before, spill-over risk is mitigated by tacitness of knowledge and speed of knowledge change, which both apply in exploration. Another instrument to govern spill-over risk is to demand

159

exclusiveness of ties. However, that would reduce the density and variety of knowledge sources, which would hinder the purpose of exploration.

While financial specific investments may be low, in exploration relative to exploitation, psychological and social investments may be high. To cope with that, given the density of ties and the frequency and openness of interaction, the size of the network must be limited. One economizes on the effort of maintaining ties not by reducing density, but by reducing the size of the network. This is consistent with the consideration, to be discussed, that especially in exploration trust is important, and for this ties need to be locally embedded. In other words, in exploration we expect dense, small, locally embedded networks.

As noted before, governance by detailed contracts is problematic, in exploration, owing to uncertainty in contract conditions and monitoring. Thus one needs to look at the alternative instruments of mutual dependence, hostages, reputation or, beyond self-interested governance, trust. Reputation is facilitated by dense network structure, to enable the gossip that is part of the reputation mechanism. The reasoning for this goes back to Simmel (1950) and Coleman (1988). Paradoxically, in exploration reputation effects are problematic and at the same time strong. Reputation is problematic since in exploration there typically is no relevant history that might form the basis for reputation. But that condition in itself also heightens the importance of reputation building: reputation being scarce, it is all the more important to build up a good one. Furthermore, good behaviour for the sake of reputation is furthered by structural uncertainty, i.e. uncertainty about future structural configurations. It is impossible to assess who may and who may not in the future yield a useful connection, or a valuable partnership. Therefore, one has to be careful in *all* ties, in view of their possible but uncertain importance and of the indirect ties they may give access to. Hostages also form an important aspect of governance in exploration, since there is much exchange of sensitive information. Mutual dependence also arises. In exploration, participants are engaged in intensive information exchange, in search of novel combinations, and here dependence is likely to be reciprocal.

Trust also is an important factor in exploration. Ex-ante trust is problematic, for similar reasons that reputation is problematic: there is little relevant history and experience. However, the open, frequent interaction typical of exploration provides a basis for building relation-specific trust. In our view, the typical trust process in relations for exploration is as follows. Trust starts from mutual need. It is well known from the trust literature that mutual need imposes pressure to develop trust. Note that therefore there is a strong connection between the governance instruments of mutual dependence and trust. We propose that trust starts with trust in competence. In exploration we are often dealing with technical professionals who respect each other's expertise, which provides initial empathy, on which they can further build trust also in intentions. The combined effects of this, mutual need, and high frequency of interaction, discussed before, may generate trust that is sufficiently fast, in relations that do not last too long. Trust building may be speeded up with the help of intermediaries (Nooteboom 1999a). The use of such intermediaries is consistent with the density of the network. Earlier, it was noted that one might need trusted intermediaries also to help understand and assess the knowledge of partners in new ties. Also, as noted before, in exploration ties are likely to be strong in terms of scope: one interacts frequently with others on multiple issues, and this yields multiple perspectives and experiences for the assessment of trustworthiness, in knowledge-based trust.

In sum, from the governance perspective there are two arguments for network density in exploration. First, it is needed to provide a reputation mechanism. Second, it is needed to provide intermediaries for trust building. Ties are weak in terms of detailed contracts, and need to be strong in terms of mutual depend-ence and empathy- or identification-based trust. Spatial proximity, wide scope and frequent interaction help trust building.

An exploration network may fail in two ways. One is that it becomes a closed clique, reducing variety in terms of both people involved and cognitive distance, and thereby gets bogged down in stagnation. Earlier discussion indic-ated the dangers of density, which may lead to lock-in and groupthink. Too much stability of network structure may arise, in the avoidance of exits and new entrants, as possible sources of spill-over and distrust. In that sense we sympathize with the thesis of the strength of weak ties in combination with low density. However, we propose that there are overriding arguments in favour of density, and arguments for ties that are strong in some dimensions, as discussed. A second way in which an exploration network may fail is that in an ongoing 'chaos' of new prototypes it achieves no convergence on a dominant design (Nooteboom 2000a).

Networks for exploitation

In a network for exploitation, a number of conditions are more or less the reverse of those that apply to a network for exploration. On the competence side, dominant designs have emerged, and technological and market uncertainty have decreased. Here, considerations of efficiency are crucial, since competition has shifted to competition on price, with new entrants in the emerging market. As a result, there is a need to utilize economies of scale, and this opportunity arises since owing to decreased uncertainty on the part of customers the market has opened up. As a result, there is increase of scale, a shake-out of producers, and resulting concentration. In addition, there is an increase of specialization that narrows the scope of ties. Investments shift to large-scale production, dis-tribution systems, and brand names, which are generally long-term, with a long economic life. This tends to lead to durable ties, which reduce cognitive distance. Cognitive distance is also reduced by codification and diffusion of knowledge that has consolidated. The drive for efficiency requires the elimination of redundant ties. This yields the need for a less dense structure. In other words, here the argument of efficiency against density, offered by Granovetter and Burt, applies, more than it does in exploration. Reduced cognitive distance, and increased codification and diffusion of knowledge lower the need for relation-specific investments in mutual understanding. This enables a less dense structure, since now one can identify what knowledge (and competences more in general) is and will remain relevant, who has those competences, and who is likely to survive in the industry. In other words, uncertainty concerning the relevance and sources of knowledge, and structural uncertainty concerning the future existence and location of those sources, have all been reduced.

On the governance side, reduced uncertainty, dominant designs, codified, diffused knowledge and a narrower scope of ties enable the specification of contracts and the monitoring of compliance, and reduce their cost. Increased competitive pressure, due to entry in the emerging market, narrows the limits of trust, and creates the need for more contractual governance. Thus there is both an increased opportunity and an increased need for contracts. This enables more arm's-length, less personal relations. This, together with a less dense structure, enables a larger size of the network. Since knowledge is less tacit and more widely diffused, and personal trust is less needed, local embedding is less needed, and at the same time there is an incentive to extend the geographical reach of ties to enlarge the market, for the sake of growth and economy of scale, and to search more widely for the most efficient contributors to the network.

Risk of spill-over may increase as the speed of knowledge change declines. This may lead to more exclusive ties, consistent with a sparser and more stable network structure. That would reduce variety and hinder exploration, but that is less of an issue now. Also, there may be less specialized knowledge left to spill over, and spill-over risk may drop out for that reason.

Concerning density, there are two opposing forces: one towards less density to eliminate redundancy, and possibly to limit spill-over, and one towards sufficient density if exploitation technology is complex. The least dense structure would be a hub-and-spoke one, with a central co-ordinator, typically an OEM, surrounded by suppliers. However, as noted before, when complexity is high, so that there are many issues of co-ordination between suppliers, the central hub may become overloaded in dealing with that complexity. A way out then is a pyramid structure, with a first tier of main suppliers who, in their turn, co-ordinate the activities of second-tier suppliers. The density of this system lies between that of a hub-and-spoke system and a maximally dense system. This structure is found, for example, in the car industry, as illustrated in Chapter 3.

Contingencies

The hypotheses concerning features of networks were based on assumptions of what generally applies to exploration and exploitation. These assumptions may not always apply. Several features may vary, especially in exploitation.

It was proposed that generally knowledge tends to be more tacit in exploration and more codified in exploitation. This is a statement of difference, not level of tacitness. The level of tacitness depends on the industry and on the type of knowledge. In exploration knowledge may arise from scientific research, and may then be highly codified. Conversely, in exploitation knowledge of 'know-how' may be highly tacit, in 'communities of practice' (Lave and Wenger 1991; Brown and Duguid 1996). There will always be combinations of tacit and codified knowledge. This is also implied by the theory of knowledge employed in this book. Knowledge that is codified into information is absorbed into a cognitive framework that is largely tacit, and in the process it is amalgamated with tacit knowledge. Often, there will be codified elements in a tacit architecture and practice of use.

The size and type of economy of scale, including division of labour, vary with industry and technology, and have implications for systemicness of technology. This, in turn, has implications for the density of structure. Specificity of investments depends on the need and opportunity of product differentiation (market) and the flexibility of technology. Required duration of relations depends on the economic life of specific investments. These all vary with the industry and technology involved. A survey of some contingencies is given in Table 5.1.

Table 5.1 Contingencies

Contingency	Effects	Sign of effect
Scientific research	Tacitness of knowledge	−
Tacitness of knowledge	Cognitive distance	+
	Spatial distance	−
	Specific investments	+
	Spill-over risk	−
Speed of knowledge change	Spill-over risk	−
Differentiation of products	Specific investments	+
Flexibility of technology	Specific investments	−
Division of labour	Systemicness	+
Systemicness	Network density, centrality	+
Economic life of investment	Duration of ties	+

163

Furthermore, instruments of governance are contingent upon industry, technology and the wider institutional environment, and their implications for contracts, reputation mechanisms, go-betweens, and trust, as discussed in Chapter 4.

Furthermore, the distinction between exploration and exploitation is a stark one, and intentionally so, to clarify the extremes. However, it is too stark to cover the complexity of reality. The theory of learning used in this book (Nooteboom 2000a) suggests that exploitation and exploration build on each other. Exploration is based on experience, when application is widened to new areas, in a process of 'generalization'. This may necessitate and enable intermediate stages in which exploration and exploitation are combined, in 'differentiation and reciprocation'. In the first, exploitation is still strong, in the preservation of central principles of architecture, and key elements of existing practice. In reciprocation exploration becomes stronger, with the adoption of major foreign elements, leading to hybrid structures, but there still is an element of exploitation, in the maintenance of elements and structural principles from established practice.

In these transitions between, and combinations of, exploration and exploitation, hybrid forms of network may arise. Thus, one could have a central exploitation network with exploratory extensions at the periphery. According to the earlier analysis that would yield a sparse core, often with high centrality, with ties that are strong in durability, cognitive proximity and size of investments, and formal governance, combined with a fringe of small but dense pockets of ties that are strong in frequency and scope, but weak in size of investments, duration and cognitive proximity, with more informal governance. Conversely, exploration networks in the transition to consolidation in dominant designs, with preparations for market expansion, may entail the emergence of more extended networks, larger-scale organizations, elimination of redundancy, emergence of centrality, larger specific investments, less informality, fewer personal relations, more distrust and more formal control. Is also possible that dual structures will arise, in a combination of networks for exploration and networks, or concentrated firms, for exploitation, where activities that have reached an exploitation stage are transferred from the former to the latter. This is observed, for example, in biotechnology, with transfer of innovations explored by small biotech companies to exploitation in large pharmaceutical companies.

Conclusion

In sum, a network for exploration has the following requirements:

1 In view of the complexity of issues, novelty and tacitness of knowledge, and speed of development, ties need to be strong in terms of scope, mutual openness and frequent interaction. In view

of tacit knowledge, frequency of interaction and the importance of trust, ties may need to be strong in terms of spatial proximity and local embedding. In view of the need for flexibility of novel combinations and variety for learning, ties need to be weak in terms of cognitive distance and duration. Specific investments may be needed to build up mutual absorptive capacity and relation-specific trust. However, these investments have a short economic life, in view of rapid change of conditions, and thereby allow for only limited duration of relations. In contrast with exploitation, the size of specific investments with long economic life, in production installations, distribution channels and brand name, is limited.

2 A dense network is needed, to hedge bets on the uncertain availability and location of sources of relevant knowledge, to maintain variety of relations, to use multiple relations for the absorption and assessment of knowledge (triangulation), and to yield an efficient reputation mechanism. Density of network is maintained in spite of short-term relations by instability of membership, with a high rate of entry and exit, which contributes to the variety needed for exploration.

3 While the risks of hold-up are limited owing to limited specific investments, high mutual openness in knowledge sharing yields a risk of spill-over. However, this risk is limited by the high degree of tacitness of knowledge, and the fact that knowledge may have changed before it can be used for competition. For governance of relational risk, contracts have limited feasibility, in both specification and monitoring, in view of uncertainty, novelty and tacitness of knowledge. Governance needs to be based more on a reputation mechanism, which is especially strong under the uncertainty of future relations. Reputation is complemented by trust based on the institutionalized standards of professional competence, which yields a basis of empathy for relation-specific intentional trust to develop.

4 The potential inefficiency of redundant relations is not salient, because competition focuses on combining complementary competences in fast development of prototypes rather than cost efficiency. The cost of setting up relations is limited due to limited size of investments.

5 There is a tendency to increase the stability of structure, with limited entry and exit, to protect existing trust relations, and to limit risks of spill-over. This limits the variety needed for exploration, yielding a risk of stagnation.

In a network for exploitation, conditions are more or less the reverse of those that apply to a network for exploration. Dominant designs have emerged, and

165

technological and market uncertainty have decreased. Here, considerations of efficiency are crucial, since competition has shifted to competition on price, with new entrants in the emerging market. Owing to increased competition on price, there is a need to utilize economies of scale, and this opportunity arises since owing to decreased uncertainty on the part of customers the market has enlarged. As a result, there is increase of scale, a shake-out of producers and resulting concentration. Investments shift to large-scale production, distribution systems and brand names, which are all long-term. The drive for efficiency requires the elimination of redundant relations. This yields a less dense structure. Increased codification of knowledge furthers diffusion and reduces the need for relation-specific investments of mutual understanding. Uncertainty declines concerning the relevance, location, accessibility, meaning and reliability of knowledge. This enables a less dense structure, since now one can identify what competences are and will remain relevant, who has those competences, and who is likely to survive in the industry. Reduced uncertainty and codified, diffused knowledge enable the specification of contracts and the monitoring of compliance. This favours the use of contracts, with less relation-specific trust, which enables more arm's-length, less personal relations. This, together with a less dense structure, enables a larger size of network. The need for trust rather than contract is less, and increased competitive pressure imposes more limits on trust.

In exploitation, some network features are variable, and depend on further contingencies. Density and strength of ties, in terms of frequency of interaction, and size of specific investments depend on how systemic versus stand-alone the technology is. Specificity of investments depends on the flexibility of technology. Required duration of relations depends on the economic life of specific investments. The need to integrate depends on the strength of economies of scale.

The different conditions for networks for exploration and exploitation are summarized in Table 5.2. Admittedly, the distinction between networks for exploration and those for exploitation is stark, and intentionally so, for the sake of clarity. Intermediate or hybrid forms of networks arise, depending on a range of contingencies, with different configurations of features.

Empirical evidence

Empirical evidence is derived from Gilsing (2003), based on studies in the development of multimedia and of biotechnology, in the Netherlands.

Multimedia

Gilsing (2003) observed two innovation patterns in the multimedia industry in the 1990s, in the Netherlands. One emerged in the early 1990s, and peaked

Table 5.2 Networks for exploration and exploitation

Network features	Exploration	Exploitation
Network structure:		
Size	Limited	Depends on systemic complexity
Density	High	Low or intermediate, depending on systemic complexity
Connectedness	High	Low
Degree centrality	Low	Often high
Betweenness centrality	Possibly high	Often high
Structural holes	Few	Many
Stability	Low	High
Structural equivalence	Possibly high	Low
Concentration of ownership and control	Low	Often high
Strength of ties:		
Frequency of interaction	High	Variable
Investments		
Size	Low	High
Specificity	High	High in case of specialties
Economic life	Short	Long
Duration of ties	Short	Often long
Openness	High	Low
Cognitive proximity	Low	High
Spatial proximity	Often high	Often low
Governance:		
Use of contracts	Low	High
Hostages	High	Variable
Reputation	High	Variable
Trust	High	Often low

in the mid-1990s, with its main focus on technological exploration. A second innovation pattern emerged from around 1995 and peaked around the start of the new century. In this pattern the focus was more on exploitation, in a quick development of technological multimedia products for a growing mass market. Earlier, in Chapter 2, it was noted that since it is difficult to combine

167

exploitation and exploration in time and place, they are usually separated in either time or place. With separation in time, a network for exploration transforms itself into a network for exploitation. That is observed in this case.

Technological exploration. Innovation started to take off after the adoption of the Internet as the worldwide standard for on-line communication, around 1990. Before the advent of the Internet, technology was scattered over a variety of separate technologies such as information, communication, audiovisual and data transmission technologies. These were mostly stand-alone. Large, R&D-intensive firms did most exploration, each in its own domain. The arrival of the Internet yielded the insight that for its full utilization a fundamental restructuring of these various technologies was required, in technological convergence. Continuous progress in the field of digitalization provided a technical opportunity for integration of technologies. This led to an increase in the number of new entrants, from the early 1990s onwards, who focused on the new opportunities. Often, these were spin-offs from large firms, by employees who could not explore their ideas within the established order of a large firm. These new entrants and spin-offs complemented the search activities of the large, R&D-intensive firms. An innovation pattern developed in combination of small, specialized multimedia firms and specialized suppliers of hardware and software. Their joint exploration activities resulted in an increasingly systemic integration of information technology, communication technology, screen display technology and language technology. No single firm had the necessary knowledge of all relevant technologies, while change in one required adaptations in others, yielding complex interdependences, which required co-operation. This created a complex search process. One had to consider first which technologies had relevance, and next how they were related. This search process took place by much trial and error of what search directions to explore and how to explore them. Knowledge was highly tacit. Uncertainties were confirmed in all the three dimensions proposed before as typical of exploration: on what knowledge would be relevant, the sources of knowledge, and who might be a player in emerging networks. As predicted for exploration networks, networks were dense and unstable, contacts were intensive, in the sense of being frequent and open, and including a variety of topics of communication (wide scope), but they were also of short duration.

Governance took place on the basis of what in the emerging industry was called a 'free souls mentality'. This was characterized by informality, with openness of communication and limited use of contracts. As predicted, this was generated by mutual need, and lack of alternatives to collaboration. Participants simply had to make it work, in mutual give-and-take. As predicted, there was an initial basis for trust on the basis of mutual respect among competent professionals struggling with connected problems. As predicted, there was also limited fear of spill-over. To keep up with the rapidly changing knowledge base, all partners had to do their part, in give-and-take, to keep up the development of their absorptive capacity, to benefit from what partners developed. It was more rational not to go for full appropriation but rather to stay connected with the exploration activities going on, and to 'live and let live' in order to keep up to date with the rapidly changing knowledge base. While the maintenance of cognitive distance was not explicitly tested, it was implicit also in the 'free souls mentality'. Also, there was no explicit test of the hypothesis of a limited need to eliminate redundant relations, but that also may be inferred from the casualness, in the 'free souls mentality', with which wide-ranging and complex patterns of interaction were undertaken. Consistent with this, it was clear that there were considerable specific investments in mutual understanding and trust building, but specific financial investments were limited in size. In sum, this stage of development gave considerable and systematic support of the hypotheses specified in Table 5.1.

Technological exploitation. Increasingly, in the mid-1990s different elements of the knowledge base of multimedia technology became more codified, for example by means of downloadable software from the Internet. In combination with a growing market for on-line applications, this led to the development of a second, more incremental innovation trajectory. As a result, a second type of pattern emerged around 1995 that consisted of firms from more traditional industries such as printing, advertising, audio-visual production, IT or PR/advertising. These industries were challenged to join the Internet bandwagon or be left behind. The emerging network structure reflected a growing division of labour: communication with customers was done by a centrally positioned 'main contractor' with a reliable reputation, surrounded by a stable set of firms with specialized competences for solving various technical issues. The focus of this network was on efficient, fast delivery of standard products such as e-mail and Web sites, enabled by an increasingly codified knowledge base. This confirms the hypothesis that towards exploitation the dominant mode of organizing entails a relatively non-dense network, with direct ties mainly between a core firm and various supplying firms, in durable relations. As discussed above, frequency of interaction is not determined by the condition of exploitation *per se*, but depends on contingencies of technology and products. Here, frequent interaction was required to accommodate fast integration and delivery processes. Supplying firms surrounding a central service provider only had direct ties among each other when needed in view of the integration process. The service network needed to deliver a 'turnkey solution' of integrated services. For the continuity of this, and to recoup the specific investments involved, the greatest parts of these networks were built up from durable relations. Governance was based mostly on mutual dependence, reputation and trust, often based on partners coming from the same region, in a local network. It was mostly reputation that prevented partners from free riding and poaching. Spill-over was controlled by exclusiveness within the hub-and-spoke network. This does not confirm the

169

corresponding hypothesis that in exploitation there would be more use of contracting and less use of trust. Apart from that, the study confirms a number of hypotheses concerning networks for exploitation. Networks had low density and high stability, and ties were strong in terms of duration, size and specificity of investment, and cognitive proximity. Openness of communication and concentration of ownership and control were not included in the observation procedure.

The case of multimedia gives an example of separation in time of exploration and exploitation. Exploitation networks developed from exploration networks. Some members from the former did not participate in the latter. For example, once dominant designs and structures for exploitation were developed, equipment producers, such as Sony, withdrew and simply sold their products to the market that was now getting into place. Others, who operated more on the side of content provision and delivery, became members also of the new network. Some, notably software providers, developed an internal spatial separation of exploration, to keep up with ongoing developments, while also participating in the commercial provision of multimedia services. In the process, one of the start-up firms in the first network (Lost Boys) grew within six years from three founders to 350 persons employed.

Biotechnology

From the early 1990s towards the early years of the twenty-first century, a 'new breed' of Dutch biotechnology firms has emerged. The number of entrants rose from four in 1992 to ten in 1998, making fifty in total. Most of these dedicated biotechnology firms (DBFs) see R&D as their core activity and they specialize, through contract research, in general platform technologies with a potential of a wide variety of applications in the pharmaceutical industry as well as in non-pharmaceutical applications such as agriculture and food. There are many technological spill-overs by means of licences to different parts of the biotechnology sector in the Netherlands as well as internationally. Especially platform technologies generate such spill-overs, in genomics, combinatorial chemistry, high-throughput screening and bio-informatics. These technologies also have a potential for application in a wide variety of non-pharmaceutical applications such as plant breeding, food processing (e.g. diagnostic kits), speciality chemicals, bio-informatics and biological catalysis. DBFs that specialize in platform technologies generally do not have the ambition to become an independent producer of pharmaceuticals. Rather, they aim to provide tools and services to pharma firms that are involved in drug discovery and development. The advantage of this model is its potential for relatively rapid commercialization with (hopefully) fast cash flows. In other words, here we see a stable separation in place of exploration and exploitation, with the DBFs doing the first and pharmaceutical companies doing the latter.

In the course of the 1990s an 'exploration–exploitation value chain' has emerged in the field of general platform technologies in the Netherlands, which is schematically depicted as follows:

Science ◄———► DBFs ◄———► Large pharma firms

Here, DBFs perform a key role in commercializing scientific knowledge. They connect a 'basic science environment', with its emphasis on the importance of new knowledge, with a 'techno-economic environment', which emphasizes economic value (McKelvey 1996). Here, DBFs are faced with a dual selection environment, which stresses economic performance on the one hand and scientific excellence on the other hand. Both parts of the value chain are considered, in turn.

Technological exploration. In contrast to the multimedia case, the knowledge base in general platform technologies is highly stand-alone, with its scientific base in molecular biology and genetic engineering. Thanks to some high-quality research at Dutch universities there were opportunities for Dutch DBFs, although mainly pertaining to a few niches. While the final outcome of this search process was formed by highly codified knowledge (through publications), the search process of scientific discovery itself was characterized by a lot of trial and error, and was highly specific to individual persons and research communities. This process entailed many tacit elements that were difficult to codify, such as the formulation of hypotheses, test set-up, accurate execution, interpretation of test results, reformulation of hypotheses and so on. It was characterized by serial, incremental improvements that led to the accumulation of tacit knowledge within stable research groups of academics and DBFs (Casper 2000). Clear spatial concentration could be observed, especially around the universities in Amsterdam, Groningen, Leiden, Utrecht, Nijmegen, Wageningen, Maastricht and Delft. The mainly tacit search process made personal contacts and frequent interaction necessary. In addition, geographical proximity enabled easy access to a talent pool of skilled workers, which enabled knowledge spill-overs by the mobility of researchers. This yields an additional argument for spatial proximity, which is well known from geography, and goes back to the work of Alfred Marshall. The importance of spatial proximity was also indicated by the fact that most patents were assigned to inventors from within the Netherlands. Frequent interaction was needed for regular checks and adaptations of the search process into the most promising search direction. In accordance with the hypotheses in Table 5.2, then, this yielded networks of small size and high density, between universities and research institutes on the one hand and DBFs on the other, with ties that were strong in terms of frequency, openness and spatial proximity. In contrast to the hypotheses, however, network structure was stable, ties were also strong in terms of duration, and were weak in terms of scope, which was limited to a narrow range of mostly scientific issues. Spill-overs within these networks were high. In contrast to the hypotheses, governance included clear (research) contracts, supported by peer control and review.

Thus, these networks contradict hypotheses in several respects. The fact that contracts were used, against expectations, suggests that in the university–DBF ties uncertainty does not preclude contracts. Perhaps this can be explained by the fact that the output of exploration is highly codified, and on the basis of shared professional knowledge there are opportunities for monitoring by peer review. According to the hypotheses set out before, the stable, lasting ties would yield too strong ties, in terms of cognitive proximity, yielding insufficient variety for exploration.

Interestingly, however, these localized, dense networks with strong ties were complemented by a non-dense periphery of ties, outside the Netherlands, with low strength in terms of stability and duration. These served to access state-of-the-art knowledge from more diverse and more varied sources. The codified nature of knowledge output allowed its access at a distance, without frequent, intensive interaction, and allowed governance by contracts in the form of licences. The relatively high turnover of these weaker ties was also enabled by the stand-alone nature of the technology. Substantial technological interdependences were absent, so that weak ties could be replaced without the risk of creating systemic frictions or bottlenecks elsewhere.

In sum, a dual network structure emerged, built up of a core of a dense, local network of strong ties, with a peripheral sparse network of weaker ties. The latter compensates for dynamic inefficiencies of the former. The dense, local, stable, durable ties enabled the development of in-depth understanding and triangulation. The peripheral ties yielded cognitive distance and variety.

From exploration to exploitation. In the second part of the exploration–exploitation chain, the network of DBFs surrounding large pharma firms was concerned with the development of commercially viable products rather than with exploring and searching for new knowledge. Here we are in the transition between exploration and exploitation. Correspondingly, one would expect to find elements of both exploration and exploitation networks. As predicted for exploitation networks, we find a sparse network, with a hub-and-spoke structure, with the pharma firm at the hub. The fact that the technology was stand-alone, and the different DBFs did not supply parts that were mutually connected, allowed the absence of links between the DBFs. The pharma firms needed to keep up to date with a rapidly changing knowledge base with all its diversity, built up from various scientific disciplines. Through the DBFs they had access to scientific research, but in a more developed form, closer to exploitation. At the same time, business opportunities pertained to niches that were difficult to define up front, making it difficult for pharma firms to decide which fields of knowledge to invest in and which to ignore. Connections with DBFs have allowed them to tap into variety without making the corresponding specific investments themselves. They were interested only in the codified output of the DBFs, not their tacit knowledge in developing that output. Since the ties were not involved in the actual testing, production and distribution of drugs, and the knowledge involved was highly codified, investments in the ties were limited in size and specificity. However, there was one-sided dependence of the DBFs. While the large pharma firms had the generalized absorptive capacity for the codified knowledge generated by multiple DBFs around them, the DBFs did have to make investments that were to some extent specific to a pharma firm, and hence they faced switching costs and limited access to alternative pharma firms. As a result, the risks of hold-up were one-sided.

In view of the codified nature of knowledge and ability to evaluate outcomes, governance was strongly based on contracts and monitoring. Research contracts were evaluated on a regular basis. Relations lasted as long as opportunities proved to be viable. They generally lasted two to five years. Since ties were aimed at exchange of research output, rather than joint involvement in either exploration or exploitation, frequency of interaction was low (between twice a month and three to four times a year). In view of opportunities for contracting, the need for personal, empathy-based trust was limited. Scope was restricted to a narrow range of issues. Openness also was limited, because there was little need, and for the DBFs there were spill-over risks of giving non-patentable knowledge, in view of the pharma firm's association with competing DBF firms.

When we look at outcomes, profitability on the side of DBFs is low, in spite of the fact that they take high risks of exploration. This has also been observed by others (Casper and Murray 2003). An explanation is that the DBFs were one-sidedly dependent on the pharma firms, for three reasons. First, as indicated they faced switching costs while the pharma firms did not. Second, the DBFs were small and many, while the pharma firms were large and few, especially after recent waves of mergers and acquisitions in pharma. In other words, the pharma firms could exert a large degree of monopsony (monopoly in market access). Third, the DBFs' appropriability of knowledge from their ties with academia was limited, owing to the latter's duty of publication. In the current structure, DBFs can expect to make profits only with more unique and imperfectly imitable competences, relative to their competitors, which requires the use of knowledge that is less public. For that, they would have to internalize some of the exploration now conducted at universities. Alternatively, the largely codified and public knowledge involved should be complemented with more tacit, firm-specific competences. In drug-related biotech, such knowledge mostly lies not so much in the scientific content of technology as in ways to use it for production. Production, however, lies more on the side of the pharma firms. Thus, another way for the DBFs to generate profits from their work would be to engage also in at least part of the production of drugs, in other words to engage

173

not only in exploration but also in some exploitation. That would also serve to yield some countervailing power with respect to the pharma firms, and would extend the range of customers for DBFs that do limit their activity to exploration. However, to move into exploitation they would have to become bigger and quite different.

In sum, this network that connects exploration with exploitation exhibits a low density of ties that are weak in terms of frequency, openness, empathy-based trust, cognitive distance and spatial distance, and are of limited strength in terms of duration. Specific investments were not large but one-sided, to the disadvantage of DBFs. Governance is highly contract-oriented. As indicated in this case, such a position between exploration and exploitation can entail high vulnerability of an intermediate position between exploration and exploitation. The DBFs were *tertius* but hardly *gaudens*.

A further lesson from the DBF–pharma case is that the earlier assumption that in exploration knowledge is typically tacit does not always apply. That assumption was important for the hypothesis that, among other things, governance would not be based on detailed contracts. In this case, knowledge was highly codified, and governance was indeed contract-based.

Development of clusters

A related analysis applies to the development of innovative clusters or industrial districts. Given the uncertainties of exploration, and corresponding tacitness of knowledge, there is a need for firms to be embedded locally, for reasons of both competence and governance. Local embedding facilitates the exchange and joint production of tacit knowledge, reputation mechanisms and relation-specific trust.

As dominant designs arise, uncertainty decreases and demand and competition increase, activities need to be disembedded to a greater or lesser extent. Depending on the nature and size of effects of scale, an increase of scale, for the sake of more efficient production, is accompanied by horizontal concentration. The growth of demand in the original market stagnates, and there is pressure to extend the market (Asheim and Isaksen 2002). With the entry into new markets, one needs to access wider distribution channels, and there is a need to adapt products and organization, which requires knowledge from outside. Increased competition brings pressure on costs, which may necessitate the relocation of production to low-wage countries.

Recall the example of Nike, given before. Nike itself conducts the more exploratory task, tapping into 'advanced' consumer markets in developed countries, and outsources production to low-labour-cost countries. Similarly, we now see some of the famous

Italian industrial districts relocating their production activities to Romania (Zuchella 2003), for efficiency (low cost) of exploitation.

For access to new markets and outside sources of information experienced MNCs may be needed. Large firms, utilizing their resources of volume and market reach, may occupy a central position in the transformation of the network. This, we suggest, is how Benetton emerged as the central player in the hub of a hub-and-spoke network. The analysis is in line with Boschma and Lambooy's (2002) analysis of developments in Italian industrial districts. They identified the role of MNCs as 'bridging enterprises', to carry activities into international markets and access outside sources of knowledge.

The question is whether the cluster is able to make such a shift to a new network structure. A potential obstacle at this stage is that the cluster is unable to go along with the codification of knowledge, expansion and transformation of the network, horizontal concentration, loosening from local context, increase of scale, and shift from personal to more formal, impersonal governance. Local embedding and local interests may contribute to such obstacles.

Note, however, that there is no single, universal outcome, in terms of network structure, type of ties and governance. The outcome depends on contingencies of the type and extent of markets (e.g. differentiated products or commodities), type of technology, the degree to which activities are systemic or stand-alone, the size and sunkenness of investments, type of knowledge, extent and type of scale effects, external economies and institutional settings (e.g. relating to competition policy, financial regimes, contracting or trust as a basis for governance). Depending on these contingencies, there are different ways to carry exploration into exploitation. In particular, the outcome depends on the extent to which exploration and exploitation are combined, which depends on the contingencies indicated above. To the extent that exploration and exploitation go together, there will be hybrid forms of networks that combine elements from the present analysis and the one in the previous section. A further analysis of this is beyond the scope of this chapter (see Nooteboom 2000a).

Whatever the outcome of the previous stage, in the subsequent stage experience gathered from expansion in differentiated markets, or invasion of radical innovations from outside, generates new options or needs, and we are back at the first stage of exploration. Here, the rigidities of established structures, which offered an advantage for exploitation, become a liability. Emerging novelties cannot achieve their potential under the systemic limitations imposed by existing structures, practices and ways of thinking. An obstacle here is that the cluster or network is locked into its previous success. If the cluster or network is unable to cope with this, it needs to be broken up, so that different elements have more scope to adapt, in different ways, to new conditions. Here, a cluster that

175

has not gone the way of integration under the wings of a large MNC, but has managed to maintain its less systemic, more modular nature, with informal governance, is at an advantage, since it offers more flexibility for reconfiguration. Here, it matters what options for reconfiguration are at hand. Here, we encounter the notion of 'Jacobs externalities' (Jacobs 1968, 1984; Boschma and Lambooy 2002). In urban regions with a large variety of different activities, and a rich, varied, complex infrastructure, with wide scope for spill-overs, new ideas and activities that become complementary in new ways, there is more scope for new exploration, in the reconnaissance of a variety of potential novel combinations.

Development of multinational corporations

It was suggested before, in the discussion of exploration and exploitation, in Chapter 2, that MNCs might use a strategy of differentiation in foreign markets not only to expand sales, but as a learning strategy, tapping into the new demands and opportunities of local business systems. That would also entail a different strategy regarding local relations. A global strategy yields a predilection for 'imposition', where one persists in the reproduction of home-country products, technology and organization, to maintain economy of scale. The choice between the two clearly depends on:

1 technical differentiability of the product;
2 demand for differentiation;
3 strength and limit of economy of scale.

Which of the two applies to the car industry? The evidence is mixed. On the one hand, the case of Rover and Honda, discussed before, indicated that Honda needed Rover to gain access to the European market. Rover yielded experience with tastes in that market and with design for them. On the other hand, more recently we see homogenization of models across multinational markets, with a given model being produced in only one location, for a wide reach of multinational markets. There are strong incentives of economy of scale. Perhaps there is convergence to a global taste.

A scale strategy, with global imposition of forms and procedures, would entail greenfield or brownfield investments or local take-overs. A multinational learning strategy would entail more local collaboration, in joint ventures or non-equity alliances. Child (2001) found this difference in strategy in a study of MNC activities in China. The latter strategy may be more difficult and expensive in the short term, but more innovative in the long term.

When the issue of cluster development and MNC strategy are combined, a possible role emerges for multinationals in the development of local clusters. MNCs may help to develop local exploration into exploitation, and provide access to international markets. To avoid local stagnation in too durable and exclusive relations, the MNC may help a local cluster to tap into the variety of more dispersed knowledge and experience. Clearly, much depends on whether the MNC takes a differentiation and adaptation strategy or a homogeneous product and imposition strategy. It also depends on its policy regarding suppliers. Does it carry along its suppliers from its home country, or from export countries where it previously developed a supplier base, in a strategy of long-term supplier relations, or does it open up to new local alliances? In his study of car assembly plants in Spain, Kamp (2003) found the first policy at Renault and the second at Volkswagen.

Keiretsu

Japanese vertical structures of *keiretsu* used to be characterized by long-term relations between end producers (e.g. of cars) and first-tier suppliers. As discussed in Chapter 4, the underlying logic was that mutual openness was needed for the full utilization of complementary competences, and for the building of trust, as we saw before, and that such openness had to be earned by mutual allowance for profit. This entailed 'price-minus' costing, where the buyer allowed for a profit margin for the supplier. This strategy is analysed in much more detail in the 'advanced' section of this chapter. Western companies have learned from this.

In a study of the auto industry in the United States and Japan, de Jong and Nooteboom (2001) found a striking similarity between Japan and the United States in the variables that characterize those relations, and in the causal relations between those variables. The study was based on a large data set on buyer–supplier relations, collected by Susan Helper and Mari Sako. The evidence clearly indicates that in the United States buyer–supplier relations have turned round from short-term, arm's-length relations, with the emphasis on low price, to more durable, co-operative relations, focused on quality by joint production of added value on the basis of complementary competences. There were only minor differences left, but on closer inspection they may be significant.

One difference was that the average level of transaction-specific investments by suppliers was lower in Japan than in the United States. This runs counter to the received view that in Japan buyer–supplier relations have more depth and are more dedicated. The second difference was that the effect of the attractiveness of the buyer on the level of those investments by the supplier was less in Japan than in the United States. The third difference was that the effect of 'future perspectives', based mostly on the level of commitment of the buyer to

177

the supplier, was higher in Japan. A fourth difference was that in the United States supply was much less exclusive: suppliers produced also, and more extensively, for competing buyers.

These differences can be explained as follows. The expected effect of buyer value on specific investments follows from the opportunity for the best suppliers to choose the most attractive buyers, and engage in more specific investments for them, leaving the less attractive buyers to the less attractive suppliers. The latter have less incentive to tie themselves down with specific investments, in order to maintain an opportunity to switch to a more attractive buyer later. If in Japan suppliers were more captive, inside *keiretsu*, with less scope for choice of customers across the boundaries of such systems, we would expect the effect of buyer value to be less. There is less incentive for suppliers to compete for the most attractive buyers by engaging in more specific investments, so that the average level of specific investments is lower. With a limited choice of buyers, suppliers can be enticed to engage in specific investments only by being offered better conditions in terms of a durable relation, guaranteed by high commitment. Thus specific investments depend only on the expected duration of the relation, i.e. future prospects, fed by buyer commitment. Summing up: Japanese relations are more durable, with more commitment, which does by itself contribute to higher levels of dedicated investments, but owing to lack of competition this does not yield a net effect of higher levels of dedicated investments.

This difference between the United States and Japan may be important. Relations need to be long enough to recoup specific investments and to build up co-operation, to achieve mutual understanding, trust and joint development. But relations may also be too long – causing undue rigidity and lack of the variety of relations that is needed for innovation, as discussed before.

Keiretsu have also been characterized by fairly strict boundaries between competing *keiretsu*, where first-tier suppliers rarely supplied to end customers in other *keiretsu*. This can be rationally explained as a strategy to block the spill-over that might otherwise result, in view of the extensive exchange of information between buyer and supplier. However, as analysed earlier, exclusiveness limits the variety in sources of cognition that is needed for learning and innovation. Furthermore, if speed of knowledge change is so fast that spill-over no longer matters, then exclusiveness is no longer needed to block spill-over.

Thus the development in the United States may have captured the advantages of co-operative relations while maintaining more choice, flexibility and variety of relations, which we would expect to favour innovation. In fact, it now seems that Japan is learning from this development in the United States. Several *keiretsu* are being broken down, or supply across the boundaries of *keiretsu* is allowed, or even encouraged, to eliminate the negative effects of exclusiveness on innovation.

178

ADVANCED

The concepts and theories used in this chapter were dealt with in preceding chapters. Therefore this chapter proceeds directly to the section on 'advanced' insights. It gives a more formal analysis, with the (light) use of game theory, of how to begin and how to end a relationship. It also gives an analysis of generic forms of buyer–supplier relations which are appropriate under different market conditions.

Opening game[3]

This section gives a more formal analysis, with the (light) use of game theory, of ways to begin a relationship, of which a more narrative account was given before. The question how to start a relationship is framed as a sequential game, to analyse reactions to possible opening moves. Use is made of the analysis of hold-up risk developed in Chapter 4, and the typology of relational strategy given there (Table 4.1), with basic strategies of *tie-down*, *offload*, *improve*, *set free* and *yield*. The sequential game is set up in the so-called *extensive form* of a *game tree* of successive choices, illustrated in Figure 5.1. It specifies opening moves that X could make, and for each of those Y's best way to react. The method recommends 'backward induction', i.e. the choice of best strategy for X, working backwards from the ways that Y would react to the best of his interest.

The starting assumption is that for both sides, X and Y, the relative value of the partner is positive: VXY > 0 and VYX > 0, so that they are in a strategically equivalent situation, and they both know it. Choice is analysed from the perspective of X. For each of the strategic options from Table 4.1, only the most probable reaction by the partner Y is specified. The most probable option for X, under certain side assumptions, is printed in bold type.

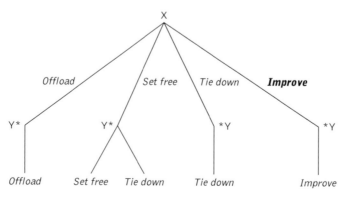

Figure 5.1 *Opening game*

Since X has a positive interest in the relation (compared with alternatives), there is no reason to consider a *loosening* action, unless it is intended as bluff to manoeuvre for a better bargaining position, but here we assume that there is sufficient information for Y to know that it would be bluffing. X might be tempted to *offload*, i.e. to go for one-sided dependence of Y, with one-sided contractual clauses binding only Y, who also carries a one-sided burden of specific investments, provision of knowledge and information for monitoring, and surrender of hostages. This would yield one-sided opportunities and incentives for opportunism for X. There is no reason for Y to accept that, since by assumption he knows his value to X. Y is likely to view such a move of X as a probe that must immediately be put down. Y would probably respond with an equal action of *offloading*, or the threat of it, which would probably deter X. In this way, the relationship would hardly get off the ground. X might consider *tying Y down*, by a one-sided increase in his switching costs, and contractual limitations on exit. This hardly makes sense: why tie a partner down at the beginning of a relationship, where one may find out that one would rather get rid of him? Y could react by setting free, feeling that X is not the type of partner he wants to have, or he might respond in kind, with tying down. In the latter case a tug-of-war arises where both sides limit each other's room for action with formal, contractual means and monitoring, and demand reciprocal hostages. X might consider *setting free*, if he wants to diversify his sources of learning across multiple relations, and is willing to allow the same for Y. How attractive this is depends on the risk of spill-over and the value of greater diversification of learning. Problems arise when this is asymmetric for the partners. If it is attractive for X but threatening for Y, then Y will probably respond by *tying down*, to prevent X from promiscuity. The option that rests for X is to *improve*, i.e. voluntarily engage in specific investments, to improve his value to Y, and to offer knowledge. The implicit or explicit threat may be to revert to *offloading* or *tying down*, if Y does not reciprocate with improvement. Y would probably reciprocate such constructive, trust generating action. Y might interpret X's move as a sign of weakness, and test this by opting for *offloading*, but X would probably retaliate quickly to deter such action. The conclusion is that one of the co-operative actions is the most attractive to X, and that the most attractive response for Y is to respond in kind.

Closing game

This section gives a more formal analysis of ways to end a relationship, of which a more narrative account was given before. The setting now is as follows. Side X wants to exit from a relation with Y, because the relative value of Y for X (VYX) has become negative owing to the emergence of a more attractive

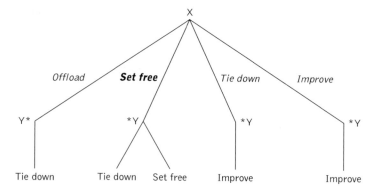

Figure 5.2 *Closing game*

potential partner. Y still needs X. The analysis of strategic choice is again presented in the frame of a sequential game, illustrated in Figure 5.2.

The least likely action for X is *tying down*. If he did choose this, Y is likely to respond with *improvement*, in an attempt to eliminate X's desire to exit. X has the option of trying again to improve the relation, but the assumption is that he no longer has faith in this. His preference will be will a loosening strategy. How would Y react if X opted for an aggressive strategy of loosening, i.e. *offloading*? Here, X would prepare his exit in secret, as far as possible, by unilaterally stopping specific investments and transfer of knowledge, and retracting hostages, and then spring the unpleasant surprise on Y. In an attempt to salvage the relation, Y may still react with *improvement*, but then runs the risk of increasing the damage, in the form of higher switching costs, if X persists in exit. If Y has no effective ways of *tying down* X, he may have no option but to *yield*. However, he may try to tie X down, with a promise of improvement if X will yield. That would cause problems for X, and this may make it attractive for X to opt for *setting free*. That would offer Y more time for *tying* down X, but X can then threaten to revert to *offloading* on Y, and Y would probably prefer to go along with *setting free*. The mutual strategy of setting free is the most likely. However, the choice for X between *offloading* and setting free depends on details of circumstance, e.g. the extent to which X can prepare his exit in secret, Y's opportunities and inclinations for tying down and for going along in setting free.

Generic strategies of outsourcing

Nooteboom (1998, 1999a) conducted an analysis of generic strategies of outsourcing, with a game-theoretic analysis. Here, that detailed formal analysis will not be reproduced but summed up verbally. Generic strategies were explored in different possible worlds, in terms of technology and markets. The viability of

181

strategies in those worlds were tested for their feasibility, in terms of constituting a 'Nash equilibrium': given the choice of strategies of buyers and suppliers, neither would want to change their strategies, given the strategy chosen by the other side.

From the literature, *Japanese practice* is approximated by the following stereotype, which is characterized here as a 'quality-based' form of contracting, and which is acknowledged to apply only to selected first-tier suppliers (Kamath and Liker 1994). There is a focus on quality and innovation rather than price; high involvement of suppliers in design and development activities; high levels of relation-specific investments; long-term relations to recoup those investments; orientation towards mutual gain ('win–win': perception of the game as positive-sum), subject to demands of quality, ongoing improvement, cost, guarantees of the recovery of investments; exchange of staff, technology and information on costs; exclusiveness – only one first-tier supplier for a given input, for the lifetime of a given model of a given product (which yields multiple suppliers of a given input across different models and products); governance based on mutual commitment, cross-ownership and trust rather than detailed contracts. It is not certain that this is a realistic characterization of Japanese practice. It was based on reports from the literature. The analysis is intended to investigate how viable this stereotype is.

In many respects, the stereotype of old *Western practice* is the opposite. Currently, in the West, a novel practice is evolving, which adopts features from Japanese practice. Traditional Western practice is approximated with the following stereotype, which is characterized as a 'cost-based' form of contracting. It is oriented primarily at lowest cost of supply; adversarial bargaining on price; no concern for mutual profit ('win–lose'; perception of the game as zero-sum); specification, design and even part of the engineering of inputs is performed by the user, as a blueprint for production by the supplier; 'closed' with respect to exchange of information on costs and technology; multiple sourcing (for a given input for a given model of a given product); 'distant' with respect to commitment in terms of investments. For the buyer, control of design, quality and cost takes precedence over utilization of supplier competence.

In the 'quality-based' form, outsourcing is driven primarily by considerations of quality, in the sense of a good fit to requirements for differentiated products, given a maximum acceptable price. The user aims to utilize as much as possible the capacities of the supplier. Therefore he leaves part of the design and engineering, as well as production, to the competence and often the initiative of the supplier, and invites him to contribute to the determination of optimal specifications. This requires specific investments, particularly on the part of the supplier, and to cover for this the user gives certain guarantees (long-term contracts, sufficient minimum volume of purchase), but then requires openness on the part of the user concerning the technology used, costs and supply to other customers, in order to control for misuse of such guarantees ('open-book contracting'). This openness is also required for effective information exchange for co-operation in development and production. Such openness may have negative effects on the bargaining position of the supplier, and, to cover for this, the user engages in 'price-minus' costing: he grants a profit margin to the supplier, deducts it from the price he can afford to pay, thus arrives at the cost at which the input is to be produced, transfers knowledge, technology and staff to the user, and jointly they invest in development in order to achieve production at this price-minus-profit cost.

For the specification of the model, returns and risks of supply relations are specified as functions of variables that represent the characteristics of a subcontracting relation. The coefficients of those variables range over values that vary between different 'possible worlds'.

The possible worlds considered are the following:

1 *Fordist world.* Here, markets and technology are stable, and products are standardized (no demand for differentiation). In this world there is no global competition, little need for product differentiation, there is a focus on price, cost and economy of scale. There is advantage in maintaining flexibility and bargaining position, with easy switching between suppliers and customers. Owing to stability and homogeneity of perceptions, preferences and technology, there is no great need for learning by transfer of new knowledge from other firms. This world is set up to represent past conditions, and is expected to favour *Western contracting*.

2 *World of quality.* Here, high quality is required, in terms of close fit with specifications of differentiated products. Owing to differentiated products there is limited economy of scale, and there is a premium on specific inputs and corresponding assets, and close co-operation between supplier and user, for optimal use of complementary competences. Turbulence, in terms of changes in markets and technology, is limited, so that learning from many outside partners is not essential. This world is set op to represent conditions during the rise of Japanese industry, and is expected to favour *Japanese contracting*.

3 *Raplex world (rapid change and complexity).* Here, there is intense competition in global markets, differentiated products (in both input and output markets), fast technological development. In this world like the previous one, there is a need for specific investments to produce differentiated products, but in addition all forms of learning from outside partners are important. Within this world, a special case is recognized, where the risk of spill-over is small from one or more of three different causes:

183

(a) *Radical speed*. Here, change is so fast that the life cycle of products is shorter than the development time of new products. Here spill-over does not matter: by the time that sensitive information reaches a competitor, through linkages in the network of one's partner, it is obsolete.

(b) *Monitoring of spill-over*. Here, there are technologies to monitor what happens to competence transferred, so that their spill-over can be controlled.

(c) *Radical differentiation*. Here, competing producers are so radically differentiated that they cannot greatly benefit from information that spills over from them.

This world was set up to represent recent developments in global markets.

Analysis of the different generic forms of outsourcing across the different worlds show, as expected, that in the Fordist world Western contracting is viable, in the sense of yielding a Nash equilibrium. Against expectation, in the world of quality, Japanese contracting does not yield a Nash equilibrium. The buyer is tempted to renege on his guarantee of a profit to the supplier, in price-minus costing, once the supplier has bound himself with specific investments. This casts some doubt on the truth of stories of 'Japanese style' buyer–supplier relations based on mutual loyalty and commitment. This form of contracting can be turned into an equilibrium, within the framework of the model, only by adding a strong reputation mechanism, whereby a buyer would be punished with a loss of reputation if he reneged on his guarantee of supplier profit.

In the raplex world neither Japanese nor Western contracting is viable. This world was set up to explore novel forms of contracting. The outcome, in a Nash equilibrium, was a form that combines elements from both. From Japanese contracting it adopts the principle of price-minus costing, high specific investments, sufficient durability of the relation to recoup them, and mutual openness and pooling of resources. However, it does not adopt the exclusiveness of relations, locked into a *keiretsu*, and allows for supply across the boundaries of a particular supply chain.

Chapter 6

Summary and conclusions

- Integrated theory
- Dyads and networks
- Goals of collaboration
- Forms of collaboration
- Governance
- Process
- Further research

SUMMARY

This chapter summarizes the main points of this book. The book aims to integrate issues of competence and governance, and perspectives from different disciplines. In the introduction, in Chapter 1, it was claimed that this is done in a coherent fashion, without eclectic confusion. The first section of this chapter summarizes the theory used, and substantiates the claim of coherence. The second discusses the results of another attempt at integration, of dyadic alliances and networks. Subsequently, this chapter summarizes the results concerning goals, structure, governance and development of inter-organizational relationships (IORs). Finally, it gives some indications for further research.

INTEGRATED THEORY

This book gives an integrated account of inter-firm collaboration, networks and strategy, by analysing the goals of inter-organizational relations, their structure, the governance of relational risk and the development of relationships and networks. An important focus is on collaboration for the purpose of learning and innovation. The book integrates issues of competence, in particular learning by interaction, and governance of the 'relational risks' involved. Thus the orientation of the book is strategic, in two senses. One of the two senses of strategy is that it deals with issues of survival in the face of competition. Learning and innovation have increasingly become crucial for that. That is the competence side. Another, military, sense of strategy is that it looks at actions and reactions of intelligent rivals. That is the governance side. The book includes the debate on how to combine exploration and exploitation. For all this, it integrates perspectives from economics, sociology, social psychology and cognitive science. The claim is that this can and has been done in a systematic, coherent fashion, in an approach that is neither over- nor undersocialized. For this, the book builds on an earlier one (Nooteboom 2000a).

The different perspectives come together in an interactionist theory of knowledge that forms the basis for 'methodological interactionism', to replace both the methodological individualism of (most) economics and the methodological collectivism of (some) sociology. Here, cognition includes perception, interpretation and value judgement, and rationality is intertwined with emotions. Among other things, this allows the inclusion of decision heuristics from social psychology. A distinction is made between rationality in the sense of calculative evaluation and adaptive rationality in heuristics of cognition and action that are conducive to survival in the face of radical uncertainty. This allows a link with evolutionary economics and evolutionary psychology. The theory is socialized in the view that people construct their cognition by interaction with both the physical and the social world. People require each other to identify and develop themselves. It is not over-socialized in that it maintains room for individuality in the proposition that knowledge construction is individualized and dependent on the paths of individual life histories.

While this theory recognizes that the claims of objective knowledge are problematic, since one cannot 'descend from the mind to inspect how knowledge is hooked on to the world', it does not lead to radical, postmodernist relativism, according to which any opinion is as good as any other, so that ultimately there is no basis for critical debate. Knowledge is seen as 'embodied realism' (Lakoff and Johnson 1999): knowledge is constructed on the basis of interaction with reality, whose existence it is reasonable to assume, at least in physical reality, even though one cannot claim to know it as it is 'in itself'. The assumption is reasonable because it is hard to understand the efficacy of knowledge if it were not valid. Since that reality is shared, to a greater or lesser extent, though more so in physical reality than in social and cultural reality, and since our capacity to construct knowledge from interaction is a capability inherited from shared evolution, there is some commonality of cognition as a basis for debate. In fact, precisely because knowledge cannot be claimed to be objective, and knowledge construction is more or less idiosyncratic, debate with others is the only basis we have for correcting our errors. This confirms the inherent sociality of cognition.

This theory of knowledge yields the notion of cognitive distance: people perceive, understand and evaluate the world differently to the extent that they have developed their cognition in different conditions, along different paths of life history. To the extent that people interact closely and for a long time,

186

especially when that happens in a closed clique, isolated from others, cognitive distance will decrease, though it will never become zero. That is called 'identification'. This leads to a cognitive theory of the firm as a 'focusing device', where a certain focus of overlapping cognition is needed for reasons of both competence and governance. For competence, organizational focus is needed to achieve a joint purpose, agenda setting, and interpretation of phenomena, with shared meanings. For governance it is needed because radical uncertainty in environmental conditions (technology, markets) and behaviour (competences, intentions) precludes complete ex-ante governance, and requires ex-post 'muddling through' in mutual adjustment, on the basis of shared norms of conduct. In other words, organizational focus is needed as a basis for trust.

The sharpness of organizational focus depends on a range of conditions. In particular, it depends on whether the emphasis of organizational strategy is on exploration, which requires a broader focus, with more ambiguity and variability of meanings and standards, or exploitation, which requires a narrower focus, with limited ambiguity and more stability of meanings and standards for the sake of co-ordination, in division of labour. The need for stability depends on how systemic rather than stand-alone the technology and organization of exploitation are (Langlois and Robertson 1995). However, focus will never be so tight as to entail identity of knowledge between people in an organization. There will always be some cognitive distance, which is a source of both error and innovation. The tightness of organizational focus determines the boundaries of the firm.

The notion of the firm as a focusing device yields a new perspective on inter-firm collaboration. By definition, focus implies myopia, whereby firms may fail to perceive and appreciate strategic opportunities and threats. To compensate for this, firms need to mobilize external sources of knowledge, at sufficient cognitive distance. This is the principle of 'external economy of cognitive scope' (Nooteboom 1992). Again, this confirms the sociality of cognition. This line of argument has important implications for the decision to integrate, in merger or acquisition, or to maintain distance between more or less autonomous firms, in an alliance. Integration has its arguments, reviewed in a later section, but next to other well-known disadvantages it has the disadvantage of reducing cognitive distance, and thereby eliminating sources of variety needed for learning and innovation. The argument also has implications for demands of exclusiveness in inter-firm relations. Such a demand may be rational, to limits risks of spill-over of competitively sensitive knowledge, through partners to competitors. The demand for exclusiveness then entails that a partner is not allowed to interact with one's competitors, in the focal area of collaboration. That, however, reduces the sources of learning that constitute the cognitive value of the partner.

Communication entails expression and absorption, or assimilation. In expression, knowledge is disembedded from a 'seamless web' (Quine and Ullian 1970) of cognition, which is largely tacit. Thus, codification of knowledge always entails abstraction in that sense of disembedding knowledge from a largely tacit web of belief, shedding highly tacit, context-specific and idiosyncratic connotations. In other words, codification and abstraction go together.[1] The web of belief also constitutes 'absorptive capacity' (Cohen and Levinthal 1990). Absorption entails re-embedding codified knowledge in the largely tacit substrate of interpretation, in the web of belief. Thus, knowledge 'received' is never identical to 'knowledge sent'. In that sense, people will never perfectly 'understand' each other. This is a source of both error and learning. In communication, expression needs to be geared to the absorptive capacity of the 'receiver'. For that, one needs communicative ability and some knowledge of how another thinks. The latter is called 'empathy'. The difference between identification and empathy is that the former entails not only knowing how another knows, but also sharing ways of knowing. In other words, crossing cognitive distance requires empathy, and reducing cognitive distance entails identification.

This leads to the notion of trust. Empathy and identification play an important role in the building of trust (McAllister 1995; Lewicki and Bunker 1996). Trust is important because uncertainty of future contingencies, intentions and competences limits control by means of contracts. This is more salient to the extent that uncertainty is larger, e.g. in innovation. Here also, this book builds on an earlier one (Nooteboom 2002). Prior to a relation there may be a basis for trust, in reputation, institutional safeguards and attribution of competences and intentions on the basis of observable characteristics (Zucker 1986), such as membership of social groups (Putnam 2000). Note that the notion of organizational focus entailed a basis for trust within organizations. Between organizations, ex-ante trust may be based on overlap of focus, from previous collaboration. To the extent that there is no prior basis for trust, it has to be built up in specific relationships. That process of trust building proceeds on the basis of the development of empathy, and may proceed to identification. In the latter, trust may go too far, in such similarity of cognition that there remains insufficient cognitive distance for learning. This may be reinforced by routinization, where partnership is taken for granted, and questions concerning possible alternatives are no longer considered, for oneself or for the partner. It is important to note here that trust does not entail the absence of difference of opinion. In fact, the strongest mechanism for building trust is to face and successfully resolve differences of opinion. Thus, trust can well be reconciled with cognitive distance. It does, however, require empathy.

Here, it is important to recognize the limits of trust, in the sense that trustworthiness will seldom be unconditional. It is unrealistic, and even unethical, to expect people, and organizations, to remain loyal under all conditions of threat to survival. On the one hand, contrary to Williamson (1993), trust does go beyond calculative self-interest, on the basis of ethics, feelings and routinization (Nooteboom 1999a, 2002). On the other hand – and this is in accordance with

Williamson (1993) — blind, in the sense of unconditional, trust is generally unwise. The trustworthiness of people, and of organizations, depends on their resistance to 'golden opportunities' for opportunism. That depends, among other things, on threats to survival. For firms, trustworthiness thus depends on the intensity of competition, and hence on markets (Pettit 1995). Trust is a four-place predicate: the trustor (1) trusts the trustee (2), in some respect (competence, intentions) (3), under some conditions (4) (Nooteboom 2002). Empathy is important for trust building, in order to assess the limits of trust in different aspects, by knowing 'what makes the partner tick'.

While the theoretical basis of this book cannot be squared with transaction cost economics (TCE), in view of its take on motivation, trust, knowledge and learning, it retains the key notion of 'specific investments', and the idea that such investments yield switching costs, and hence are a source of dependence, which may cause a 'hold-up' problem. Indeed, the theory used in this book extends the typology of specific investments with two types. One is relation-specific investments in mutual understanding, needed to cross cognitive distance, and the other is relation-specific investment in the building of trust. They are related, since they both involve the building of empathy, but the purpose is different: the first is a matter of competence, and the latter is a matter of governance. Both investments, in mutual understanding and in trust, are relation-specific, to a greater or lesser extent, since mutual understanding and trust in one relationship will often not be transferable to another. However, it does seem possible to develop a generalized ability to cross cognitive distance, in building communicative and absorptive capacity, to understand people who think differently.

DYADS AND NETWORKS

The large literatures of on the one hand inter-firm alliances and on the other hand social networks have not been well connected. The alliance literature has largely concentrated on dyadic relations, with an emphasis on characteristics of the partners involved, with some network effects added on in an *ad hoc* fashion. It has looked at managerial issues of firm strategy, in goals and forms of collaboration, relational risks and their governance. The focus has been on 'relational embeddedness'. Social network theory has focused on 'structural embeddedness' in networks: the effects on a more generalized, network level, of network structure and type of ties. This has often coincided with neglect of the characteristics of participants in the network.

Simmel (1950) already indicated the fundamental changes that take place in going from two to three actors (Krackhardt 1999). Then, the dependence of each actor becomes less, with a third actor present. Opportunities arise for coalition formation, bridging positions, intermediation and reputation effects. Bridging positions can be advantageous, in playing off against each other the agents that the boundary spanner connects (*tertius gaudens*). However, such positions can also constrain actions of the boundary spanner, when he has to satisfy conflicting expectations or norm sets.

This book makes an attempt to better connect relational and structural embeddedness. In the strategic analysis of the goals, forms and governance of relations it tries to take into account effects of networks and their structure. In the analysis of networks it tries to build in managerial considerations of strategy, goals, risks and governance of relational risk. The theory set out earlier fits this endeavour well, in its social, interactive view of knowledge and learning. In a later section, a summary is given of how relational and structural embeddedness interact.

Many goals of collaboration entail collaboration between multiple partners, beyond dyads, such as consortia, associations, industrial districts or clusters, franchising, supply chains and Japanese *keiretsu*. Whatever the number of partners, collaboration is embedded in wider structures that affect competence, relational risk and governance (Das and Teng 2002).

As discussed in the network literature, structural embeddedness has implications for competence, as proposed in the thesis of the 'strength of weak ties', and for governance, as in the notion of 'social capital' (Granovetter 1973; Coleman 1988; Burt 1992; Uzzi 1997; Gabbay and Leenders 1999). Concerning competence, density of structure and strength of ties have implications for the effectiveness and efficiency of knowledge search. Concerning governance, they have implications for reputation mechanisms, network institutions (customs, norms and rules), coalition formation, and trust building. In governance, there is also an important role for 'go-betweens' (Shapiro 1987; Nooteboom 1999a).

Concerning relational risk, this book distinguishes the following types:

1 value and its loss, depending on network structure and position;
2 'hold-up' risk, due to lack of alternative options for partnership or to specific investments;
3 risk of spill-over of strategically sensitive knowledge to competitors;
4 social/psychological risks of reputation and legitimation.

Resources that determine the value of a partner may go beyond its intra-firm resources, for the access he yields to outside resources, as a gatekeeper or boundary spanner. Loss of resources or relational risk may arise from hostile take-over or hold-up of a partner by a competitor. If A has relations with B, and has a competitor C on whom B depends, then A runs a risk. These are network effects that go beyond dyadic relations.

Risks of reputation and legitimation are, virtually by definition, effects of networks. Spill-over risk also is mainly a network effect, in the risk that commercially sensitive knowledge spills over through an alliance partner to a competitor. The size of risk, and modes of its governance, depend on network structure (density, type of ties, connectedness, structural holes) and network position of the players involved (centrality, 'betweenness', structural equivalence). There is a distinction between intra- and inter-network spill-over. The former may be limited to a tight clique, and be hardly threatening, while the latter may threaten the whole of the clique. Risks of 'hold-up', as a result of switching costs, may apply to individual relationships, but also to a network as a whole. Next to relation-specific investments there are network-specific investments. Thus, there are clear connections between relational and structural embeddedness. However, though certainly not absent from the literature, those connections are insufficiently developed. The following features merit attention.

First, the analysis of network effects on learning is not well founded in theories of learning and innovation. For innovation and learning variety and cognitive distance are required between partners, and this has implications for network structure and ties. Knowledge search should take into account uncertainty concerning the relevance and sources of knowledge, and the stability of their position in a network (Nooteboom and Gilsing 2003). In knowledge transfer one should take into account problems of absorption and communication in 'crossing cognitive distance' (Nooteboom 1999a, 2003).

Second, in governance, opportunities have been missed to connect network effects with insights from the notion of transaction costs and specific investments. The specificity of investments in dyadic relations, and opportunities for alternative use, in other relationships, depend on density and strength of ties in multiple relationships.

Third, analysis of alliances and networks can be better connected to the analysis of industrial or regional 'clusters' and regional innovation systems (Fornahl and Brenner 2003), taking into account externalities of location and agglomeration (Jacobs 1968, 1984; Krugman 1991; Maskell and Malmberg 1999).

Fourth, there has been neglect of the dynamics, i.e. the development, of networks and clusters (Nooteboom and Klein Woolthuis 2003).

This book aims to contribute to an improvement on all these counts. This leads, among other things, to the following:

1 an extension of the dimensions of network structure and strength of ties, to deal better with both competence and governance, in Chapter 3;
2 criticism of the thesis of the strength of weak ties, in Chapter 5;
3 analysis of the dynamics of networks and clusters, in Chapter 5.

GOALS OF COLLABORATION

In this book, possible goals of collaboration have been grouped into three classes: efficiency, competence and positioning. They are specified in Table 2.1.

Efficiency is mainly aimed at exploitation, i.e. the efficient utilization of existing assets and competences. Here, use is made of mostly standard concepts of static efficiency derived from economics (efficiencies of scale, scope and time). Relatively new is the consideration of 'threshold effects' that arise in many consumer services (Nooteboom 1982), and of economies of scale in transaction costs (Nooteboom 1993b). Competence is mainly aimed at exploration, i.e. learning, innovation and the development of new competences. Here, use is made of theories of innovation and the theory of learning set out above. Positional advantage is aimed at entering new markets and at protecting existing ones. Exploitation in novel markets, or more generally in novel contexts, may lead to exploration. This proposition derives from a theory of discovery (Nooteboom 2000a) that is summarized in the advanced section of Chapter 2 (p. 59). Positional advantage in the protection of markets (cartels, blocking competition), diminishes public welfare, but may offer advantage to individual firms.

Most goals allow for more than two participants, in networks, or even imply multiple participants by definition. This applies, in particular, to joint support systems (E2), risk spreading (E4), combination of products (E5), externalities of location (C3), cartels (P8) and blocking entry or exit (P9). Different forms for network collaboration are discussed in Chapter 3. The development of networks, for exploration and exploitation, is discussed in Chapter 5.

FORMS OF COLLABORATION

One important question of form is whether partners in collaboration should integrate, in a merger or acquisition (MA), or should maintain their formal independence, in alliances. Chapter 3 offers a number of considerations, listed in Table 3.1. Most of the arguments in favour of integration (MA) concern governance. When potential conflict from risks of dependence, hold-up and spill-over is high, integration may be needed. The argument derives largely from transaction cost economics: the generalized authority of an employment relationship allows more enforcement of duties, in information provision for monitoring and in conflict resolution, than relations between formally independent firms. Most of the arguments in favour of alliances concern competence (learning), which has been neglected by TCE. The arguments derive largely from the theory of knowledge and learning indicated before. For learning one needs to maintain cognitive variety, with multiple partners who each have access to their own varied sources of experience and knowledge, and sufficient cognitive distance between them, to employ 'external economy of cognitive scope'. This yields a prediction that runs counter to TCE. When uncertainty is high, in terms of complexity and change of technology and markets, the need for that is high, so that firms should not integrate more, as predicted by TCE, but less. This is confirmed in empirical research (Colombo and Garrone 1998). Some of the arguments in favour of maintaining distance, in alliances, are adopted from TCE: independence and responsibility for own survival yield higher incentives for effort. An argument that goes back to Adam Smith, and is used also in TCE, is that specialization in production yields economies of scale. Another argument, taken from the theory of evolution and innovation, and from the literature on industrial districts, is that a network of more independent actors gives more flexibility of configuration, in the exploration of Schumpeterian novel combinations. An argument against MA from the business literature is that full integration of different organizational structures, procedures, and cultures often is highly problematic, and is an important cause of failure. This argument gains additional theoretical weight from the notion of organizations as epistemic and normative focusing devices, used in this book. Large, bureaucratic firms may want to rejuvenate themselves by taking over a successful small, entrepreneurial firm. This may also be in the interest of the small firm, if its success yields growth and requires formalization of management that the entrepreneur is unable or unwilling to provide. How-ever, entrepreneurial momentum may be stifled in the assimilation into the large firm. Brand name considerations can go both ways. One may want to integrate to better control risks of brand name deterioration in careless or opportunistic use by external partners. On the other hand one may need to let an external brand name maintain its organizational identity. Finally, an argument for an alliance is that it entails a smaller step than an MA, and leaves open more options, including a further step to an MA in a later stage, when its advantages become more apparent and problems turn out to be limited.

There are also reasons of default, where the most desired form is not available, and the other form is the only option. This may, for example result in an alliance between airlines, because reasons of national interest, in landing rights or identity, block an MA.

The conditions in favour of an MA arise most strongly between partners in the same industry and market, for three reasons. First, potential conflict is highest there, in a zero-sum game between competitors, where activities substitute rather than complement. Second, advantages of scale in the integra-tion of similar activities are highest. Third, differences in organizational structure and culture that raise obstacles to integration are likely to be smallest. Fourth, for the same reason cognitive distance is smallest, so that the disadvantage of reducing such distance, in the identification that arises in integration, carries less weight.

Next to these considerations that are rational from the perspective of the firm, there are social-psychological considerations of management that go against the interests of the firm. One is that an MA is more instantaneous and spectacular than the careful build-up of an alliance, and thereby appeals to macho behaviour and the drive to make a dramatic impact in the market for management. A second is that managers may be afraid of losing their position when they are taken over, so that they take over as a pre-emptive move. A third is mere fashion and bandwagon effects: managers imitate what seems to be the thing to do.

As a result of such less rational motives (from the firm perspective), and lack of appreciation of the arguments listed in Table 3.1, there has been an inclination towards MA where an alliance would have been better.

An equity joint venture presents a third alternative, between the options of MA and a non-equity alliance. It gives most of the advantage of stronger control of an MA, with fewer problems of integration, and somewhat more flexibility in the disentanglement of the relation. It can shield off spill-over problems that might arise when competitors of an alliance partner have relations with other parts of a firm than the one the alliance partner has relations with. Sometimes, a joint venture may be used as an intermediate step, to assess the potential value and problems of integration of an MA, before taking up that option. Of course, the down side of a joint venture is that it entails substantially higher set-up costs than a non-equity alliance. A well-known dilemma in the control of a joint venture is whether there should be a balance or a clear majority in ownership/control. The advantage of a clear majority is greater efficiency and speed in decision making. The disadvantage is that a minority partner may lack incentives and may be overly suspicious of opportunism (the 'Calimero effect'). However, this problem can be solved by separating owner-ship and control, with one partner taking on management, and the other having equal power for ex-post control. These roles might also alternate between the partners.

Beyond dyadic relations, in networks, potential configurations of collabora-tion explode. To categorize them in a way that allows the combination of competence and governance perspectives, Chapter 3 proposes the following dimensions of network structure and strength of ties:

Identity and characteristics of firms in the network:
1 ownership of the firm;
2 control of the firm;
3 legal form;
4 industries in which it is active.

These features are relevant e.g. for risks of hostile take-overs of partners by competitors.

Network structure:
1 number of participants (network size);
2 density/sparseness;
3 connectedness (mutual reachability of participants through direct and indirect ties);

4　degree of centrality (number of direct ties a participant has);
5　betweenness centrality (number of positions a firm takes between others);
6　structural holes (gaps in direct ties within the network);
7　isolation (lack of ties to other networks);
8　stability (frequency of exit and entry);
9　structural equivalence (firms having similar patterns of ties);
10　concentration of ownership and control in the network.

The only feature that is comparatively new here, in view of standard social network literature, is stability. For governance stability may be desirable, to alleviate risks of 'hit and run' entry and exit, to limit spill-over risk and to maintain trust. For competence it may not be desirable, since it blocks the turnover of network membership that generates variety for the sake of learning and exploration (March 1991).

Type and strength of ties:
1　scope;
2　investments in the tie:
　　(a)　size;
　　(b)　specificity;
　　(c)　economic life;
3　frequency of interaction;
4　duration;
5　openness of (internal) communication;
6　cognitive proximity;
7　spatial proximity.

Comparatively novel elements here, in view of standard social network theory, are scope, specific investments, duration, and cognitive and spatial proximity. Scope refers to what the tie means and includes: a relation of authority, ownership, control, monitoring; a flow of goods, services, information, personnel, money, and the percentage of total activity of the firms included in the relation. Specific investments and duration yield a connection with TCE and they are related. As argued in TCE, one is willing to engage in specific investments only if a relation is likely to last sufficiently long to recoup that investment. How long the relation should last depends on the economic life of the investment. Cognitive distance yields a connection with theory of knowledge and learning, and is relevant for competence. Spatial proximity yields a link with geography, and refers to externalities of location. On the competence side this includes the role of distance in the transfer and joint production of tacit knowledge, labour pools,

195

and variety as a source of novel combinations. On the governance side it includes local reputation mechanisms, gossip and personal interaction that support trust building.

GOVERNANCE

Chapter 4 offers an audit of hold-up risk in dyadic relations, first published in Nooteboom (1996). This gives a method of assessing the size and probability of relational risk, and their symmetry on two sides of the dyad. This method can be used for the diagnosis of risk in existing relations, and for the (re)design of relationships. Size of risk is what one may lose if a relation breaks, and it is the sum of switching costs (e.g. due to specific investments) and the opportunity cost of the value of the partner relative to the best alternative. This includes the 'shadow of the future', i.e. the potential future value of an ongoing relationship. Together they constitute the maximum to which one can be held up. The probability of incurring this loss, owing to the breakdown of a relationship or hold-up, depends on the opportunities, incentives and inclinations for opportunism of the partner. Opportunities depend on the closeness of contracts and the monitoring of their compliance. Incentives include the dependence that the partner, in his turn, has on the relationship, hostages and reputation effects. Inclinations refer to trust, going beyond material, calculative self-interest. The latter element is the only new one, compared with TCE, but an important one, in view of the denial, in TCE, that trust can viably go beyond calculative self-interest (Williamson 1993).

Including the results of that analysis, but going beyond them, to include not only hold-up risk but also spill-over risk, and to include network effects, Chapter 4 offers a toolbox of instruments of governance, listed in Table 4.2, together with their drawbacks.

The first option is one by default: avoid hold-up risk by not engaging in specific investments, do not yield hostages, and do not surrender strategically sensitive information. That prevents the risks of dependence in hold-up and spill-over. However, it also obstructs the process of value addition in collaboration. It may serve the goal of static efficiency, but blocks the goals of product differentiation, innovation and learning. Product differentiation, in collaboration to produce specialties, requires specific investments to the extent that technology is not so flexible as to allow for a variety of product forms with a given investment. Crossing cognitive distance, needed for learning, entails investments in absorptive and communicative capacity that are at least partly relation- and/or network-specific. To employ opportunities in complementary competences one needs to surrender knowledge, even if that entails a risk of spill-over, if only because otherwise the partner cannot assess what he could contribute.

196

The second option, of integration, with its advantages and disadvant; compared with alliances, has been discussed in the summary of Chapter 3, in ... previous section (p. 192). The remaining instruments pertain to alliances.

The number of partners is an instrument in several ways. One can limit dependence on a single partner, in a given field of activity, by maintaining several alternatives to fall back on in the event of failure or hold-up. It maintains bargaining position. However, the down side is a multiplication of specific investments. Also, one may thereby create a spill-over risk for all partners in that activity, since partners in the same activity tend to be competitors, and as a result they may be wary of disclosing all information needed for productive collaboration. To control spill-over risk for oneself, one may demand exclusive-ness, i.e. limit the partner's access to one's competitors. However, this may lead the partner to demand a higher share of added value, to compensate for less access to others. More important, it would eliminate the variety of relevant sources of knowledge and experience of the partner, which would detract from his value as a source of learning. In view of this drawback, it is important to look critically at spill-over risk. The issue is not whether knowledge spills over, but whether the net result is gain or loss of knowledge. Second, risk is less to the extent that the knowledge involved is tacit. Third, it is not the mere leakage of information that matters, but the possibility of competitors to absorb it, i.e. to understand it and to implement it in effective competition. If by the time a competitor is able to do this the knowledge involved has changed, one no longer cares. In other words, under conditions of fast knowledge change the problem of spill-over drops out (Nooteboom 1998). If, finally, knowledge will spill-over anyway, regardless of ties, the risk of giving information in any specific tie is irrelevant.

Contracts may be used to constrain a partner's action space, and thereby limit opportunities for opportunism. However, contracts can seldom be complete, and this problem increases with uncertainty concerning future conditions that affect contract execution. Contracts are also useless when monitoring perform-ance is difficult. Both problems arise especially when the goal of collaboration is innovation. When in innovation detailed contracts are used anyway, they may form a straitjacket that eliminates all scope for innovation. Contracts may also set a vicious cycle of distrust in motion, which may be difficult to turn round to trust building.

There are several instruments to limit a partner's incentives to opportunism. One is to increase the partner's dependence on the relationship, by increasing one's value to him, relative to his alternatives. Value enhancement indicates that relation-specific investments may have two contrary effects on hold-up risk. The direct effect is that one makes oneself more dependent on the partner. But if the investment is used to make oneself more uniquely valuable to the partner, the second-order effect is that the partner also becomes more dependent. Thus

197

the net effect of a specific investment may be in doubt (Nooteboom *et al.* 2000). This second-order effect may lead to a 'race to the top': a virtuous cycle of mutual specific investment, to create mounting added value. Another instrument is to take hostages, typically in the form of sensitive information. Another is to employ a reputation mechanism. Reputation is enhanced by network density and strong ties.

The down side of these instruments is as follows. As indicated, the attempt to make the partner dependent by improving one's unique value to him may require specific investments which also increase one's own dependence. Second, one's value may not be robust under changes of technology and the entry of more attractive new players in the field. Third, to the extent that one's value lies in the network one is in, one does not have complete control over it. The down side of hostages is that they may die a natural death. The problem with reputation mechanisms is that they may not be in place. A reputation mechanism has several requirements. One is that defection can be reliably observed and convincingly communicated to potential future partners of a partner (without being perceived as malicious gossip). A second is that the culprit must not be able to escape to new communities not reached by the reputation mechanism.

The advantage of trust, going beyond enforcement (limiting opportunities for opportunism) and calculative self-interest (limiting incentives to opportunism), is that it appeals to more intrinsic motivation that requires less monitoring. As a result it is also more robust under changing conditions. Trust is both a consequence and an antecedent of strong ties. It is not an instrument in the usual sense. It cannot be bought or installed on demand. If it is not already present, it has to be built up. One can, however, design a relation such that trust is given a chance to build up. Trust can also be seen as an instrument in the sense that one selects a partner for the ex-ante trust one has, as a friend or family member, as the result of previous experience, reputation, or characteristics such as membership of trusted communities. One problem with trust is that when not in place ex-ante it can take a long time to build up. A second problem lies in the saying that 'trust comes on foot and departs on horseback'. It takes long to build up and is easily destroyed. Third, trust is also subject to limits. As argued earlier, those limits depend on the temptations and pressures of survival that a partner faces. Fourth, trust may go too far, becoming too much routinized, unconditional and blind. This increases vulnerability and may create rigidities that limit learning and innovation.

One may also employ go-betweens. They may be used to help solve the 'revelation problem' in knowledge exchange, to guard hostages, to eliminate misunderstanding in the build-up of trust (where mishaps may be seen not as accidents or failures of competence but as evidence of opportunism), to monitor performance, to control spill-over and to serve as a sieve of gossip and an amplifier in reputation mechanisms. They may help to speed up the trust-building process. A problem with go-betweens is that when they are not in place they are not easily or quickly built up.

Finally, one may build network structure, or find a position in an existing network, to limit relational risk. Note that many of the earlier instruments for alliances carry network effects. Number of partners, exclusiveness, reputation and go-betweens are network effects by definition. Several are affected by network density and strength of ties. In addition, one may, for example:

1 form coalitions to deter or punish opportunism;
2 reduce network stability to break down opportunistic coalitions;
3 create structural holes and weaken the strength of ties to limit spill-over.

The instruments in Table 4.2 constitute a toolbox, from which one should carefully select an appropriate mix of tools to suit a range of conditions. There is no universally best design and governance of relationships. Some examples of relevant conditions are the following:

1 To the extent that technology is flexible, investments are less relation-specific and the hold-up problem is less.
2 When knowledge is tacit, or when it changes fast, as in innovation, spill-over risk is less.
3 When specific investments (including the building of knowledge or skill) are 'deeper' in the sense that they have a longer economic life, relations (in employment or between firms) need to last longer.
4 Under greater uncertainty, as in innovation, contracts are less feasible.
5 When appropriate legal institutions, in the form of laws and their implementation (police, the judiciary), are not in place, contracts are not feasible.
6 When price competition is intense, trust is more limited.
7 When appropriate institutions (ethics, social groups) are lacking, trust is less.
8 When ex-ante trust is lacking, it takes time to build up.
9 Reputation mechanisms and appropriate go-betweens may not be in place.
10 Under easy hire and fire and limited protection against MA, more integrated firms are viable, as opposed to more networked business structures (Nooteboom 2000b).

Clearly, a mix of instruments has to be internally consistent. Contracts and trust can be complementary, but detailed contracts, with the purpose of constraining opportunism, often do not mix well with trust. Under innovation, where detailed contracts are problematic, an attractive instrument is mutual

199

dependence on the basis of high, relation-specific value. Since this is not by itself sufficiently robust, it may have to be complemented by trust. High mutual dependence stimulates trust building, which is a good complement to mutual dependence.

PROCESS

The fact that both the form of relations and their governance depend on conditions, as discussed above, shows that relationships should adapt as conditions change, as they always will. Thus, relationships should be seen not as entities that are set up once and for all, but as processes of adjustment. The question of how to adapt relations, and how to end them, is as important as, and arguably more difficult than, the question of how to set them up.

Take, for example the strategy of mutual dependence. As noted above, this may not be robust under change of technology and markets, and the entry of new players. Often, alliances start in mutual dependence, and then one party loses value relative to the other. This may be because it does not keep up its learning, or because the partner no longer needs its special competence. Then, a new balance should be sought, or the alliance is likely to break down or shift to one partner taking over the other, in an MA.

Important in the process of alliances is the process of trust. When trust is not in place ex-ante, it has to be built up. Some of the literature suggests that since by assumption trust is not in place, the relationship should start on the basis of control, until empathy grows as a basis for trust (McAllister 1995; Lewicki and Bunker 1996). Empathy is needed to assess the degree, foundations and limits of trustworthiness. However, as argued above, beginnings on the basis of control or 'deterrence' may yield an obstacle to the building of trust. An alternative is to start with small steps that entail little risk, and yield fast results, for trust to develop (Shapiro 1987). However, that may take too long, especially under current conditions, where competition is often a race to the market. Then, go-betweens may help to speed up trust building.

Important, in the process of trust building and relationship development, is the notion of *voice* (Hirschman 1970). This is related to the insight of Zand (1972) that in the trust process openness is crucial, in the surrender of some control and acceptance of some control by the partner, and giving information that allows him to exert it, such as information for the purpose of monitoring. This also engenders the empathy needed for trust building. Voice entails the reporting of fear and apprehension, to allow a process of working things out. This openness may prevent the attribution of opportunism from events that are, in fact, the result of mishap or gaps in competence. It allows recognition of conflict, and the joint solution of trouble, which is one of the best ways of deepening trust.

200

Relations may even be ended in a voice mode, where intentions to exit are announced in time, for partners to divorce with a minimum of switching costs and other damage, in the prevention of reputational loss, mutual return of hostages, a stop on specific investments, and the preparation of new relations.

In the dynamics of networks, Chapter 5 contested the well-know thesis of 'the strength of weak ties' (Granovetter 1973; Burt 1992), which claimed that for exploration networks structure should be sparse (non-dense) and that ties should be weak. At first glance, the thesis is plausible, in claiming that for exploration one needs loose, disintegrated structures that allow for flexibility, in the reconfiguration of patterns of activity, for Schumpeterian 'novel combinations', as proposed also in the theory of discovery used in this book (Nooteboom 2000a). However, loose structure can go together with density of ties that are strong in some sense. In fact, Chapter 5 argues that in exploration structure should be dense for reasons of both competence and governance.

For competence, structure should be dense to hedge bets, under the high uncertainty of especially radical innovation, concerning the relevance, source and availability of sources of knowledge, and for the interpretation and triangulation of uncertain knowledge. Ties have to be strong in terms of specific investments for building mutual absorptive and communicative capacity, for the transfer and mutual development of knowledge that in exploration is often highly tacit. Ties also need to be strong in terms of openness. In view of uncertainty, the need to recoup and build these investments, and the speed needed in innovation, interaction has to be frequent. However, ties should not last long, to maintain the flexibility of configuration needed in exploration. Ties need not last long because the size of specific investments is typically small, in exploration, and their economic life is short, in view of rapid obsolescence of the knowledge assets involved.

For governance, in view of the uncertainty of exploration, in both contract specification and monitoring of compliance, contracts are problematic, and one has to go more for mutual dependence and reputation. The first entails ties that are strong in frequent interaction and in a certain amount of specific investment in mutual understanding. Reputation requires dense network structure.

Dense structure, for reasons of both competence and governance, does yield redundancy, as argued by the proponents of the thesis of the strength of weak ties. However, as argued above, this redundancy may be needed to hedge bets in the uncertainties of exploration. Second, in exploration the cost per tie is limited, in view of the limited size of relation-specific investments. Third, in exploration the focus of rivalry lies not on cost but on technological and commercial viability, so that relational costs are less relevant. In early exploration, relevant reputations may not yet obtain. However, uncertainty concerning relevant potential future partners enhances the need to be trustworthy in relationships in general (one never knows who one may need in future). In

201

exploration, players are often professionals, in science and technology, and there often is mutual respect for competence, which may yield the basis for competence trust, which may then yield empathy, on which intentional trust can be built.

In principle, density of network structure and openness of communication entail a spill-over risk. However, speed of knowledge change and the often high tacitness of knowledge, in exploration, reduce that risk. In the dense network spill-over may take place anyway, so that secrecy in individual relations is not useful. In any case, the need for complementary knowledge is so high that closure with respect to information exchange is not an option.

The analysis suggests that in networks for exploitation features will, in general, be the opposite. Less dense network structure is needed to eliminate redundancy, which now matters, with more focus on cost. Increased price competition limits trust. This may yield hub-and-spoke or pyramidal structures. Uncertainty has decreased, and knowledge has become more codified and diffused, which improves conditions for (specification and monitoring of) contracts. Investments increase, and their economic life increases, in the set-up of efficient, often specialized, large-scale production and distribution. They are also specific to the extent that technology is not flexible and strategy is aimed at differentiated products. Then, relations must last longer to recoup such investments. The extension of markets yields opportunities for expansion, and the pressure of competition makes it attractive to utilize such opportunities. Codification and diffusion of knowledge allow co-ordination across larger distances, to allow for that. Less emphasis on personalized trust reduces the need for localized relations and reputation mechanisms.

Table 5.2 summarized the proposed differences between networks for exploration and for exploitation. Empirical research on the emergence of multimedia has largely confirmed these hypotheses (Gilsing 2003). The multimedia case illustrated how the problem of combining exploration and exploitation can be solved by separation in time, where a network for exploration is transformed into a network for exploitation. Empirical research of biotechnology gave an illustration of how exploration and exploitation can be combined by separation in place. There was an exploration network of universities and Biotech firms, and a network for transferring the results of exploration to exploitation by pharma firms. The study of exploration networks contradicted some of the predictions (Gilsing 2003). One of the contradictions was that contracts played an important role. This could be traced to the fact that, contrary to one assumption, knowledge was not tacit but highly codified, which enabled more use of contracts. Contrary to another prediction, relations had long duration. However, this was seen as a weakness, within the networks, and compensation was found in less durable relations, on the periphery of the networks, to tap in outside variety for the sake of ongoing innovation. In other words, while some of the predictions were falsified, observations did confirm some of the underlying logic. The network for transferring the results from exploration to exploitation, from biotech firms to pharma firms, as one would expect, showed a mix of characteristics of both types of network. The lack of profitability of the biotech firms, linking universities with pharma firms, gave an illustration of how an intermediary position can fail to yield advantage (a *tertius* who is far from *gaudens*).

Chapter 5 also proposes how the dynamics of networks and clusters may work. In brief, the hypothesis is that they evolve from networks for exploration to networks for exploitation, and back again, in a cycle of structural change (Nooteboom and Klein Woolthuis 2003). In conformance with the logic set out above, in early stages of exploration a cluster may require a dense, localized network. As exploration consolidates in a dominant design, knowledge becomes more codified and diffused, the market widens and price competition increases, a cluster needs to be disembedded from local conditions, to increase its market reach. This appears to be confirmed in empirical research (Ashheim and Isaksen 2002; Zuchella 2003). From the analysis, a further prediction is that at a yet later stage of renewed innovation, in novel combinations, clusters have to be broken up, arise again from local embedment, and that a location with a wide variety of activities yields an advantage, in 'Jacobs externalities' (Jacobs 1968, 1984). Finally, Chapter 5 gave an analysis of developments of Japanese *keiretsu*, which are opening up to non-exclusive relations between end producers and first-tier suppliers, crossing boundaries between *keiretsu*.

FURTHER RESEARCH

While this book takes into account network effects on dyadic relationships, from the perspective of individual firms, it does not treat governance on the 'higher' level of a network or cluster as a whole. This suggests one area for further research. From a policy perspective that is important for finding out how, if at all, clusters can be governed as a whole.

Going in the other direction, the logic of collaboration developed in this book might be tried on the 'lower' level of interaction between people in 'communities of practice' (Lave and Wenger 1991; Brown and Duguid 1996) within firms (Bogenrieder and Nooteboom 2003), as briefly indicated in Chapter 2. In a different direction, it might be applied to public administration, in relations between public bodies, public–private relationships, and political processes of alliance formation, elections, etc.

In the research area of 'business systems' or 'varieties of capitalism' (e.g. Whitley 1999), there is a need to move from the comparative statics of forms of organization in different institutional systems to the dynamics of their emergence and change. This is especially needed to understand how business systems may change under the influence of internationalization, where different institutional systems meet and may mingle, even if that does not lead to global convergence,

203

and to understand why it would not do so. For that, there is a need to unravel the causal mechanisms in the mutual causation between organizations and institutional systems. The intermediate level of IORs and networks is likely to be crucial for such understanding, in a similar way that the intermediate level of 'communities of practice' is needed to understand the mutual causality between organization and the people in it.

Some parts of the analysis are empirically much better founded than others. Goals, forms and governance of dyadic relations are fairly well founded. However, the analysis in Chapter 5, of differences in networks for exploration and for exploitation requires much more systematic and extensive empirical testing. The same applies to the related development of networks and clusters. Only limited connections have been made with geography. There is a need for more conceptual, theoretical and empirical analysis of how local institutional conditions, their historical roots and MNCs affect cluster dynamics. If theoretically different stages of cluster development can be argued, how universal are they, in view of such effects? If the notions of cluster governance and cluster dynamics are combined, with their institutional contingencies, is there any perspective for public cluster policy?

This book did not go into details of cross-national alliances, in the context of the internationalization of firms.

Only a modest use was made of decision heuristics from social psychology, mainly to understand trust processes. Much more use can be made of social psychology, for a further understanding of processes of collaboration and interaction that implement but also shift the order of organizations.

In sum, this book has only scratched a number of surfaces. Hopefully it contributes a basis and some directions for several lines of further research.

▐ Appendix

Specification of variables

The specification of variables in the empirical study by Nooteboom *et al.* (1997) which were not specified in Chapter 4 is as follows.

Value partner

%S: percentage of total sales to the buyer, as a cardinal measure of value alter
RVA: remaining indicators of value alter ($\alpha = 0.70$):

1 Because we supply this customer we are able to build up technological know-how that is also useful for other customers.
2 Because we supply this customer we obtain market knowledge that would otherwise be difficult to access.
3 Our firm is involved in an early stage in the development of new components for this customer ('early supplier involvement').
4 This customer involves us in the testing of components and/or in prototyping.

Switching costs

DA: dedicated assets ($\alpha = 0.83$):

1 Our firm employs significantly more people than if we did not supply this customer.
2 Our firm must have people with specific expertise in house to be able to supply this customer.
3 Our firm has had to create extra capacity to supply this customer.
4 We had to make investments to satisfy the specific supply conditions of this customer (e.g. for 'just-in-time').

PAS: physical asset specificity ($\alpha = 0.70$):

1 To produce for this customer, highly specific machines, apparatus or instruments are needed.
2 Most of the machines, apparatus or instruments needed for production for this customer can also be used for other customers, if necessary.

KAS: knowledge specificity ($\alpha = 0.68$):

1 We have had to invest much time in acquiring the procedures desired for this customer (e.g. in the area of logistics and quality control).
2 Much specific technological know-how is required to effectively supply this customer.
3 Much knowledge of the internal organization of this customer is required for effective co-operation.

LS: location specificity:

1 The location of our firm plays an important role in the relation with this customer.

SW: switching costs ego = ASE asset specificity ego ($\alpha = 0.84$) = dedicated assets + physical asset specificity + knowledge specificity + location specificity

Room for opportunism

LO: legal ordering ($\alpha = 0.79$):

1 The contract with this customer is as complete as possible.
2 The contract forms the core of our relation with this customer.
3 In this relation it is not so important to have a good contract.

PO: private ordering ($\alpha = 0.71$):

1 The customer shares in the payment for specific machines and apparatus that we must make for the production for him.
2 The customer shares in the payment for the investments in specific tools and/or measurement apparatus that we must make for the production for him.
3 Guarantees are given for minimal custom over an agreed period of time.
4 We give guarantees for supply for an agreed period of time.

RO: restriction of room for opportunism ($\alpha = 0.79$) = legal ordering + private ordering

Incentive

VE: value ego ($\alpha = 0.76$):

1 Our supply performance to this customer cannot be assessed on its merits if one looks only at the price.
2 This customer is aware that our supply performance cannot be assessed on its merits if one looks only at price.
3 Our supply to this customer is clearly custom-made.
   We provide an important source of information on new technologies for this customer.
4 Our firm is involved in an early stage in the development of new components for this customer ('early supplier involvement').
5 This customer involves us in the testing of components and/or in prototyping.

GR: growth ($\alpha = 0.68$):

1 The relation between our firm and this customer has continually improved in the course of time.
2 Our supply to this customer has increased strongly in the course of time.

FP: future perspective ($\alpha = 0.67$):

1 In this relation it is assumed that contracts will in general be renewed.
2 For the foreseeable future we do not expect a break with this customer.
3 We see the relation with this customer as a long-term relation, in which one must invest, and in which both sides are willing to make concessions if it is really necessary.

CON: continuity ($\alpha = 0.78$) = growth + future perspective

Notes

1 INTRODUCTION

1 Renewed, i.e. after the globalization that occurred in pre-First World War imperialism.

2 This implies that the notion of resources 'bites in its tail' (is recursive): by including competences to acquire and develop resources, resources include their own use and renewal. Nooteboom (2000a) elaborated the notion of competence, on different levels in an organization, in terms of nested scripts.

3 Such a perspective is usually taken, also, in theories of corporate governance, with shareholders in the seat of the principal. Taking that approach, one fixes shareholder value as the basic value of firms from the start. One can also take a more balanced view of different 'stakeholders', in a balancing of their interests (Nooteboom 1999b).

4 It is not the intention to imply that stability of relations is always a good thing economically, in the sense that it is always conducive to efficiency and welfare. A certain amount of stability may be needed to recoup specific investments, which may in turn be needed to achieve high added value and innovativeness. However, relations can become too stable and exclusive and thereby yield rigidities. The question therefore is how to develop relations that have optimal duration: neither too short nor too long.

5 The distinction between extension/reference (or in German: *Bedeutung*) and intension/sense (*Sinn*) goes back to Frege (1892).

2 GOALS

1 This is not necessarily bad. Maximum flexibility to buy and sell, hire and fire, may detract from motivation to long-term investment in firm-specific competence, teamwork and knowledge sharing within companies (cf. Nooteboom 2000b).

2 If revenue for a spherical unit of production is proportional to volume v, which is proportional to the cube of radius r (r^3, so that r is proportional to volume to the power 1/3), and total cost is proportional to the square of the radius, then unit cost is proportional to $1/r$. The ratio of unit cost between two installations, with $r1$ and $r2$ then is $r2/r1 = (v2/v1)^{1/3}$. Thus, if $v2/v1 = 2$, the unit cost ratio is 0.8.

3 This case was constructed by the author of this book, from interviews with management and consultants from Arthur Andersen.

4   This case was constructed from discussions in a course on organizational learning that the author of this book gave for consultants from Cap Gemini.

4 GOVERNANCE

1   This method is taken from Nooteboom (1996).

5 PROCESS

1   The source of this is a private communication from someone on the Italian side.
2   This section is based on Nooteboom and Gilsing (2003).
3   This and the following section are derived from Nooteboom (1999a).

6 SUMMARY AND CONCLUSIONS

1   Contrary to Boisot (1995), they do not constitute independent dimensions of cognition and communication.

References

Abernathy, W. J. (1978) *The Productivity Dilemma: Roadblock to Innovation in the Automobile Industry*, Baltimore MD: Johns Hopkins University Press.
—— and J. M. Utterback (1978) 'Patterns of industrial innovation', *Technology Review*, 81: 41–7.
Albert, M. (1993) *Capitalism against Capitalism* (translated from the French), London: Whurr.
Amin, A. (1989) 'Flexible specialisation and small firms in Italy: myths and realities', *Antipode*, 21: 13–34.
—— and M. Dietrich (1991) 'From hierarchy to "hierarchy": the dynamics of contemporary corporate restructuring in Europe', in A. Amin and M. Dietrich (eds) *Towards a New Europe? Structural Change in the European Economy*, Aldershot: Edward Elgar: 49–73.
Anderson, E. and H. Gatignon (1986) 'Modes of foreign entry: a transaction cost analysis proposition', *Journal of International Business Studies*, fall: 1–26.
Archer, M. S. (1995) *Realist Social Theory: The Morphogenetic Approach*, Cambridge: Cambridge University Press.
Argyris, C. and D. Schön (1978) *Organizational Learning*, Reading MA: Addison Wesley.
Ashheim, B. T. and A. Isaksen (2002) 'Regional innovation systems: the integration of local "sticky" and global "ubiquitous" knowledge', *Journal of Technology Transfer* (forthcoming).
Axelrod, R. (1984) *The Evolution of Co-operation*. New York: Basic Books.
Bakos, J. Y. and E. Brynjolfsson (1993) 'Information technology, incentives and the optimal number of suppliers', *Journal of Management Information Systems*, 10 (2): 37–53.
Barkow, J., L. Cosmides and J. Tooby (1992) *The Adapted Mind: Evolutionary Psychology and the Generation of Culture*, Oxford: Oxford University Press.
Bartlett, C. A. and S. Goshal (1989) *Managing across Borders: Transnational Solutions*, Boston MA: Harvard Business School Press.
Bateson, G. (1973) *Steps to an Ecology of Mind*, London: Paladin Books.
Bazerman, M. (1998) *Judgement in Managerial Decision Making*, New York: Wiley.
Beamish, P. W. (1985) 'The characteristics of joint ventures in developed and in developing countries', *Columbia Journal of World Business*, 20 (3): 13–19.

210

Beije, P. (1998) *Technological Co-operation between Customer and Subcontractors*, ERASM research report 98-39, Rotterdam: School of Management, Erasmus University.

Berger, J., N. G. Noorderhaven and B. Nooteboom (1995) 'The determinants of supplier dependence: an empirical study', in J. Groenewegen, C. Pitelis and S. E. Sjöstr (eds) *On Economic Institutions; Theory Applications*, Aldershot: Edward Elgar: 195–212.

Bettis, R. A., S. Bradley and G. Hamel (1992) 'Outsourcing and industrial decline', *Academy of Management Executive*, 6 (1): 7–16.

—— and C. K. Prahalad (1995) 'The dominant logic: retrospective and extension', *Strategic Management Journal*, 16 (1): 5–14.

Birley, S., S. Cromie and A. Myers (1991) 'Entrepreneurial networks: their emergence in Ireland and overseas', *International Small Business Journal*, 9 (4): 56–74.

Blackler, F. (1995) 'Knowledge, knowledge work and organizations: an overview and interpretation', *Organization Studies*, 16 (6): 1021–46.

Bleeke, J. and D. Ernst (1991) 'The way to win in cross-border alliances', *Harvard Business Review*, November–December: 127–35.

Bogenrieder, I. and B. Nooteboom (2003) 'Learning groups: what types are there?', *Organization Studies* (forthcoming).

Boisot, M. (1995) *Information Space: A Framework for Learning in Organizations, Institutions and Culture*, London: Routledge.

Boschma, R. A. and J. G. Lambooy (2002) *Knowledge, Market Structure and Economic Co-ordination: The Dynamics of Italian Industrial Districts*, Utrecht: Faculty of Spatial Sciences, Department of International Economics and Economic Geography, University of Utrecht.

Bradach, J. L. and R. G. Eccles (1984) 'Markets versus hierarchies: from ideal types to plural forms', *Annual Review of Sociology*, 15: 97–118.

Brown, J. S. and P. Duguid (1996) 'Organizational learning and communities of practice', in M. D. Cohen and L. S. Sproull (eds) *Organizational Learning*, London: Sage: 58–82. First published in *Organization Science*, 2 (1) 1991.

Bruner, J. S. (1962, 1979) *On Knowing: Essays for the Left Hand*, Cambridge MA: Belknap Press.

—— (1987) 'Social contagion and innovation: cohesion versus structural equivalence', *American Journal of Sociology*, 92: 1297–335.

Burt, R. S. (1992) *Structural Holes: The Social Structure of Competition*, Cambridge MA: Harvard University Press.

Cantwell, J. A. and L. Piscitello (1999) 'The emergence of corporate international networks for the accumulation of dispersed technological capabilities', *Management International Review*, special issue, 1: 123–47.

Carter, R. (2002) 'Empirical work in transaction cost economics: critical assessments and alternative interpretations', PhD dissertation, University of Cambridge.

Casper, S. (2000) 'Adaptiveness, technology policy, and the diffusion of new business models: the case of German biotechnology', *Organization Studies*, 21 (5): 887–914.

—— and F. Murray (2003) 'Technical communities in science: how the organization of scientific labour markets impacts the competitiveness of biotechnology Clusters', paper, workshop on 'National business systems in the new global context, Competing Explanations of Economic Development and Organization', 8–11 May, Oslo.

211

Chesbrough, H. W. and D. J. Teece (1996) 'When is virtual virtuous? Organizing for innovation', *Harvard Business Review*, January–February: 65–73.

Child, J. (2001) 'Trust and international strategic alliances', in C. Lane and R. Bachmann (eds) *Trust within and between Organizations*, Oxford: Oxford University Press: 241–72.

—— (2002) 'A configurational analysis of international joint ventures', *Organization Studies*, 23 (5): 781–815.

—— and D. Faulkner (1999) *Strategies of Co-operation; Managing Alliances, Networks and Joint Ventures*, Oxford: Oxford University Press.

Chiles, T. H. and J. F. McMackin (1996) 'Integrating variable risk preferences, trust transaction cost economics', *Academy of Management Review*, 21 (7): 73–99.

Choo, C. W. (1998) *The Knowing Organization*, Oxford: Oxford University Press.

Cohen, M. D. and P. Bacdayan (1996) 'Organizational routines are stored as procedural memory', in M. D. Cohen and L. S. Sproull (eds) *Organizational Learning*, London: Sage: 403–30. First published in *Organization Science*, 5 (4) (1994).

Cohen, M. D. and D. A. Levinthal (1990) 'Absorptive capacity: a new perspective on learning innovation', *Administrative Science Quarterly*, 35: 128–52.

Coleman, J. S. (1988) 'Social capital in the creation of human capital', *American Journal of Sociology*, 94: 95–120.

Colombo, M. G. and P. Garrone (1998) 'Common carriers' entry into multimedia services', *Information Economics and Policy*, 10: 77–105.

Contractor, F. J. and P. Lorange (1988) *Co-operative Strategies in International Business*, Lexington MA: Lexington Books.

Cook, S. D. D. and D. Yanow (1996) 'Culture and organizational learning', in M. D. Cohen and L. S. Sproull (eds) *Organizational Learning*, London: Sage: 430–5. First published in *Journal of Management Enquiry*, 2 (4) (1993).

Cosmides, L. and J. Tooby (1992) 'Cognitive adaptations for social exchange', in H. Barkow, L. Cosmides and J. Tooby (eds) *The Adapted Mind*, Oxford: Oxford University Press: 163–228.

Cusumano, M. A. and T. Fujimoto (1991) 'Supplier relations management: a survey of Japanese, Japanese-transplant US auto plants', *Strategic Management Journal*, 12: 563–88.

Damasio, A. R. (1995) *Descartes' Error: Emotion, Reason and the Human Brain*, London: Picador.

Daniels, J. and L. Radebaugh (1995) *International Business*, 7th edn, Reading MA: Addison Wesley.

Das, T. K. and B. S. Teng (1998) 'Between trust and control: developing confidence in partner co-operation in alliances', *Academy of Management Review*, 23 (3): 491–512.

—— (2001) 'Trust, control risk in strategic alliances: an integrated framework', *Organization Studies*, 22 (2): 251–84.

—— (2002) 'Alliance constellation: a social exchange perspective', *Academy of Management Review*, 27 (3): 445–56.

Deutsch, M. (1973) *The Resolution of Conflict: Constructive and Destructive Processes*, New Haven CT: Yale University Press.

Dore, R. (1983) 'Goodwill and the spirit of market capitalism', *British Journal of Sociology*, 34: 459–82.

—— (1989) *Taking Japan Seriously*, Stanford CA: Stanford University Press.

Dosi, G., C. Freeman, R. Nelson, G. Silverberg and L. Soete (1988) *Technical Change and Economic Theory*, London: Pinter.

Doz, Y. L. and G. Hamel (1998) *Alliance Advantage: The Art of Creating Value through Partnering*, Boston MA: Harvard Business School Press.

Dyer, J. H. (1996) 'Specialized supplier networks as a source of competitive advantage: evidence from the auto industry', *Strategic Management Journal*, 17: 271–91.

Dyer, J. H. and W. G. Ouchi (1993) 'Japanese-style partnerships: giving companies a competitive edge', *Sloan Management Review*, 35: 51–63.

Edelman, G. M. (1987) *Neural Darwinism: the Theory of Neuronal Group Selection*, New York: Basic Books.

—— (1992) *Bright Air, Brilliant Fire; On the Matter of Mind*, London: Penguin.

Edmonson, A. (1999) 'Psychological safety and learning behaviour in work teams', *Administrative Science Quarterly*, 44: 350–83.

Eldredge, N. and S. J. Gould (1972) 'Punctuated equilibria: an alternative to phyletic gradualism', in T. J. M. Schopf (ed.) *Models in Paleobiology*, San Franciso: Freeman Cooper: 82–115.

Essers, J. P. J. M. (2003) 'Incommensurability and organization' (in Dutch), PhD thesis, Rotterdam: School of Management, Erasmus University.

Etzioni, A. (1988) *The Moral Dimension: Towards a New Economics*, New York: Free Press.

Faulkner, D. (1995) *International Strategic Alliances; Co-operating to Compete*, Maidenhead: McGraw-Hill.

Fey, C. F. and P. W. Beamish (2001) 'Organizational climate similarity and performance: international joint ventures in Russia', *Organization Studies*, 22 (5): 853–82.

Fiol, C. M. and M. A. Lyles (1985) 'Organizational learning', *Academy of Management Review*, 10 (4): 803–13.

Fornahl, D. and T. Brenner (eds) (2003) *Co-operation, Networks and Institutions in Regional Innovation Systems*, Cheltenham: Edward Elgar.

Frank, R. H. (1988) *Emotions within Reason: The Strategic Role of the Emotions*, New York: Norton.

Freeman, L. C. (1978–9) 'Centrality in social networks: conceptual clarification', *Social Networks*, 1: 215–39.

Frege, G. (1892) 'On sense and reference' (in German), *Zeitschrift fur Philosophie und philosophische Kritik*, 100: 25–50.

Frey, B. S. (2002) 'What can economists learn from happiness research? *Journal of Economic Literature*, 40 (2): 402–35.

Fukuyama, F. (1995) *Trust, the Social Virtue and the Creation of Prosperity*, New York: Free Press.

Gabbay, S. M. and R. Leenders (eds) (1999) *Corporate Social Capital*, Deventer: Kluwer.

Gambetta, D. (1988) 'Can we trust trust?', in D. Gambetta (ed.) *Trust: Making Breaking of Co-operative Relations*, Oxford: Blackwell: 213–37.

Gargiulo, M. and M. Benassi. (1999) 'The dark side of social capital', in R. T. A. J. Leenders and S. M. Gabbay (eds) *Corporate Social Capital Liability*, Dordrecht: Kluwer: 298–322.

Geringer, M. J. and L. Hebert (1989) 'Control performance of international joint ventures', *Journal of International Business Studies*, summer: 235–54.

Gersick, C. J. G. (1991) 'Revolutionary change theories: a multi-level exploration of the punctuated equilibrium paradigm', *Academy of Management Journal*, 16 (1): 10–36.

Giddens, A. (1984) *The Constitution of Society*, Cambridge: Polity Press.

Gilsing, V. A. (2003) 'Exploration, exploitation and co-evolution in innovation networks', PhD thesis, Rotterdam: School of Management, Erasmus University.

Glimstedt, H. (1999) 'Constructing the global, reconstructing the local: reflexive actors and economic action in the internationalized context', unpublished paper.

Gouldner, A. W. (1960) 'The norm of reciprocity: a preliminary statement', *American Sociological Review*, 25 (2): 161–78.

—— (1985) 'Economic action social structure: a theory of embeddedness', *American Journal of Sociology*, 91: 481–510.

Grandori, A. (1997) 'An organizational assessment of interfirm co-ordination modes', paper, EGOS colloquium, 3–5 July, Budapest.

Granovetter, M. S. (1973) 'The strength of weak ties', *American Journal of Sociology*, 78 (6): 1360–81.

Granstrand, O., P. Patel and K. Pavitt (1997) 'Multi-technology corporations: why they have distributed rather than distinctive core competences', *California Management Review*, 39 (4): 8–25.

Grey, C. and C. Garsten (2001) 'Trust, control, post-bureaucracy', *Organization Studies*, 22 (2): 229–50.

Griffin, R. W. and M. Pustay (1996) *International Business*, Reading MA: Addison Wesley.

Gulati, R. (1995) 'Does familiarity breed trust? The implications of repeated ties for contractual choice in alliances', *Academy of Management Journal*, 30 (1): 85–112.

Hagedoorn, J. (1993) 'Understanding the rationale of strategic technology partnering: interorganizational modes of co-operation and sectoral differences', *Strategic Management Journal* 14: 371–85.

—— and G. Duysters (2002) 'Learning in dynamic inter-firm networks: the efficacy of multiple contacts', *Organization Studies*, 23 (4): 525–48.

—— and J. Schakenraad (1994) 'The effect of strategic technology alliances on company performance', *Strategic Management Journal*, 15: 291–309.

Håkansson, H. (ed.) (1982) *International Marketing and Purchasing of Industrial Goods: An Interaction Approach*, Chichester: Wiley.

—— (1987) *Industrial Technological Development: A Network Approach*, London: Croom Helm.

—— (1989) *Corporate Technological Behaviour: Co-operation and Networks*, London: Sage.

—— (1977) 'Influence tactics in buyer–seller processes', *Industrial Marketing Management*, 5: 319–32.

—— and I. Snehota (1995) *Developing Relationships in Business Networks*, London: Routledge.

Hansen, M. T. (1999) 'The search-transfer problem: the role of weak ties in sharing knowledge across organization subunits', *Administrative Science Quarterly*, 44: 82–111.

Hedberg, B. L. T. (1981) 'How organizations learn and unlearn', in P. C. Nystrom and W. H. Starbuck (eds) *Handbook of Organizational Design*, New York: Oxford University Press: 3–27.

——, P. C. Nystrom and W. H. Starbuck (1976) 'Camping on seesaws: prescriptions for a self-designing organization', *Administrative Science Quarterly*, 21: 41–65.

Heide, J. B. and A. Miner (1992) 'The shadow of the future: effects of anticipated interaction and frequency of contact on buyer–seller co-operation', *Academy of Management Journal*, 35: 265–91.

Helper, S. (1987) 'Supplier relations innovation: theory application to the US auto industry', PhD thesis, Cambridge MA: Harvard University.

—— (1990) 'Comparative supplier relations in the US and Japanese auto industries: an exit/voice approach', *Business Economic History*, 19: 1–10.

—— (1991) 'Strategy and irreversibility in supplier relations: the case of the US automobile industry', *Business History Review*, 65: 781–824.

—— and D. I. Levine (1992) 'Long-term supplier relations and product–market structure', *Journal of Law, Economics and Organization*, 8 (3): 561–81.

Henderson, R. M. and K. B. Clark (1990) 'Architectural innovation: the reconstruction of existing product technologies and the failure of established firms', *Administrative Science Quarterly*, 35: 9–30.

Hennart, J. F. (1988) 'A transaction cost theory of equity joint ventures', *Strategic Management Journal*, 9: 361–74.

Hill, C. W. L. (1990) 'Co-operation, opportunism and the invisible hand: implications for transaction cost theory', *Academy of Management Review*, 15 (3): 500–13.

Hirschman, A. O. (1970) *Exit, Voice and Loyalty: Responses to Decline in Firms, Organizations and States*, Cambridge MA: Harvard University Press.

Hodgson, G. M. (2002) 'The legal nature of the firm and the myth of the firm–market hybrid', *International Journal of the Economics of Business*, 9 (1): 37–60.

Holland, J. H. (1975) *Adaptation in Natural and Artificial Systems*, Ann Arbor MI: University of Michigan Press.

Jacobs, J. (1968) *The Economy of Cities*, London: Weidenfeld and Nicolson.

—— (1984) *Cities and the Wealth of Nations*, London: Penguin.

Jaffe, A. F. (1986) 'Technological opportunity and spill-overs of R&D: evidence from firm's patents, profits and market value', *American Economic Review*, 76: 984–1001.

Jarillo, J. C. (1988) 'On strategic networks', *Strategic Management Journal*, 9: 31–41.

Johanson, J. and J. Vahlne (1977) 'The internationalization process of the firm: a model of knowledge development and increasing foreign market commitment', *Journal of International Business Studies*, spring–summer: 23–32.

—— (1990) 'The mechanism of internationalization', *International Marketing Review*, 7 (4): 11–24.

Johanson, J. and L-G. Mattsson (1987) 'International relations in industrial systems: a network approach compared with the transaction cost approach', *International Studies of Management and Organization*, 17 (1): 34–8.

Johnson-Laird, P. N. (1983) *Mental Models*. Cambridge: Cambridge University Press.

De Jong, G. and B. Nooteboom (2001) *The Causality of Supply Relationships: A Comparison between the US, Japan, Europe*, ERIM Report series ERS-2001-73-ORG, Rotterdam: Erasmus University.

Kamath, R. R. and J. K. Liker (1994) 'A second look at Japanese product development', *Harvard Business Review*, November–December: 154–70.

Kamp, B. P. G. (2003) 'Formation and evolution of international business networks', PhD dissertation, Tilberg: University of Tilburg.

215

Killing, J. P. (1983) *Strategies for Joint Ventures*, New York: Praeger.

Klein Woolthuis, R. (1999) 'Sleeping with the enemy: trust, dependence and contracts in inter-organizational relationships', PhD dissertation, Enschede, Netherlands: Twente University.

——, B. Hillebrand and B. Nooteboom (2002) 'Trust, contract and relationship development', article under review.

Knight, F. (1921) *Risk, Uncertainty and Profit*, Boston MA: Houghton Mifflin.

Kogut, B. (1988) 'A study of the life cycle of joint ventures', in F. J. Contractor and P. Lorange (eds) *Co-operative Strategies in International Business*, New York: Lexington Books: 169–240.

Krackhardt, D. (1999) 'The ties that torture: Simmelian tie analysis in organizations', *Research in the Sociology of Organizations*, 16: 183–210.

Krugman, P. R. (1991) *Geography and Trade*, Cambridge MA: MIT Press.

Kuhn, T. S. (1970) *The Structure of Scientific Revolutions*, 2nd edn, Chicago: University of Chicago Press.

Laage-Hellman, J. (1997) *Business Networks in Japan: Supplier–Customer Interaction in Product Development*, London: Routledge.

Lakoff, G. and M. Johnson (1999) *Philosophy in the Flesh*, New York: Basic Books.

Lamming, R. (1993) *Beyond Partnership*, New York: Prentice Hall.

Langlois, R. N. and P. L. Robertson (1995) *Firms, Markets and Economic Change*, London: Routledge.

Lave, J. and E. Wenger (1991) *Situated Learning; Legitimate Peripheral Participation*, Cambridge: Cambridge University Press.

Lazaric, N. (1998) 'Trust and organizational learning during inter-firm co-operation', in N. Lazaric and E. Lorenz (eds) *Trust and Economic Learning*, Cheltenham: Edward Elgar: 209–26.

—— and E. Lorenz (1998) 'The learning dynamics of trust, reputation and confidence', in N. Lazaric and E. Lorenz (eds) *Trust and Economic Learning*, Cheltenham: Edward Elgar: 1–22.

Leenders, R. T. A. J. and S. M. Gabbay (1999) 'Corporate social capital: the structure of advantage and disadvantage', in R. T. A. J. Leenders and S. M. Gabbay (eds) *Corporate Social Capital Liability*, Dordrecht: Kluwer: 1–14.

Lewicki, R. J. and B. B. Bunker (1996) 'Developing and maintaining trust in work relationships', in R. M. Kramer and T. R. Tyler (eds) *Trust in Organizations: Frontiers of Theory Research*, Thousand Oaks CA: Sage: 114–39.

Lippman, S. and R. P. Rumelt (1982) 'Uncertain imitability: an analysis of interfirm differences in efficiency under competition', *Bell Journal of Economics*, 13: 418–38.

Lorange, P. and J. Roos (1992) *Strategic Alliances*, Oxford: Blackwell.

Lorenzini, G. and C. Baden-Fuller (1993) 'Creating a strategic centre to manage a web of partners', paper, IMP conference, Bath, September.

Los, B. (1999) 'The empirical performance of a new interindustry technology spill-over measure', in P. P. Saviotti and B. Nooteboom (eds) *Technology and Knowledge; From the Firm to Innovation Systems*, Cheltenham: Edward Elgar.

Lounamaa, P. H. and J. G. March (1987) 'Adaptive co-ordination of a learning team', *Management Science*, 33: 107–23.

Macaulay, S. (1963) 'Non-contractual relations in business: a preliminary study', *American Sociological Review*, 28: 55–67.

Macneil, I. (1980) *The New Social Contract: An Enquiry into Modern Contractual Relations*, London: Yale University Press.

Maguire, S., N. Philips and C. Hardy (2001) 'When "silence = death", keep talking: trust, control and the discursive construction of identity in the Canadian HIV/AIDS treatment domain', *Organization Studies*, 22 (2): 285–310.

March, J. (1991) 'Exploration and exploitation in organizational learning', *Organization Science*, 2 (1): 101–23.

Marshall, A. (1920) *Principles of Economics*, 8th edn, London: Macmillan.

Maskell, P. and A. Malmberg (1999) 'Localised learning and industrial competitiveness', *Cambridge Journal of Economics*, 23: 167–85.

McAllister, D. J. (1995) 'Affect- and cognition-based trust as foundations for inter-personal co-operation in organizations', *Academy of Management Journal*, 38 (1): 24–59.

McKelvey, M. (1996) *Evolutionary Innovations: The Business of Biotechnology*, Oxford: Oxford University Press.

McKinsey and Co. (1988) *Making Choices for the Eighties* (in Dutch), Amsterdam: McKinsey.

Mead, G. H. (1934) *Mind, Self and Society, from the Standpoint of a Social Behaviorist*, Chicago: University of Chicago Press.

Merleau-Ponty, M. (1964) *Le Visible et l'invisible*, Paris: Gallimard.

Ministry of Economic Affairs (1991) *Partners in Production: Subcontracting in Innovation* (in Dutch), The Hague: Ministry of Economic Affairs.

Mintzberg, H. (1983) *Structure in Fives: Designing Effective Organizations*, Englewood Cliffs NJ: Prentice Hall.

Mody, A. (1993) 'Learning through alliances', *Journal of Economic Behavior and Organization*, 20: 151–70.

Mokyr, J. (1990) *The Lever of Riches: Technological Creativity and Economic Progress*, Oxford: Oxford University Press.

Mol, M. (2001) *Outsourcing, Supplier Relations and Internationalization: Global Sourcing Strategy as a Chinese Puzzle*, ERIM PhD series in Management 10, Rotterdam: Erasmus University.

Mowery, D. C. and R. N. Rosenberg (1993) 'The US national system of innovation', in R. R. Nelson (ed.), *National Innovation Systems*, Oxford: Oxford University Press: 29–75.

Murakami, Y. and T. P. Rohlen (1992) 'Social-exchange aspects of the Japanese political economy: culture, efficiency and change', in S. Kumon and H. Rosorsky (eds) *The Political Economy of Japan*, III *Cultural and Social Dynamics*, Stanford CA: Stanford University Press: 63–105.

Neisser, U. (ed.) (1987) *Concepts and Conceptual Development*. Cambridge: Cambridge University Press.

Nelson, R. R. (ed.) (1993) *National Innovation Systems: a Comparative Analysis*, New York: Oxford University Press.

—— and Winter, S. (1977) 'In search of useful theory of innovation', *Research Policy*, 6: 36–76.

—— (1982) *An Evolutionary Theory of Economic Change*, Cambridge: Cambridge University Press.

Nonaka, I. and H. Takeuchi (1995) *The Knowledge-creating Company*, Oxford: Oxford University Press.

Noorderhaven, N. G. (1996) 'Opportunism and trust in transaction cost economics', in J. Groenewegen (ed.) *Transaction Cost Economics and Beyond*, Boston MA: Kluwer: 105–28.

217

Nooteboom, B. (1982) 'A new theory of retailing costs', *European Economic Review*, 17: 162–86.

—— (1992) 'Towards a dynamic theory of transactions', *Journal of Evolutionary Economics*, 2: 281–99.

—— (1993a) 'An analysis of specificity in transaction cost economics', *Organization Studies*, 14 (3): 430–51.

—— (1993b) 'Firm size effects on transaction costs', *Small Business Economics*, 5: 283–95.

—— (1996) 'Trust, opportunism and governance: a process and control model', *Organization Studies*, 17 (6): 985–1010.

—— (1998) 'Cost, quality and learning-based governance of buyer–supplier relations', in M. G. Colombo (ed.) *The Changing Boundaries of the Firm*, London: Routledge: 187–208.

—— (1999a) *Inter-firm Alliances: Analysis and Design*, London: Routledge.

—— (1999b) 'Exit and voiced-based systems of corporate control', *Journal of Economic Issues*, 33 (4): 845–60.

—— (2000a) *Learning and Innovation in Organizations and Economies*, Oxford: Oxford University Press.

—— (2000b) 'Institutions and forms of co-ordination in innovation systems', *Organization Studies*, 21 (5): 915–39.

—— (2002) *Trust: Forms, Foundations, Functions, Failures and Figures*, Cheltenham: Edward Elgar.

—— (2003) 'Problems and solutions in knowledge transfer', in D. Fornahl and T. Brenner (eds) *Co-operation, Networks and Institutions in Regional Innovation Systems*, Cheltenham: Edward Elgar: 105–25.

—— and I. Bogenrieder (2002) *Change of Routines: A Multi-level Analysis*, ERIM research report, Rotterdam: School of Management, Erasmus University.

—— and V. A. Gilsing (2003) *Exploration, Density and Strength of Ties: A Competence and Governance Approach*, ERIM research report, Rotterdam: Erasmus Institute for Research in Management, Erasmus University.

—— and R. Klein Woolthuis (2003) 'Cluster dynamics', article under review.

—— J. Berger and N. G. Noorderhaven (1997) 'Effects of trust and governance on relational risk', *Academy of Management Journal*, 40 (2): 308–38.

—— G. de Jong, R. W. Vossen, S. Helper and M. Sako (2000) 'Network interactions and the role of mutual dependence: a test in the car industry', *Industry and Innovation*, 7 (1): 117–44.

North, D. C. (1990) *Institutions, Institutional Change and Economic Performance*, Cambridge: Cambridge University Press.

—— and R. Thomas (1973) *The Rise of the New World: A New Economic History*, Cambridge: Cambridge University Press.

Nussbaum, M. C. (2001) *Upheavals of Thought: The Intelligence of Emotions*, Cambridge: Cambridge University Press.

Ohmae, K. (1989) 'Global logic of strategic alliances', *Harvard Business Review*, March–April: 143–54.

Oinas, P. and E. J. Malecki (2000) 'Technical trajectories in time and space: from national and regional to spatial innovation systems', paper, Erasmus University.

Oliver, A. L. (2001) 'Strategic alliances and the learning life-cycle of biotechnology firms', *Organization Studies*, 22 (3): 467–89.

Oliver, C. (1990) 'Determinants of international relationships: integration and future directions', *Academy of Management Review*, 15 (2): 241–65.

Osborn, R. N. and C. C. Baughn (1990) 'Forms of interorganizational governance for multinational alliances', *Academy of Management Journal*, 33 (3): 503–19.

Ouchi, W. G. (1980) 'Markets, bureaucracies, clans', *Administrative Science Quarterly*, 25 (1): 129–43.

Pagden, A. (1988) 'The destruction of trust and its economic consequences in the case of eighteenth-century Naples', in D. Gambetta (ed.) *Trust: the Making and Breaking of Co-operative Relations*, Oxford: Blackwell: 127–41.

Parkhe, A. (1993) 'Strategic alliance structuring: a game theoretic and transaction cost examination of inter-firm co-operation', *Academy of Management Journal*, 36: 794–829.

Pascal, B. (1670, 1977) *Penseés*, Paris: Gallimard.

Pavitt, K. (1984) 'Sectoral patterns of technical change: towards a taxonomy and a theory', *Research Policy*, 13: 343–73.

Peirce, C. S. (1957) *Essays in the Philosophy of Science*, Indianapolis IN: Bobbs-Merrill.

Penrose, E. (1959) *The Theory of the Growth of the Firm*, New York: Wiley.

Pettit, P. (1995) 'The virtual reality of *homo economicus*', *Monist*, 78 (3): 308–29.

Pfeffer, J. and G. R. Salancik (1978) *The External Control of Organizations: A Resource Dependence Perspective*, New York: Harper and Row.

Piaget, J. (1970) *Psychologie et epistémologie*, Paris: Denoël.

—— (1974) *Introduction a l'épistémologie génétique*, Paris: Presses Universitaires de France.

Piore, M. J. and C. F. Sabel (1983) 'Italian small business development: lessons for US industrial policy', in J. Zysman and L. Tyson (eds) *American Industry in International Competition: Government Policies and Corporate Strategies*, Ithaca NY: Cornell University Press.

—— (1984) *The Second Industrial Divide*, New York: Basic Books.

Polanyi, M. (1962) *Personal Knowledge*, London: Routledge.

—— (1966) *The Tacit Dimension*, London: Routledge.

—— (1969) *Knowing and Being*, London: Routledge.

Popper, K. R. (1970, 1976) 'Normal science and its dangers', in I. Lakatos and A. Musgrave (eds) *Criticism and the Growth of Knowledge*, Cambridge: Cambridge University Press, 51–8.

Porter, M. E. and M. B. Fuller (1986) 'Coalitions and global strategies', in M. E. Porter (ed.) *Competition in Global Industries*, Boston MA: Harvard Business School Press: 315–44.

Powell, W. W. (1990) 'Neither market nor hierarchy: network forms of organization', in B. A. Staw and L. L. Cummings (eds) *Research in Organizational Behavior*, XII, Greenwich CT: JAI Press: 295–336.

Prahalad, C. and G. Hamel (1990) 'The core competences of the corporation', *Harvard Business Review*, May–June.

Putnam, R. D. (2000) *Bowling Alone; the Collapse and Revival of American Community*, New York: Simon and Schuster.

Quine, W. V. (1960) *Word and Object*, New York: Wiley.

—— and J. S. Ullian (1970) *The Web of Belief*, New York: Random House.

Quinn, J. B. (1982) *Strategies for Change*, Homewood IL: Irwin.

—— (1992) *Intelligent Enterprise*, New York: Free Press.

REFERENCES

Reitman, V. (1997) 'To the rescue: Toyota's fast rebound after fire at supplier shows why it is tough', *Wall Street Journal*, 8 May: A15–16.

Ring, P. and A. van de Ven (1992) 'Structuring co-operative relationships between organizations', *Strategic Management Journal*, 13: 483–98.

—— (1994) 'Developmental processes of co-operative interorganizational relationships', *Academy of Management Review*, 19 (1): 90–118.

Romanelli, E. and M. Y. Tushman (1994) 'Organizational transformation as punctuated equilibrium: an empirical test', *Academy of Management Journal*, 37 (5): 1141–66.

Rosch, E. (1977) 'Human categorization', in N. Warren (ed.) *Advances in Cross-cultural Psychology* I, New York: Academic Press.

Sahal, D. (1981) *Patterns of Technological Innovation*, Reading MA: Addison Wesley.

Sako, M. (1992) *Prices, Quality, and Trust: Inter-firm Relations in Britain and Japan*, Cambridge: Cambridge University Press.

Schein, E. H. (1985) *Organizational Culture and Leadership*, San Francisco: Jossey Bass.

Scher, M. J. (1996) 'The relational access paradigm and Japanese interfirm networks; why outsiders seldom win: outcomes and policy implications', paper, EMOT workshop (European Management and Organization in Transition, of the European Science Foundation), Turin, 15–16 November.

Semlinger, K. (1991) 'New developments in subcontracting: mixing market and hierarchy', in A. Amin and M. Dietrich (eds) *Towards a New Europe? Structural Change in the European Economy*, Aldershot: Edward Elgar: 96–115.

Shapiro, S. P. (1987) 'The social control of impersonal trust', *American Journal of Sociology*, 93: 623–58.

Simmel, G. (1950) 'Individual and society', in K. H. Wolff (ed.) *The Sociology of Georg Simmel*, New York: Free Press.

Simon, H. A. (1983) *Reason in Human Affairs*, Oxford: Blackwell.

Six, F. (2001) 'The dynamics of trust and trouble', paper, seminar on 'Trust and Trouble in Organizations', Rotterdam: Erasmus University, 4–5 May.

Smircich, L. (1983) 'Organization as shared meaning', in L. R. Pondy, P. J. Frost, G. Morgan and T. C. and Dridge (eds) *Organizational Symbolism*, Greenwich CT: JAI Press: 55–65.

Stoelhorst, J. W. (1997) 'In search of a dynamic theory of the firm', PhD dissertation, Enschede: Twente University.

Storper, M. (1997) *The Regional World: Territorial Development in a Global Economy*, New York: Guilford Press.

Spender, J. C. (1989) *Industry Recipes*, Oxford: Blackwell.

Sydow, J. (2000) 'Understanding the constitution of interorganizational trust', in C. Lane and R. Bachmann (eds) *Trust in and between Organizations*, Oxford: Oxford University Press: 31–63.

Teece, D. J. (1986) 'Profiting from technological innovation: implications for integration, collaboration, licensing and public policy', *Research Policy*, 15: 285–305.

—— (1988) 'Technological change and the nature of the firm', in G. Dosi, C. Freeman, R. Nelson, G. Silverberg and L. Soete (eds) *Technical Change and Economic Theory*, London: Pinter.

Telser, L. G. (1980) 'A theory of self-enforcing agreements', *Journal of Business*, 53: 27–44.

Thompson, J. D. (1967) *Organizations in Action*, New York: McGraw-Hill.

Tooby, J. and L. Cosmides (1992) 'The psychological foundations of culture', in J. H. Barkow, L. Cosmides and J. Tooby (eds) *The Adapted Mind*, Oxford: Oxford University Press: 19–136.

Tushman, M. L. and P. Anderson (1986) 'Technological discontinuitties and organizational environments', *Administrative Science Quarterly*, 31: 439–65.

Tushman, M. L. and E. Romanelli (1985) 'Organizational evolution: a metamorphosis model of convergence and reorientation', in B. A. Staw and L. L. Cummings (eds) *Research in Organizational Behavior*, Greenwich CT: JAI Press, 171–222.

Tversky, A. and D. Kahneman (1983) 'Probability, representativeness, and the conjunction fallacy', *Psychological Review*, 90 (4): 293–315.

Uzzi, B. (1996) 'The sources and consequences of embeddedness for the economic performance of organizations: the network effect', *American Sociological Review*, 61 (4): 674–98.

—— (1997) 'Social structure and competition in interfirm networks: the paradox of embeddedness', *Administrative Science Quarterly*, 42: 35–67.

Vandevelde, A. (2000) 'Reciprocity and trust as social capital' (in Flemish), in A. Vandevelde (ed.) *Over vertrouwen en bedrijf*, Leuven: Acco: 13–26.

Vermeulen, F. and H. Barkema (2001) 'Learning through acquisitions', *Academy of Management Journal*, 44 (3): 457–76.

Vernon, R. (1966) 'International investment and international trade in the product cycle', *Quarterly Journal of Economics*, 80: 190–207.

Vygotsky, L. (1962) *Thought and Language*, ed. and trans. E. Hanfmann and G. Varkar, Cambridge MA: MIT Press.

Wegner, D. M., T. Giuliano and P. Hertel (1985) 'Cognitive interdependence in close relationships', in W. Ickes (ed.) *Compatible and Incompatible Relationships*, New York: Springer: 253–76.

Weick, K. F. (1979) *The Social Psychology of Organizing*, Reading MA: Addison Wesley.

—— (1995) *Sensemaking in Organizations*, Thousand Oaks CA: Sage.

—— and F. Westley (1996) 'Organizational learning: affirming an oxymoron' in S. R. Clegg and W. R. Nord (eds) *Handbook of Organization Studies*, London: Sage: 440–58.

Weigelt, K. and C. Camerer (1988) 'Reputation and corporate strategy: a review of recent theory and applications', *Strategic Management Journal*, 9: 443–54.

Welch, L. S. and R. Luostarinen (1988) 'Internationalization: evolution of a concept', *Journal of General Management*, 14 (2): 34–55.

Wenger, E. and W. M. Snyder (2000) 'Communities of practice: the organizational frontier', *Harvard Business Review*, January–February: 139–45.

Whitley, R. (1999) *Divergent Capitalisms: The Social Structuring and Change of Business Systems*, Oxford: Oxford University Press.

Williamson, O. E. (1975) *Markets and Hierarchies*, New York: Free Press.

—— (1985) *The Economic Institutions of Capitalism: Firms Markets, Relational Contracting*, New York: Free Press.

—— (1993) 'Calculativeness, trust, and economic organization', *Journal of Law and Economics* 36: 453–86.

—— (1999) 'Strategy research: governance and competence perspectives', *Strategic Management Journal*, 20: 1087–108.

Willinger, M. and E. Zuscovitch (1988) 'Towards the economics of information-intensive production systems: the case of advanced materials', in G. Dosi, C. Freeman, R. Nelson, G. Silverberg and L. Soete (eds) *Technical Change and Economic Theory*, London: Pinter: 239–55.

Wittgenstein, L. (1953, 1976) *Philosophical Investigations*, Oxford: Blackwell.

Womack, J., D. Jones and D. Roos (1990) *The Machine that Changed the World*, New York: Rawson.

Wuyts, S., M. G. Colombo, S. Dutta and B. Nooteboom (2003) *Empirical Tests of Optimal Cognitive Distance*, ERIM research report, Rotterdam: Erasmus Institute for Research in Management, Erasmus University.

Zand, D. E. (1972) 'Trust and managerial problem solving', *Administrative Science Quarterly*, 17 (2): 229–39.

Zuchella, A. (2003) *Geographic Co-location and Global Value Chains: Cluster Dynamics and Strategic Innovations in Cluster-based Firms*, Pavia: University of Pavia.

Zucker, L. G. (1986) 'Production of trust: institutional sources of economic structure', in B. A. Staw and L. L. Cummings (eds) *Research in Organizational Behaviour*, VIII, Greenwich CT: JAI Press: 53–111.

Name index

Abernathy, W. J. 52
Albert, M. 145
Alitalia 147
Amin, A. 46
Andersen, E. 137
Anderson, E. 37, 84, 151
Anderson, P. 62
Archer, M. S. 31, 70
Argyris, C. 53
Arrow, K. 93
Arthur Andersen 56, 57
Asheim, B. T. 174, 203
Axelrod, R. 122

Bacdayan, P. 57
Baden-Fuller, C. 76
Bakos, J. Y. 105
Barkema, H. 78
Barkow, J. 29
Bartlett, C. A. 63
Bateson, G. 53
Baughn, C. C. 75
Bazerman, M. 13
Beamish, P. W. 28, 45
Beije, P. 24
Benetton 76, 175
Berger, J. 121, 138, 140
Bessemer 41
Bettis, R. A. 6, 25, 52
Birley, S. 132
Blackler, F. 12, 57
Bleeke, J. 45, 82, 84, 151, 153
BMW 151
Boeing 62
Bogenrieder, I. 16, 57, 203
Boisot, M. 209n
Bosch 88
Boschma, R. A. 175, 176
Bradach, J. L. 113
Brenner, T. 191
Bridgestone 44
Brown, J. S. 12, 20, 21, 46, 57, 136, 163, 203
Bruner, J. S. 12
Brynjolfsson, E. 105
Bunker, B. B. 22, 73, 111, 114, 146, 188, 200

Burt, R. S. 7, 48, 69, 72, 86, 93, 150, 155, 156, 190, 201

Camerer, C. 109
Cantwell, J. A. 63
Cap Gemini 57
Casper, S. 171, 173
Chesbrough, H. W. 6
Child, J. 37, 42, 74, 176
Chiles, T. H. 113
Choo, C. W. 18
Clark, K. B. 52, 61
Cohen, M. D. 9, 27, 32, 57, 188
Coleman, J. S. 7, 73, 104, 160, 190
Colombo, M. G. 28, 192
Contractor, F. J. 37, 75
Cook, S. D. 56
Corus 82
Cosmides, L. 29, 30
Cromie, S. 132
Cusumano, M. A. 87, 115

DAF 42, 118
Damasio, A. R. 11
Daniels, J. 44, 58
Das, T. K. 69, 70, 110, 190
de Jong, G. 115, 177
Deutsch, M. 112, 146, 149
Dietrich, M. 46
Dore, R. 87
Dosi, G. 31, 52
Douglas 62
Doz, Y. L. 37, 70
Duguid, P. 12, 20, 21, 46, 57, 136, 163, 203
Dunhill 39
Dutta, S. 28
Duysters, G. M. 156
Dyer, J. H. 87, 115

Eccles, R. G. 113
Edelman, G. M. 32
Edmondson, A. 26
Eldredge, N. 62
Enichem 49
Ernst, D. 45, 82, 84, 151, 153

Essers, J. P. 17, 33, 34
Etzioni, A. 31

Faulkner, D. 37, 42, 49, 74, 151
Fey, C. F. 28
Fiol, C. M. 53
Fokker 40
Ford, Henry 46
Fornahl, D. 19
Frank, R. H. 30
Fraunhofer Institute 23
Freeman, L. C. 68
Frege, G. 208n
Frey, B. S. 18
Fuji 42, 120, 152–3
Fujimoto, T. 87, 115
Fukuyama, F. 116, 131
Fuller, M. B. 37, 44

Gabbay, S. M. 94, 190
Gambetta, D. 133
Garrone, P. 28, 192
Gatignon, H. 37, 84, 151
Geringer, M. J. 45, 84, 151
Gersick, C. J. 52
Giddens, A. 31, 70
Gilsing, V. A. 145, 166, 191, 202
Glimstedt, H. 63, 65
Goshal, S. 63
Gould, S. J. 62
Gouldner, A. W. 113
Grandori, A. 135
Granovetter, M. S. 7, 73, 85, 155, 156, 190, 201
Granstand, O. 25
Griffin, R. W. 58

Hagedoorn, J. 45, 75, 156
Hakansson, H. 9
Hamel, G. 3, 37, 70
Hansen, M. T. 73, 111
Hebert, L. 45, 84, 151
Hedberg, B. L. 53
Heide, J. B. 122
Heineken 41
Helper, S. 87, 115, 177
Henderson, R. M. 52, 61
Hennart, J. F. 37
Hill, C. W. L. 109
Hirschman, A. O. 104, 113, 148, 200
Hodgson, G. M. 17
Holland, J. H. 53
Honda 42
Hoogovens 82

ICI 49
Isaksen, A. 174, 203

Jacobs, J. 43, 176, 191, 203
Jaffe, A. F. 28
Jarillo, J. C. 37
Johanson, J. 9, 58
Johnson, M. 31, 32, 186
JVC 47

Kahneman, D. 15
Kamath, R. R. 88, 115, 182
Kamp, B. P. 67, 69, 89, 177
Killing, J. P. 37, 45, 84, 151
Klein Woolthuis, R. 110, 191, 203
KLM 147, 148
Knight, F. 98
Kogut, B. 45
Krackhardt, D. 92, 93, 189
Krugman, P. R. 43, 191
Kuhn, T. 17, 33, 34, 35

Laage-Helman, J. 9
Lakoff, G. 31, 32, 186
Lambooy, J. G. 175, 176
Lamming, R. 37, 87, 89, 91, 115, 121
Langlois, R. N. 19, 55, 80, 135, 187
Lave, J. 151, 163, 203
Lazaric, N. 109
Leenders, R. 94, 190
Levine, D. I. 87
Levinthal, D. A. 9, 27, 32, 188
Levi-Strauss, C. 57
Lewicki, R. J. 22, 73, 111, 114, 146, 188, 200
Liker, J. K. 88, 115, 182
Lippman, S. 9, 100
Lorange, P. 37, 42, 44, 68, 75, 120, 152
Lorenzini, G. 76
Los, B. 28
Lounama, P. H. 14
Luostarinen, R. 58
Lyles, M. A. 53

Macauley, S. 139
Malecki, E. J. 94
Malmberg, A. 43, 191
March, J. G. 14, 53, 54, 195
Marshall, A. 43
Maskell, P. 43, 191
Matsushita 47
Mattson, L-G. 9
McAllister, D. J. 22, 73, 111, 114, 146, 188, 200
McDonald's 44, 59
McKelvey, Maureen 171
McKinsey 91
McMakin, J. F. 113
Mead, G. H. 12
Merck 148
Merleau-Ponty, M. 11, 31
Miner, A. 122
Mintzberg, H. 18, 22
Mitsubishi 42, 118
Mody, A. 45
Mokyr, J. 41
Mol, M. 25
Mölnlycke 152
Mowery, D. C. 8
Murray, F. 173

NEDCAR 42, 118
Nelson, R. R. 17, 21, 31, 52
Nike 41, 174
Nonaka, I. 12

Nooteboom, B. 5, 12, 14, 16, 18, 20, 21, 22, 25, 31, 34, 37, 43, 51, 57, 60, 75, 85, 100, 111, 113, 115, 116, 132, 140, 145, 156, 158, 161, 164, 175, 177, 181, 186, 187, 188, 189, 190, 191, 192, 196, 197, 198, 199, 201, 203, 205
North, D. C. 20
Nussbaum, M. C. 11

Oce van der Grinten 138
Ohmae, K. 37, 45, 46
Oinas, P. 94
Oliver, C. 2
Osborn, R. N. 75
Ouchi, W. G. 87, 115

Pagden, A. 132
Pascal, B. 34
Peaudouce 152
Peirce, C. S. 32
Penrose, E. 8
Pettit, P. 189
Peugeot 91
Pfeffer, J. 9
Philips 3–4, 6, 41, 45, 47, 78, 84, 88, 148
Piaget, J. 12
Piore, M. J. 85
Piscitello, L. 63
Polanyi, M. 11, 116
Popper, K. 32, 35
Porter, M. E. 37, 44
Powell, W. W. 7
Prahalad, C. 3, 52
Pustay, M. 58
Putnam, R. D. 113, 188

Quine, W. V. 187
Quinn, J. B. 62

RABO 80–1
Radebaugh, L. 44, 58
Reitman, V. 101
Renault 70, 89, 177
Ring, P. 112
ROBECO 81
Robertson, P. L. 20, 55, 80, 135, 187
Romanelli, E. 52
Roos, J. 42, 44, 68, 120, 152
Rosch, E. 14
Rosenberg, P. N. 8
Rover 42, 151, 176
Rumelt, R. P. 9, 100

Sabel, C. F. 85
Sahal, D. 52
Sako, M. 177
Salancik, G. R. 9
Schakenraad, J. 45
Schein, E. H. 19, 62, 151
Scher, M. J. 118
Schon, D. 53
Schumpeter, J. 19, 21
Scott 152
Semlinger, K. 108
Shapiro, S. P. 115, 116, 147, 190, 200

Seimens 88
Silicon Valley 85
Simmel, G. 92, 93, 150, 160, 189
Simon, H. 11, 116
Six, F. 146
Smircich, L. 18
Smith, Adam 2, 193
Snehota, I. 9
Snyder, W. M. 57
Socrates 22
Sony 3–4, 45, 47
Spender, J. C. 52
Stoelhorst, J. W. 9, 37, 43
Storper, M. 63
Sydow, J. 114, 117
Syntens 23

Takeuchi, H. 12
Teece, D. J. 6, 9, 25, 52, 135
Telser, L. G. 122
Teng, B. S. 69, 70, 110, 190
Thomas, R. 20
Thompson, J. D. 18
Tooby, J. 29, 30
Toyota 44, 101
Tushman, M. Y. 52, 62
Tversky, A. 15

Ullian, J. S. 187
Utterback, J. M. 52
Uzzi, B. 7, 190

Vahlne, J. 58
Van de Ven, A. 112
Vandevelde, A. 114
Vermeulen, F. 78
Vernon, R. 59, 63
Volkswagen 70, 89, 177
Volvo 42, 118
Vossen, R. W. 198
Vygotsky, L. 12

Wegner, D. M. 12
Weick, K. F. 18, 56
Weigelt, K. 109
Welch, L. S. 58
Wenger, E. 57, 151, 163, 203
Westley, F. 56
Whirlpool 45, 84
Whitley, R. 3, 31, 203
Williamson, O. E. 5, 20, 28, 80, 105, 113, 188, 189, 196
Willinger, M. 135
Winter, S. 17, 21, 31, 52
Wittgenstein, L. 32
Wuyts, S. 28

Xerox 42, 44, 120, 152–3

Yanow, D. 56

Zand, D. E. 115, 148, 200
Zuchella, A. 175, 203
Zucker, L. G. 113, 116, 188
Zuscovitch, E. 135

225

Subject index

absorptive capacity 9, 25, 32, 150, 188; cognitive distance and 27; and tacit knowledge 22–3, 51, 157
acquisitions *see* mergers and acquisitions
activity theory 11–12, 17, 18, 54, 57
adaptation 151–4, 174
agglomeration 43
aircraft industry 40, 50, 62
airline industry 81, 147–8
alliances 28, 69, 70, 78, 107–8, 192, 193; reasons for 79, 81
allopatric speciation 62–3
aluminium 44
anchoring/adjustment heuristic 14, 146
anti-trust regulation 8
appropriability of knowledge 26, 173
assembly lines 46
assembly plants 70, 71
associations 39, 76
atmosphere 125, 128
attribution 14, 15
automobile industry 10, 42, 44, 50, 70, 108–9, 115, 134, 151, 176; assembly lines 46; product cycles 62; supply systems 88, 89–91, 177
availability heuristic 13, 15
awareness 11, 116

bauxite 25, 78, 123
benchmarking 25, 78, 123
biotechnology 28, 50, 170–1; exploration/ exploitation networks 171–4, 202–3
blame 15
boundary spanners 84, 93, 112, 150–1, 190
brand names 50, 59, 80, 161, 193
business process engineering 39
business studies 7
business systems 3, 203–4
buy group 100
buyer–supplier relationships 115, 121, 139–40, 177–8, 184; network structure 87–92; pyramid 71–2, 87–9, 162, 202; vertical co-operation 91–2

calculation 154
calculative rationality 13, 116, 186

Calimero syndrome 84, 110, 146–7, 151, 194
Camorra 133
capacity: dedicated 99; excess 49; utilization 38, 39, 49; *see also* absorptive capacity
cartels 44, 70
Cartesianism 11
causal ambiguity 100
chips (semiconductors) 6, 78
clans 131
clusters 84, 174–6, 177, 190, 203
coalitions 70
co-evolution 31
cognition 11, 12, 18, 186; complementary 21–2; construction of 31, 32; variety of 32
cognitive abilities 29, 30
cognitive dissonance 13, 16
cognitive distance 18, 21–2, 54, 94, 162, 186–7, 193; crossing 42, 53, 150–1, 196; empirical tests 27–9; mathematical model 27; and mutual understanding 42–3, 69
cognitive institutions 20
cognitive proximity 73
cognitive science 7, 12
communities of practice 12, 21, 46, 57–8, 136, 150–1
compact discs 3
competence/s 5, 32, 38, 42–3, 64, 79, 185, 187, 190; complementary 3, 42, 63; core 6, 9, 25, 78, 82, 83–4, 92; exploration and 37, 156–8, 192; information benefits 69; and network structure 195, 201–2; organizational 89; resources 8–10; technological 89
competition 3, 9, 10, 38, 64, 134, 157, 166, 174
complexity 3, 162, 183; of knowledge 158
consortia 39, 43, 76, 128, 190
consultancy 55, 56, 57–8
consumer credit 80–1
consumer electronics 6, 50, 78
consumer services 59–60
contracts 103, 105, 108, 135–6, 139, 162, 173, 197, 199–200; trust and 110–11, 117
control 67, 72, 83, 97, 151; benefits 69; concentration 74–5; of risk 104–6, 146
co-operation 3, 76, 133, 136
co-operatives 41, 76

corporate venturing 92
costs 37, 47; of contact 51; of contract 51; of control 105; fixed 39, 49; of governance 102, 108, 122, 123; opportunity 7, 25, 107, 133; of redundant ties 157; of search 51, 59; set up 40, 49, 194; sunk 7, 10, 16, 49; threshold 40, 46, 49–50, 51, 59–60, 192; transaction 51, 131–2; transport 41; *see also* switching costs
creative destruction 135
culture *see* organizational culture
cycle of discovery 60–3, 64

default 14, 81, 193, 196
dependence 25, 28, 105, 109, 196, 200; gross 138; mutual 18, 108, 109, 114–15, 152, 158, 160, 169, 198, 200; net 138, 139; value and 152–3, 197–8
differentiation 59, 61, 63, 133, 164, 176, 196
diffusion of knowledge 23, 48
discovery 52, 60–3
distance: death of 74, 94–5; psychological 58; *see also* cognitive distance
distribution channels 50, 80, 122, 161, 174
diversity 21–2
division of labour 2, 20, 46, 169
dominant design 52, 156, 161, 165, 203
dominant logic 52
durability of ties 45, 73, 76, 77, 158–9, 161–2, 171, 172, 202
dyads 7, 92–3, 189–90, 191
dynamic capabilities 6

economics 7, 17–18, 33–4, 186; evolutionary 31; industrial 7; institutional 20; *see also* transaction cost economics
economies of scale 7, 37–9, 46–8, 59, 80, 122, 176, 193; engineering 47; in exploration/exploitation networks 161, 163, 166; opportunism and 108, 125–6; threshold costs 40, 50, 59–60; and value 122
economies of scope 7, 38, 39, 40, 48–9, 80, 81
economies of time 49–52
effects: band-wagon 47, 48, 83, 194; car queue 49; contagion 47, 48; experience 51; institutional 8; snob 48; snowballing 47; telephone 47; time 39–40, 49–52
efficiency 7, 64, 79, 157, 161–2, 166, 192; allocative 37; innovative 37; productive 37; static 37–41
electronic data interchange (EDI) 122
embeddedness 155; local 160, 174, 175; relational 7, 189; structural 7, 189, 190
emotions 11, 126
empathy 13, 22, 147, 188, 189, 200
employment 86
endowment effect 15
entrepreneurship 19, 78, 132, 193
entry barriers 10, 44, 131
evolution 13, 29–30, 31, 32
evolutionary psychology 29–30, 150, 186
exchange rate 40
exclusiveness 105, 107–8, 169, 178, 187, 197
exemplars 14

exit 104, 113, 117, 132, 154–5, 180–1
exit barriers 10, 44, 49, 76, 134, 136
expectations 14, 146
exploitation 37, 153; and exploration 56, 60–3, 92, 164; learning for 53–5; networks for 85, 161–2, 165–6
exploration 37, 85, 86, 153, 163–4, 187, 192; clusters 174–6; exploitation and 56, 60–3, 92, 164; learning for 53–5; networks for 156–61, 164–5, 166–74, 201, 202
external corporate venturing 92
external economy of cognitive scope 27–9, 63, 120, 187, 192
externalities 43, 195; Jacobs 176, 203; network 4, 47–8, 80

factor analysis 137–8; Cronbach's alpha 137, 140; factor loadings 137
falsification 32–3
fashion industry 41, 62, 76
first mover advantage 47
fitness 20, 30
flexibility 23, 25, 43, 79, 85, 120, 145
flexible knowledge 99
flexible specialization 85
focal awareness 11
Fordism 46, 183; post-Fordism 46
foreign direct investment (FDI) 43, 58, 63, 70
framing 15, 30; gain/loss frames 16
franchising 76, 190
free riding 26, 58, 70, 169

game theory: backward induction 179; closing game 180–1; extensive form 179; game tree 179; Nash equilibrium 127, 182, 184; opening game 179–80; positive sum 182; repeated games 154; win–win 182; zero-sum 82
generalization 63, 164
geography 7, 43, 171
global strategy 59, 176
globalization 3, 59
go-betweens 84, 93, 110, 116–17, 150, 151, 190, 198–9
governance 5, 24–6, 69, 76–7, 97–8, 185, 187, 190, 192, 195, 201; bilateral 83, 116; contingencies 109–11, 131–3, 163–4; of exploration networks 158–61, 165, 168; instruments of 106–9, 128–30, 196–200; legal 125, 128, 131; problems of 133–7; trilateral 116

heat loss 47
heuristics 12–16, 29, 186; anchoring/adjustment 14, 146; availability 13, 15; of discovery 61; representativeness 13, 14
hierarchy 28, 71–2
hold-up risk 72, 107, 110, 173, 189, 190, 191; audit of 101–4; due to specific investments 25, 28, 98–9, 165, 189, 196; in transaction cost economies 19, 25, 28, 78
hostages 109, 117, 118–19, 123, 124, 126, 154, 160, 198; value of 98, 102
hub-and-spoke 71, 162, 169, 202
hunter–gatherer societies 29–30

227

ICT (information and communications technology) 3, 25–6, 29, 46, 168; distance and 74
identification 13, 15, 22, 133, 147, 158, 159, 187, 188
import restrictions 43, 44
incentives for opportunism 103, 123, 196
inclination for opportunism 103, 109, 125, 126, 196
incommensurability 17, 22, 33–5
incubators 80
incumbents 10
industrial districts 43, 74, 75, 84, 85, 174–6
industries: aircraft 40, 50, 62; airline 81, 147–8; banking 80–1, 81–2; brewing 41; building 115; business process 39; cement 62; chemical 49; computer 62; consumer electronics 6, 78, 85; defence 43; electrical/electronic 140; fashion 41, 62, 76; financial services 62, 122; gas 134; leather 48; machine 62, 85; meat 48; offshore 124; oil 49, 55, 124; pharmaceutical 28, 40–1, 62, 172–3; process 47, 49; PVC 49; retailing 39; shoe 85; steel 49, 82; telecommunications 44, 62, 143; textile 85; white goods 45, 84; *see also* automobile industry, biotechnology industry
industry recipe 52
information 11, 13, 78, 109, 126; benefits 69, 156; revelation of 93–4, 104, 117
information and communications technology *see* ICT
innovation 23–4, 52–3, 56, 110, 185, 199–200; and cognitive distance 21–2, 28–9; incipient 131; incremental 134, 135; life cycle theory 52, 63; radical 28, 61, 85, 86, 131, 136, 145, 201; spatial systems 94; transfer of technology 23–4
institutional arrangements 85
institutional environment 8, 20, 31
institutions 20–1; cognitive 20; evolution and 31; legal 110; regulative 20, 132
integration: horizontal 39, 81–2, 174; reasons for 78–83; semi- 17; vertical 46; vertical disintegration 39, 81; *see also* mergers and acquisitions
interaction 7, 70; frequency of 158, 159, 160–1, 169, 171, 201
interactionism 12, 18, 31–3, 186–7
intermediate communities 116
intermediation 117, 189
internationalization 43–4, 58–9, 119–20, 122; learning by 63, 65
Internet 168, 169
investment 10; brownfield/greenfield 176; *see also* foreign direct investment, specific investments

Japanese companies 6, 42, 118, 124, 152; outsourcing 182
joint ventures 75, 76, 83–4, 120, 194
just-in-time delivery 39, 94, 99, 122

keiretsu 115, 124, 177–8, 190
King Saul effect 41
knowledge 121, 158, 191; activity theory of 11–12, 18, 29, 31–2, 54, 57; canonical 57; codified 12, 27, 163, 166, 172, 173, 187–8, 202; complementary 156–7; documented 121; interactionist theory 186–7; of management 54;

procedural 57; production of 12, 31–2, 53; search for 168, 171, 190, 191; sharing 53, 56, 57–8; tacit 12, 22–3, 23–4, 51, 94–5, 131, 163, 165, 173; transfer of 23–4, 94–5, 100, 110, 191

landing rights 81
latent variables 137
learning 28–9, 51, 53–5, 72, 185, 191, 192; communities of practice 57–8; by internationalization 63, 65; levels of 53, 56–7
legal form 67, 72
licensing 76, 86–7, 94, 117; cross-licensing 40–1
life cycle theory of innovation 52, 63
Likert scale 137
logistic curve 48
logistics 39

mafia 133
maieutics 22, 23
management 33–4, 54, 84; macho behaviour 147, 193; managerial hubris 83, 193–4
marketing 50, 54
markets 3, 6, 131, 134; access to 38, 41, 64; clusters and 174, 175
mergers and acquisitions 76, 107–8, 187; reasons for 78–83, 192–4
methodological collectivism/individualism 31
methodological interactionism 31–3, 186
modular system 20, 55
monopoly 134, 173
monopsony 173
motivation, intrinsic/extrinsic 18
multimedia, exploration and exploitation networks 166–70
multinational corporations 63, 175, 176–7
myopia 21, 27, 42, 145, 187
myths 14

negotiation 148–9
network analysis 7
network density 70–1, 85–6; in exploitation 162, 169; in exploration 153–4, 157–8, 161, 165, 201, 202
network structure 67, 190, 191, 194–5, 199, 200; centrality of 68, 71–2, 73, 164, 195; connectedness 68, 71, 194; externalities 4, 80; innovative properties 84–6; isolation of 34, 72, 195; size of 70, 160, 162, 166; stability of 72, 145, 195; structural equivalence 72; structural holes 72, 104, 195, 199
networks 2, 7, 9; firm characteristics 194; goals of 37; personal 132
novel combinations 52, 85, 159, 165, 193

open-book contracting 115, 183
openness 182–3; trust and 115–16, 149, 155, 177; *see also* voice
opportunism 19, 105, 108, 112, 113, 115–16, 122, 148, 197–9; control of 146, 197–8; incentives for 103, 123, 196; intent towards 103, 125, 126–7, 196; opportunities for 103, 125–6, 196
organization 16–20, 74; virtual 74, 75–6

organizational change 62
organizational co-ordination 16, 18
organizational culture 19, 21, 113
organizational focus 19–20, 62, 187, 188
organizational learning 53–5, 57–8
ownership 67, 123; concentration of 74–5, 195; of joint ventures 84, 151, 194

paradigms 14, 17, 22, 33
parent firms 76, 92
patents 28, 29, 51, 86
performance 45
pharmaceutical industry 28, 40–1, 62, 172–3
philosophy of science 31, 33–4
piggyback exports 58, 70
poaching 169
portfolio 40, 42
positional advantage 9, 37, 38, 43–4, 64, 79, 120–1, 192
postmodernism 32
power 72, 73; trust and 150
pragmatic/pragmatist view of knowledge 32
price-minus costing 88, 115, 177, 183, 184
principal-agent theory 17–18, 19
prisoner's dilemma 83
product cycles 59, 62, 63
product–market collaboration 42, 152–3
production–product collaboration 42
production technology 39
prospect theory 15, 155
prototypes 14, 52, 159
psychology: evolutionary 29–30, 150, 186; social 7, 13–16, 18, 186
public administration 85, 203
punctuated equilibria 52, 62–3

quality 122, 182, 183
queuing theory 59, 60
quid pro quo 113, 133

rationality 116, 186; adaptive 13, 186; bounded 11; calculative 13, 116, 186; procedural 97; substantive 97
realism 32, 33–4, 186
reciprocation 30, 61, 62, 113–14, 164
recursiveness 127, 141
redundant ties 86, 157, 201, 202
regional innovation systems 43, 84, 94, 191
relativism 32
representativeness heuristic 13, 14
reputation mechanisms 95, 104, 110, 158, 160, 165, 184, 198; go-betweens 117; and self-interest 109, 126
research and development (R&D) 25, 54, 122, 134, 170; cross-licensing 40–1; internationalization 63
resource dependence 9
resources 7, 9; access to 121; joint utilization 48; risk and 97, 98, 101, 103, 190; value and 199
return on investment (ROI) 45
revelation problem 93–4, 117, 198
risk 15, 24; audit of 119–30, 196; avoidance of 107; political 40; psychological/social 24, 26, 148, 149; relational 98–104, 107, 116, 126,

127, 190, 199; spreading 40; value and 97, 105; see also hold-up risk, spill-over risk
rivalry 2
role models 14
routinization 11, 17, 116, 153, 188

satisficing 11
scientific knowledge 171
scope 161, 173, 195
seasonal effects 39
selection 31, 32
self-confidence 15
self-interest 16, 108–9, 126–7, 146; gift giving 113, 114
semiconductors 6, 50, 78
service facilities 49–50
social capital 94, 190
social constructivism 32
social network theory 189, 190, 195
socialization 31, 136, 147
sociology 7, 12, 18, 70, 186; and trustworthiness 149–50
spatial proximity 69, 73, 74, 161, 158, 171, 195
specialization 2, 46, 161, 193
specific investments 110, 158–60, 163, 166, 174, 178, 182, 202; hold-up risk due to 25, 28, 98–9, 165, 189, 196; knowledge-specific 139; location-specific 138; and mutual dependence 152, 158, 159, 169, 198; network-specific 104, 191; relation-specific 10, 25, 145–6, 159, 189; transaction-specific 10, 28, 139
spill-over risk 26, 84, 104, 111, 118, 121, 149; and exclusiveness 108, 159–60, 197; in mergers/acquisitions 78, 82; and network structure 157, 165, 190–1, 202; and tacit knowledge 100, 110, 159, 162
stakeholders 9
stand-alone firms 20, 55
standards 40, 44, 55–6, 63, 135, 183
stockholders 40
strategy 185–6; global 59, 176
strategy, relational: improving 106, 180, 181; loosening 106, 180, 181; off loading 106, 180, 181; setting free 106, 180, 181; tying down 106, 180, 181; yielding 106, 181
strength of weak ties 73, 85, 145, 156, 157, 164, 190, 201
structural holes 72, 104, 195, 199
structuration 31, 70
subsidiary awareness 11, 116
suppliers 71–2, 87–8, 89, 121, 139; see also buyer-supplier relationships
supply chains 2, 39, 49, 190
supply pyramid 71–2, 87–9, 162, 202
supply tiers 72, 87–8, 120, 178; vendor selection 88
survival 29–30, 61, 185
switching costs 76, 98, 102–3, 105, 123–5, 173, 189, 196
system of shared meanings 18
systemic firms 19–20, 55, 60

technological guideposts 52
technological paradigms 52

229

technological regimes 52
technological trajectories 52
technology 50, 131, 134; flexible 99, 110; new
    developments 3, 6; platform 6, 78, 170–1;
    sensors 3; spill-over of 119, 120, 136, 152–3,
    154, 169, 170; see also ICT
technology–design collaboration 42
tertius gaudens 93, 150, 190
third parties 67–8, 84, 92–3, 109; gatekeepers
    112; mediation 116; see also boundary spanners,
    go-betweens
ties 55, 68, 72, 173, 195; openness of 69, 73;
    scope of 69, 73–4, 195; strength of 73, 75,
    85–6, 111, 153–4, 158, 164–5, 171–2,
    195; see also durability of ties, frequency of
    interaction, spatial proximity, strength of weak
    ties
time effects 39–40, 49–52
trade associations 41, 73
transaction cost economics (TCE) 5–6, 18, 19,
    105, 196; and hold-up 25, 28; and mergers/
    acquisitions 78, 79, 192–3; and opportunism
    125, 126; and specific investments 10, 99–100,
    139, 189
triads 92–3, 189
trust 110–11, 111–16, 132, 140–1, 142, 188–9,
    196, 198, 200; behavioural 15, 95, 111;
    benevolence 14, 112; characteristics-based 113;

competence and 111, 112, 150–1, 160–1, 165;
    dedication 112; ex-ante 188, 198, 199; guardians
    of 116; in honesty 112; identification-based 114;
    institutional 111; institutions-based 111, 113,
    116; intentional 111–12, 150; and intermediaries
    117; knowledge-based 114; in loyalty 139;
    mistrust 108, 147, 150; organizational 111,
    112, 150; process-based 114; relation-specific
    124–5, 158–9, 160–1; robustness of 112;
    routine-based 116; sociality and 29–30, 113,
    146–7
trustworthiness 13, 14, 15, 113, 126–7, 149, 189,
    200, 201

uncertainty 15, 131, 134, 188, 192, 201; in
    exploration networks 156, 157, 160, 201;
    reduction of 15, 162, 166; risk and 97, 98, 110

value 81, 119–22, 197; dependence and 152–3,
    197–8; relative 102, 179–80; and resources 199
variety 21, 173; of cognition 32
venture capital 92
video-recorders 3–4, 47–8
virtual organizations 74, 75–6
voice 104, 113, 117, 132, 148, 154, 200–1

weakness of the will 14
word of mouth 48